Berlitz HANDB

D1168031

TURKEY

Contents

FAMILY FRIENDLY SYMBOL 👪

This symbol is used throughout the Handbook to indicate a sight, hotel, restaurant or activity that is suitable for families with children.

Top 25 Attractions

1   **Hagia Sofia and the Blue Mosque** Two potent symbols of Christendom and Islam sit opposite each other in power and glory *(see p.65)*

2   **The Blue Voyage** Take a calming and leisurely cruise on a traditional wooden yacht anywhere between Bodrum and Antalya *(see p.26)*

Ephesus The most impressive classic site in Turkey, also the most visited and best preserved 2nd- to 4th-century AD Roman city *(see p.124)*

4 İstanbul's Archaeology Museum
The matriarch of the city's museums exhibits classical artefacts *(see p.70)*

5 Antakya Archaeological Museum
A collection of whimsical mosaics and frescoes from Roman villas *(see p.167)*

6 Pergamon Stunningly authentic 8th- century Greek city on a dramatic hilltop *(see p.114)*

7 Shopping in the Grand Bazaar
Full of verve, this was İstanbul's 15th-century commercial hub *(see p.70)*

8 Aphrodisias A shrine and temple to love, dating from the 1st century *(see p.128)*

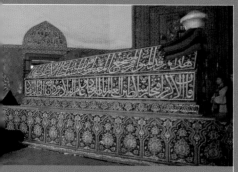

9 **Bursa** The first capital of the Ottomans, Bursa is packed with thermal spas *(see p.96)*

10 **Troy** See centuries' worth of ruins in the land described in Homer's *Iliad* and *Odyssey* *(see p.104)*

12 **Trekking the Lycian Way** This classic waymarked trail runs over the Taurus Mountains *(see p.31)*

11 **Oil wrestling at Edirne** Turkey's national sport comes to an oily finale every July *(see p.98)*

13 **Antalya Archaeology Museum** Beautiful displays of Lycian, Pamfilian and Pisidian artefacts *(see p.158)*

15 **Castle of St Peter, Bodrum** This 14th-century castle is now a museum of underwater archaeology *(see p.132)*

14 **Gallipoli Peninsula**
A tragic, moving and fascinating World War I battle point evoking poignant memories *(see p.95)*

16 **İstanbul's Palaces** Topkapı and Dolmabahçe palaces are the city's two most grandiose *(see p.69 and p.72)*

17 **Hot-air ballooning over Cappadocia** Disneyworld meets the moon's surface in a virtuoso geological performance *(see p.201)*

18 **Hierapolis (Pamukkale)**
Travertine terraces and ancient hot springs have delighted onlookers for decades (see p.128)

19 **Akdamar Church** A 1,100 year-old Armenian church in the middle of Lake Van, recently renovated as a 'museum' (see p.240)

20 **Nemrut Dağı (Mount Nimrod)**
Mystical and massive statuesque remains from the Commagene kingdom (see p.233)

21 **Konya** Visit the ancestral home of the Whirling Dervishes for authentic performances *(see p.188)*

22 **Gaziantep Archaeological Museum** Magnificent Roman mosaics skilfully showcased *(see p.234)*

23 **Museum of Anatolian Civilisations** Highlighting Neolithic and Palaeolithic ingenuity *(see p.180)*

24 **Sumela Monastery** This Greek Monastery was once a sanctuary for Christian pilgrims *(see p.219)*

25 **Safranbolu** A time-warp 19th-century Ottoman town with intact wooden mansions *(see p.213)*

Turkey Fact File

Renowned for its shimmering beaches, Turkey also offers Alpine mountains, freshwater lakes and lush pastures. The country straddles two continents: Anatolian Turkey lies in Asia and is delineated from European Turkey by the Bosphorous Straits. The country is divided into 81 provinces with a marked contrast between the more developed western regions and the country's traditional and conservative eastern provinces.

 BASICS
Name: Republic of Turkey (Türkiye Cumhuriyeti)
Population: 72.5 million
Area: 783,562 sq km (302,535 sq miles)
Language: Turkish (official), Kurdish, Arabic, minority dialects
Religion: majority Sunni Muslim (95 percent) some Alevis; abstract minorities
Capital City: Ankara
Largest City: İstanbul
President: Abdullah Gül
Prime Minister: Recep Tayyip Erdoğan
Government: Representative Parliamentary Republic

Republic established: 1923 by Mustafa Kemal Atatürk
National Anthem: The March of Independence
National Carrier: Turkish Airlines (THY)
Climate: dry (semi-arid) in lateral mountain ranges, moderate (Mediterranean) in coastal regions

 CURRENCY
Turkish Lira (TL)
100 kuruş = 1TL
£1 (GBP) = 2.31TL
$1 (US) = 1.53TL
€1 (Euro) = 2.10TL

 TIME ZONE
GMT +2
EST +7

TELEPHONE NUMBERS

Country Code (calling to Turkey):
+90
International calls (from Turkey):
00 + country code + number
Police (in urban areas): 155
Jandarma (in rural areas): 156
Ambulance: 112
Fire: 110
Internet domain: .tr

AGE RESTRICTION

Driving: 18
Drinking: none
Age of Consent: 16

Smoking is banned in all public
buildings and transport. People
comply on urban transport but the
law is widely flouted in indigenous
pockets where law makers and
keepers will probably also smoke.

ELECTRICITY

220–240 volts officially, but often
lower in practice

OPENING HOURS

Banks: 9am–noon, 1–5pm (state
banks), 9am–5pm (private banks)
Shops: 10am–5pm
Malls: 10am–10pm
Museums: close on Mon but
Topkapı Palace closes on Tue
Normal Museum hours:
9am–noon, 1.30–5.30pm
Hospitals: (for outpatients)
9am–noon, 1–5pm

POSTAL SERVICE

Post offices are marked by the letters
PTT; they are usually open Mon–Sat
9am–12.30pm and 1.30–5pm.
There are also small PTT kiosks in
tourist areas where you can buy
stamps (only available at PTT outlets),
post letters and buy phonecards.
Delivery can be slow, but local
couriers guarantee next-day service;
try **Aras Kargo** (www.araskargo.
com.tr) and **Yurt İçi Kargo** (www.
yurticikargo.com), two good couriers
with local offices everywhere.

Trip Planner

WHEN TO GO

Climate

Turkey's climate can be divided into three distinct zones:

• The Marmara (including İstanbul), Aegean and Mediterranean regions covering the western and south-western parts of the country have a Mediterranean climate with hot, humid summers and mild but damp winters. Summer temperatures can reach an uncomfortable 40°C.

• The Black Sea region is Turkey's dampest region with excess rainfall, moderate temperatures and mists and fog even in summer.

• The Central and Eastern Anatolian regions experience extremely hot, dry summers and cold, snowy winters that often close roads for days.

The glorious beaches that fringe Turkey are some of the country's biggest draws

Public Holidays	
1 January	New Year's Day
23 April	National Sovereignty and Children's Day
19 May	Commemoration of Atatürk and Youth and Sports Day
30 August	Victory Day
29 October	Republic Day
Ramazan	The holy month of Ramazan (Ramadan) comprises 40 days of fasting determined by the setting and rising sun, falling back by about 11 days in each successive year
Şeker Bayram	The three-day Sugar Feast immediately follows Ramazan as a joyous breaking of the fasting period
Kurban Bayram	The Feast of the Sacrifice is a four-day affair, taking place 40 days after the Sugar Feast above

Springtime wild flowers in bloom at Ephesus

High and Low Season

For sun and beach lovers, the best time to visit is between May and October, when prices will also be at their highest. July and August are excruciatingly hot and humidity makes anything requiring exertion impossible. March or April are the perfect months to see wild flowers. Remember that Turkey is mountainous, and even in summer high passes will be cold.

Expect prices to be about 15 or 20 percent lower between October and April, but bargain in any season. Smaller hotels or pensions may close in October and not reopen until April. Some larger hotels may say they are open but not be prepared for visitors. It pays to check this carefully.

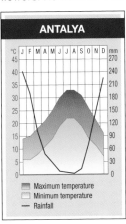

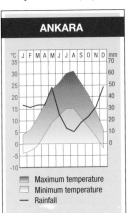

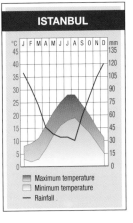

ESSENTIAL EVENTS

Intricately adorned camels, ready for wrestling heats at Selçuk

January

Camel Wrestling, Selçuk
Held any time during the month, with initial heats staged in the Selçuk, İzmir and Aydın areas of the Aegean and Mediterranean.

February

Camel Wrestling, Selçuk
Winners of the local heats compete in title fights.

March

International Film Festival, İstanbul (30 Mar–10 Apr)
Celebrating its 30th year in 2011, this is a prestigious and star-studded smorgasbord of international and Turkish film.

April

ANZAC Days, 24 and 25 Apr Çanakkale and Gallipoli Peninsula
The Australian and New Zealander lives lost in these Turkish battlefields are commemorated annually with a dawn service.

May

International Yachting Week, 15–20 May, Marmaris
Sailing enthusiasts from around the world compete off the coast of Marmaris. The event attracts brokers, buyers and chandlers.
Conquest of İstanbul, 29 May, İstanbul
This event celebrates the capture of the city in 1543 by Mehmet the Conqueror.

June

Çanakkale-Troia Film Festival, 4–9 June, Çanakkale
Due to be held for the first time in 2011, boosted by the enormous success of other film galas in Turkey.
International Classical Music Festival, 15 June, İstanbul
Catch a series of first-rate concerts as international orchestras perform at several well-publicised venues around the city.

Grease Wrestling, 25 June–1 July, Edirne
The final championships for traditional oiled wrestling are held at Kırkpınar.

Aspendos Opera and Ballet Festival, mid June to mid July, Aspendos
Open-air performances under the stars to thrill opera and ballet fans.

Navy Days, 1 July, throughout Turkey
This event celebrates the end of the Capitulations, or concessions, over-generously granted to foreign powers. Mostly involves sea games, visits to Naval ships and cleaning up beaches.

Hacı Bektaş Veli Commemoration, 16–18 Aug, Hacı Bektaş
A Bektaşi and Alevi ritual featuring singing, dancing and Sufi ceremonies.

Turkish Grand Prix, 21 Aug, İstanbul
The city's racing circuit hosts a leg of the famous Formula One motor race.

Golden Orange Film Festival, 4–11 Oct, Antalya
This film extravaganza has been going for almost 50 years and is a world-class festival with stars in attendance.

St Nicholas Symposium, Demre and Antalya
Conference and pilgrimage to Patara keeping the spirit of the famous saint's life alive.

Mevlâna Festival, 17 Dec, Konya
A once-a-year opportunity to see the authentic Whirling Dervish troupe performing in their ancestral home.

15

Trip Planner

Crowds pack out the Mevlâna festival for the chance to see the real Whirling Dervishes

ITINERARIES

Turkey is a large country and distances that look a breeze on the map can take hours to traverse. For Europeans, a long weekend in İstanbul is feasible; and a one-week trip suits those on charter package holidays. But long-haul, adventurous visitors will relish the two or three weeks required to absorb the culture and everything Turkish. The tours below factor in shopping and downtime.

Three days in Christian and Jewish İstanbul

Day 1: Sultanahmet. View the Hagia Sophia, the remarkable 6th-century AD Byzantine basilica and the Mosaic Museum, once the Palace of Byzantine Royalty, with pastoral mosaic themes from the 5th century AD. Explore the Basilica Cistern, a subterranean water depot dating from the 6th century AD.

Day 2: Karaköy and Chora. Take a morning tour of the Jewish Quin-centennial Foundation Museum of

Turkish Jews in Karaköy, followed by an afternoon visit to the Church of St Saviour in Chora, which dates from the 11th century AD and has stunning Byzantine frescoes and mosaics.

Day 3: Balat and Fener. Explore the Armenian and Jewish neighbour-hoods on the Golden Horn. Sites of note include the 15th- century Ahrida Synagogue; the Church of the Holy Angels with its sacred spring; Aya Yorgi Metokhi Church; the Greek Orthodox Patriarch; Fener's red-brick Greek High School for Boys; the 1877 iron Church of St Stephen of the Bulgars and the Church of Pamma-karistos (now the Fethiye Mosque). Not all are open to the public but historical atmosphere lingers and these sites can all be seen on foot.

14 days for Archaeology Buffs

Days 1–3: İstanbul. Take in the city's highlights: Topkapı Palace, the Grand Bazaar, Hagia Sophia and a Bosphorous cruise.

Day 4: İzmir. From here, take a tour to Bergama (Pergamum).

Day 5: Ephesus. Take a whole day to tour classical Ephesus, the museum in Selçuk and, further afield, the house of the Virgin Mary.

Catching the ferry at İzmir

***Days 6–8:* Priene, Miletus, Didyma.**
Delve into these classical Roman
sites and cities.
***Days 9–10:* Bodrum.** Enjoy a break
in this lively seaside town.
***Days 11–12:* Antalya.** Visit the
Archaeological Museum and the
city's quaint 'old town', with narrow
streets and wattle houses. Day tour
to Aspendos.
***Days 13–14:* Turkey's Lake District.**
Base yourself in Eğirdir and take trips
to Termessos and Sagalossos.

**Three weeks on Alexander
the Great's Campaign Trail**

***Days 1–2:* İstanbul.** See the main
sights and the statue of Alexander in
the Archaeology Museum.
***Day 3:* Troy.** Cross the Hellespont to
Troy, where Alexander marched with
his armies.
***Day 4:* Sardis.** This city's riches
attracted Alexander.
***Day 5:* Ephesus.** Tour of the site that
Alexander much admired.
***Day 6:* Priene.** Visit this ancient stop
on Alexander's westward route and
the Temple of Apollo at Didyma.
***Day 7:* Bodrum.** The town's Carian
fortifications were besieged by
Alexander.
***Day 8:* Xanthos.** Travel to Lycian Xan-
thos, which was taken by Alexander.
***Days 9–11:* Göcek to Antalya.** Enjoy
a three-day cruise visiting coastal
cities, especially Phaselis, which
welcomed Alexander.
***Day 12:* Antalya.** Tour Antalya and
investigate the Roman sculptures
in the Archaeology Museum. Climb
to Termessos, the Pisidian city
bypassed by Alexander.

The Temple of Artemis at Sardis

***Day 13:* Aspendos and Perge.** Visit
these strategic bases for Alexander.
***Day 14:* Sagalassos.** Visit this city,
which was captured by Alexander on
his way to Persia.
***Day 15:* Gordium.** Tour the Phrygian
capital, where the legendary Gordian
knot was severed by Alexander.
***Days 16–17:* Cappadocia.** Explore
the region that Alexander tried to rule
from afar.
***Day 18:* Taurus Mountains.** Retrace
Alexander's route along Roman
roads through the Taurus Mountains,
eventually descending through the
Cilician Gate.
***Day 19:* Issus.** Visit the Issus battle-
field where Alexander defeated
Persian ruler Darius III and see the
Antakya and Roman mosaics.
***Days 20–21:* İstanbul.** Return to the
start point of your route.

BEFORE YOU LEAVE

Visa and Entry

All visitors to Turkey must hold a valid passport, which should be machine-readable, if possible, and have at least six months' validity remaining on both entering and exiting Turkey.

Only Germans are exempt from needing a visa. These are usually given for 90 days and will be multiple entry and stamped in your passport. If you are on a cruise ship, you will be issued a day-return visa by the crew. Overstaying is not recommended even by one day: this can be costly.

Some visas are obtained from the Turkish embassy or consulate in your country and others can be obtained at the border on landing in Turkey. They all require a fee. After you disembark, be sure to obtain a visa before you go through passport control and have the correct fee handy. They don't offer change or accept credit cards.

The criteria for tourist visas and entry is complicated and governed by nationality. Log on to www.konsolosluk.gov.tr for information, e-applications and Turkish Foreign Office links with English-language options.

Embassies and Consulates

UK: Rutland Lodge, Rutland Gardens, Knightsbridge, London SW7 1BW, United Kingdom; tel: 020-7591 6900; www.turkishconsulate.org.uk
USA: 2525 Massachusetts Avenue, Washington, DC District of Columbia 20008, USA; tel: 202-612 6700; www.washington.emb.mfa.gov.tr
Canada: 197 Wurtemburg Street, Ottawa, ON K1N 8L9, Canada; tel: 888-

Nationality	Visa Required
UK	✓
US	✓
Canada	✓
Australia	✓
New Zealand	✓
Ireland	✓
South Africa	✓

566 7656; www.turkishembassy.com
Australia: 60 Mugga Way, Red Hill, Canberra, ACT 2603, Australia; tel: 2-6295 0227; http://canberra.emb.mfa.gov.tr
New Zealand: 15–17 Murphy Street, Level 8, Thorndon, Wellington, New Zealand; tel: 4-472 129 092; http://wellington.emb.mfa.gov.tr
Ireland: 11 Clyde Road, Ballsbridge, Dublin 4, Ireland; tel: 1-668 5240; email: turkconsec@eircom.net
South Africa: 1067 Church Street, Hatfield, 0028, Pretoria, South Africa; tel: 12-342 6053; www.turkishembassy.co.za

Vaccinations and Insurance

There are no specific vaccinations formally required. But keeping tetanus, polio and other jabs up to date is a good idea. Tuberculosis is found in pockets. It is not necessary to return home if you are bitten by a dog; some do carry rabies but serum is readily available. If you are allergic to bee stings or snake venom, bring your own suction pack. This could be life-saving.

It is imperative to have a travel insurance policy that includes medical insurance and, if possible, repatriation. This should be a priority.

It is wise to be on your guard with dogs and other animals; a minority carry rabies

Booking in Advance

Major airlines and scores of holiday companies feature trips to Turkey; Turkish Airlines is also part of the Star Alliance, providing code-sharing opportunities. Turkish hotels, holiday clubs and pensions have websites in English and often offer online booking, which can yield big discounts. Always ask and don't be afraid to bargain.

Tourist Information

Turkish Tourism Ministry: www.tour ismturkey.com and www.kultur.gov.tr
UK: 29–30 St James' Street, 4th Floor, London SW1A 1HB; tel: 0207-839 7778; www.gototurkey.co.uk and www.tourismturkey.org
USA: New York: 821 United Nations Plaza, New York, NY 10017; tel: 212-687 2194; email: ny@tourism turkey.org. Washington, DC: 1717 Massachusetts Ave NW, Washington, DC 20036; tel: 202-612 6800; www.turkishembassy.org

Useful Websites

www.neredennereye.com
www.todayszaman.com
www.tourismturkey.org
www.turkeycentral.com
www.turkeytravelplanner.com
www.turkishculture.org
www.twarpage.com

Maps and Books

Maps and street plans are not readily available. The tourism ministry's overall map of Turkey is the best country-wide. Street plans are available from local tourism offices or the provincial governors' offices (valilik).

Good books to read prior to arriving in Turkey include the following:
Osman's Dream by Dr Caroline Finkel. A scholarly book on all aspects of the Ottoman Empire.
Lords of the Horizons by Jason Goodwin. A good all-round assessment of the Ottoman centuries.
Snow by Orhan Pamuk. Turkey's first Nobel Laureate in Literature delves into the political attitudes of Kars.
Portrait of a Turkish Family by İrfan Orga. Poignant narrative detailing an Ottoman family's descent into poverty.
The Bastard of İstanbul by Elif Şafak. Turkey's top female author eschews xenophobia in her best-known book.

Trip Planner

Packing List

- lightweight, natural-fibre clothes
- light headscarf for visiting mosques
- sunscreen (available locally)
- mosquito repellent (available locally)
- comfortable walking shoes
- sun hat (available locally)
- good-quality boots if you are trekking

UNIQUE EXPERIENCES

Coastal Activities

For those who dream of gilded, wish-you-were-here coastline, Turkey surpasses all expectations. Dozens of glorious beaches redefine the perfect seaside holiday. Traditional yachts offer relaxed cruising possibilities, diving and sky sports will inspire spirited adventurers and intrepid climbers will revel in scaling cliffs and rock faces.

Turkey's mountainous lateral backbone is intersected by deep rift valleys that plummet to the sea, shaping dramatic coastlines with secret coves and undiscovered bays. The secluded inlets that once allowed civilisations, like that of the Lycians, to remain cut off and resist invaders, are now pristine jewels where pleasure boats can moor and swimmers may be the first in the waters for hundreds, maybe thousands, of years.

The same geological development that caused the silting up of cities such as Ephesus (see p.124) and Patara (see p.149), leaving them literally high and dry, deposited shimmering golden beaches that trim the Aegean and Mediterranean shorelines. Everywhere, the waters are safe for swimming, the subtropical climate meaning that you can take a dip from May until October.

Being moist and more temperate, the Black Sea region is less enticing for sun worshippers and the water is quite brackish. On a warm day, however, it is refreshing to go for a dip on the more unspoilt beaches at picturesque coastal villages such as Ünye or Giresun (see p.215).

The Aegean and Mediterranean coastal areas are alive with sports and activities that are in, on and under the

Yachts anchored off the island of Kekova

The crystal-clear waters are very inviting

Mediterranean coast. Even if your stomach churns, navigating the updraughts is a thrilling experience.

In recent years, Turkey has begun to promote the potential of extreme sports like canyoning and rock climbing. With the most challenging cliff faces rising directly from sea level in the Mediterranean region, there are ample opportunities to push your skills to the limit and ramp up endurance thresholds. Scaling the vertical face of a rock is intense and challenging. But hardy tourists are choosing nature-defying activities and adding a new buzz to coastal tourism. Possibilities include an Adventure Forest, a fantastic Climbing Garden, and a complete rock-climbing course.

water. The one not to miss is the simplest, a leisurely cruise on a wooden yacht, or *gulet*, where sailors can delight in the ocean breezes.

Alternatively, many visitors come to Turkey exclusively to dive, and, although most coastal towns have diving opportunities, the unofficial sub-aqua capital of Turkey is Kaş, where nine local diving school operators focus on safety, diving protocol and respect for the aquasphere. A bonus is that diving continues pretty well year-round. Few know that Olympos (*see p.153*) also has many exciting diving areas. Whether it is wrecks, underwater caves or fascinating aquatic life, crystal-clear waters provide unparalleled aqua vision for divers and snorkellers.

Far above the waves, paragliding has taken off as a 'passenger' sport, especially at Fethiye and Kaş on the

Golden Beaches

Apart from being family-friendly and relaxing, the best thing about a beach holiday is that you can do it on your own. No guides, instructors or tour

On or Off: Topless Bathing

Turkey is a religiously conservative society but topless bathers are spotted on every coastal beach, where dress codes are less inhibited than in fashionable urban centres or demure villages. Local trendy Turks worship the sun and want the whole body experience when it comes to tanning. Discreet topless bathing is generally fine for Turkish women but the impression tends to be that it is less acceptable for foreigners. This doesn't usually stop anyone, however, and the more touristed beaches, epic holiday clubs and inclusive resorts overflow with topless flocks from six to 60.

operators are needed to pack your sunscreen, grab a beach umbrella and spend the day improving your tan. Many beaches are attached to hotels and resorts, but almost all public beaches *(Halk Plajı)* can be reached on local minibuses. Beaches are government property and open to all, but many still charge a fee for entrance. For information about individual beaches, charges and how to get there, the local tourist office will advise.

Aegean beaches are frequented mainly by Turks who have been summering or retiring in Akçay, Ayvacık, Ayvalık or Foça for decades. Tourists have taken a long time to discover the brilliant sands at places like Sarımsaklı, 8km (5 miles) from Ayvalık. Its name means 'garlicy' but all you will find here is the purest whitest sand and enough accommodation and activities for an agreeable independent holiday for all the family. Yeni (new) Foça has some upmarket resorts with their own beachfront that are ideal for an all-inclusive holiday. 🚻

Further down the coast, near İzmir, Ilıca has a majestic sweep of sand gently sloping into the sea. One cannot pretend that this is not in the thick of resortland but the **Sheraton Çeşme Resort and Spa** (Şifne Caddesi 35, Ilıca, Çeşme, İzmir; tel: 0232-723 1240; www.sheratoncesme.com) attracts health visitors who want to combine a beach holiday with hydrotherapy and treatments in the hotel's natural geothermal springs. 🚻

Didyma and Altınkum, south of İzmir, are some of the most fashionable beaches in Turkey. Many English expatriates have relocated here and there

The stunning Ölüdeniz beach

is definitely something of a 'blighty' atmosphere. But it is lively; there are three bucket-and-spade beaches that nudge the seaside and numerous watersports. It is best to get here early to secure a sunbed and umbrella. 🚻

In the chic resort of Bodrum, the city beach is a little disappointing, although romantic for an evening stroll. But for swimming and lapping up the sun, Bitez or Gümbet are dream beaches, just a short distance from town by city transport. 🚻

Twelve km (7 miles) from Dalyan, a huge spit cradles the beach at İztuzu, which has somewhat crusty sand. The protected loggerhead turtle favours this warm sand to lay eggs between May and September, when the beach turns into a turtle maternity ward and humans must vacate the sands well before dark. The best way to get here is by boat from the centre of Dalyan.

Ölüdeniz on the **Mediterranean** coast is Turkey's premier billboard beach, an incredible lagoon nestled under the striking cliffs at Babadağ and catering to bronzed bathers and package travellers. Favourable updraughts make it a perfect location for paragliding and marvelling at the bird's-eye view before a gentle landing on the soft, warm sands.

Patara is the quintessential beach of all beaches with 18km (11 miles) of sweeping, restless white sand. The water is exceptionally shallow and suitable for get-wet kids and waders. There is only one café on the beach that rents umbrellas. The entrance charge seems expensive, but is worth it for the spotless WC. It is tempting to head off to infinity on the sands, but wandering solo too far from the entrance into the more lonely stretches of beach is not recommended.

The most dramatic beach in Turkey is at the mouth of a dramatic gorge, the descent 200 steps down (and up again) a plunging rock face at Kaputaş (between Kaş and Kalkan) to the divine beach and pristine swimming. The water is very cold and children need supervision due to heavy swells and a shelf that drops off steeply underwater. The coastal *dolmuş* (minibus) runs frequently along the main road above the beach.

After Kemer, heading west along the Mediterranean coast, there are lovely stretches of sandy beach, picnic tables and barbecues at big (*büyük*) and little (*küçük*) Çaltıcak, just before entering the tunnel on the Antalya highway. The Beydağlar mountains tower above and the setting is magical. These beaches charge a fee, and at weekends this is the place to glimpse a slice of Turkish life, as extended families pile in, lugging enormous picnics, to swim, sun and grill meat.

Antalya's Konyaaltı beach has a European flavour with cafés and kiosks spaced along a jaunty boardwalk bordering the seashore. The sand is grainy but this is a city beach and can be reached by a local bus service.

Alanya's broad sandy beaches at İncekum, once romantically gifted to Cleopatra, stretch for miles and teem with activities and water sports. The swimming is safe, if crowded, but this remains one of Turkey's most attractive beaches. The further east you go, the more peaceful and people-free it becomes.

Holiday-makers aboard a *gulet (see p.26)*

Sailing

The **Blue Voyage** (aka Blue Cruise) was inspired by a dissident intellectual, Cevat Şakir Kabaağaçlı, exiled to Bodrum in the 1920s. He enjoyed his banishment and the exquisite beauty of the sparkling, secluded bays enough to write a book about it, eventually becoming recognised by the book's title, the *Fisherman of Halicarnassus*. From an unknown backwater, Bodrum grew into a sophisticated, upmarket tourist haven. There is nothing to top the experience of the legendary Blue Cruise, exiling yourself for a day or more. The most pleasant way to enjoy it is to have at least three or four days on board to unwind, enjoy the breezes, swimming, snorkelling and superlative cuisine. Bodrum, Marmaris, Göcek and Antalya are the main hubs for hiring a *gulet*, a traditional wooden sailing ship that sleeps up to 12 people. The size of the *gulet* determines its legal 'payload.' Many of the classic sailing *gulets* are still built in Bodrum. Note, however, that most *gulets* now journey under motor and not sail.

A reliable charter company in Bodrum is **Kaya Güneri Yachting** (Atatürk Bulvarı 107, Konacık; tel: 0252-319 0485; www.kayaguneri yachting.com) and, in Fethiye, **V-Go Yachting and Travel Agency** (İskele Meydanı, under Hotel Dedeoğlu, Fethiye; tel: 0252-612 2113; www.boat cruiseturkey.com) is recommended. **Costa Turca** in Marmaris (Şirinyer Mah., Durmazlar Sokak 20; tel: 0252-417 6420; www.costaturca.com) fulfils dreams with their luxurious *gulets*. If chartering from the UK, **Westminster**

Classics sails exceptional cultural charters out of Bodrum on *gulets* (www.wct99.com).

It is customary to start and return to the same destination; there will be a surcharge for one-way voyages or for a drop-off en route, with the exception of exclusive, high-end charters. If money is no object, you can charter Turkey's most princely ocean-going beauty, *Papa Joe*, from **Blue Point Yachting** (tel: 0252-316 9556; www.mspapajoe.com and www.bluepointyachting.com).

If you are a sailor, why not charter a yacht and be your own skipper? This is known as a 'bareback' charter and an excellent operator is **Pupa Yachting** (Neyzen Tevfik Caddesi 242/7, Bodrum; tel: 0252-316 7715; www.pupa.com.tr). They also have centres in Marmaris and Göcek.

Windsurfing is a possibility at Alacatı

Surfing and Kiteboarding

On the Aegean coast, Alacatı and Çeşme are upbeat resort areas favoured by summering Turks. Very strong winds have given Alacatı an edge as the most exciting 'surfin' Türkiye' centre; try **Alaçatı Wind Surf School** (tel: 0232-716 0511).

Kite surfing, not found everywhere in Turkey, raises adrenalin levels at Akyaka, near Muğla, with **Winds of Gökova Kiteboarding** (Sahil Sokak 2, Akyaka, Muğla; www.gokovaruzgar.com) a good place to gear up.

Diving

Of all the coastal attractions, diving has most captured the imagination of tourists. Forget the seasons: divers suit up off Kaş even on New Year's Day. Alanya and Antalya also have excellent diving facilities, but divers of all abilities converge on Kaş with its many diving schools and well-equipped dive boats. Many like the après-dive nightlife too. There are numerous wrecks, sea slugs (venomous), playful turtles, dolphins, stingrays and octopuses to be seen underwater. Try not to touch, even if turtles nudge you. The water is clear down to 40m (130ft) and local young and creative artisans have 'sunk' an underwater art exhibition close to the shore off the Kaş Peninsula (*Yarımadı*). A World War I Turkish air-force plane has even been implanted underwater, a relic of a bizarre sort.

Bougainville Adventure Diving (İbrahim Serin Caddesi 10, Kaş; tel: 0242-836 3737; www.bougainville-turkey.com), **Kaş Diving** (Küçük Çakıl Mahallesi 41, Kaş; tel: 0242-836 4045) and **Nautilus Diving** (Terzi Sokak

Dive with turtles at Kaş

Coastal Activities

Top Tips

- The Mediterranean sun is strong. Use sunscreen even if you are away from the coast, especially paragliding or at high altitudes where oxygen is thin.
- *Gulets* take up to 12 passengers. Join a cruise even if you are solo: it is easy to meet new friends.
- Plan a day trip on a *gulet* if you don't have time for a three- or four-day cruise. It is still fun and all *gulet* tours include a splendid spread and a barbecue for lunch.
- Mosquitoes can be a problem wherever you go. Take repellent and a net.
- For risky activities like diving, paragliding or canyoning, leave your hero profile behind; rent or buy the best gear you can afford and go with a group. Follow the advice of group leaders or dive masters.

2/A, Kaş; tel: 0242-836 4115; www.
nautilusdiving.org/home) are the local
professional diving schools, catering
for novices up to experts. Diving is
safe, regulated and respects international standards; be sure to pack your
PADI, CMAS or BSAC certificates and
your diving log. Costs begin at about
€25 but a package of dives is much
more economical. Around Alanya
there is exciting underwater topography and many undersea caverns to
explore. **Dolphin Dive** (İskele Caddesi 23, Alanya; tel: 0242-512 3030;
www.dolphin-dive.com/en) has all the
equipment and skills for both beginners and experienced divers.

Non-Turks are not allowed to dive
solo in Turkish waters, so joining one
of the licensed diving schools makes
sense. Known to the select few, Olympos (see p.153) has a diving school,
Olympos Diving (Olympos, Antalya;
tel: 0242-892 1316; www.olymposdiv
ing.com). There are 20 outstanding
diving areas offshore that give this
place of legendary summits and mountain gods a new sub-aqua persona.

Paragliding
Paragliding is, quite literally, one of
the most uplifting activities imaginable; to drift peacefully, then wheel
like a bird, is the experience of a life-
time even for repeat gliders. Additionally, it is eco-friendly. Parachutes and
harness are provided but a reasonable
pair of legs to gain momentum before
up-currents waft you skywards helps.
Expect to pay around €75 per flight.

Fethiye's Mt Babadağ offers paragliding and Kaş has two reputable
operators, **Natura Blue Sports**

Events (Likya Caddesi 1/A, Kaş; tel:
0242-836 2580; www.naturablue.com)
and the all-round eco-specialists,
**Dragoman Outdoors Activities
Centre** (Uzun Çarşı 15, Kaş; tel: 0242-
836 3614; http://en.dragoman-turkey.
com/t/12). There are also safe landing
pads on the harbour.

Climbing and Zipwiring
The craggy mountains, deep gorges
and harsh coastal terrain have
endowed Turkey with the ideal setting for extreme sports and character
building (or stretching) activities.
Specialist companies like **Olympos Rock Climbing** (Kadir's Tree
Houses, Olympos, Antalya; tel: 0242-
892 1316; www.kadirstreehouses.com
and www.olymposrockclimbing.com)
have qualified instructors and run
courses to ensure you know about
rope technique, route planning,
equipment and climbing techniques
whether you are just curious, an

Kadir's Tree Houses are a good climbing base

enthusiast or a skilled climber. This is the holiday for those who love the stimulus of challenging nature. An introductory course begins at €34.

Climber's Garden (tel: 0242-441 3421; www.climbersgarden.com) at Geyikbayırı, 25km (13 miles) north of Antalya, offers budget-conscious rock-climbing adventures, making use of the limestone rocks, dramatic crags and various rock faces and pitches. Routes can accommodate all grades of climbers but the virgin territory tempts those looking for a first ascent. It is open year-round, but July and August will be unbearably hot, even in the tent and bungalow accommodation.

Bordering Olympos National Park, **Adventure Forest** (Çifteçeşmeler Mah., Comaklar Mevkii, Göynük Kanyon Yolu, Beldibi; tel: 0242-824 8749; www.yuksekparkur.com/eng/index.html;

Take advantage of Turkey's crags and peaks

Nov–Mar Sat–Sun only, summer daily 9.30am–4pm; charge) has you soaring through pine forests on zipwires, even playing Jane and Tarzan swinging from vines. Harness, safety equipment and orientation courses are provided.

What to Expect on a Blue Cruise

Gulets typically accommodate 12 to 16 people in shared cabins. The foredeck is for stretching out on sun beds or keeping watch for dolphins or other sea life. The aft deck is fitted out with seating, cushions and a dining table. Meals are shared here and most cruises provide a hearty breakfast, a lunch of pasta, maybe a moussaka, with salad and fruit.

Dinner begins with Turkey's famous starters (*meze*), followed by barbecues of meat and plenty of fish. Salads and rice or potatoes are the usual garnishes. Tea and coffee will be ad-lib. There are usually about three crew members and one will cook. It is best to ascertain whether alcoholic drinks will be included in the daily charter price or extra. It is also

advisable to check that port/harbour taxes are included, and Turkish VAT.

Gulets sail for three or four hours each day, then anchor in restful bays and coves for swimming, snorkelling or shore excursions. Poor sailors need not worry about being queasy. *Gulets* anchor overnight but captains may weigh anchor before dawn if forecasts are for high seas or winds.

An air-conditioned cabin makes all the difference to a successful charter. Cabins get hot at night and mosquitoes may make sleeping on deck less romantic, despite what brochures say. However, nothing tops sitting on deck, enjoying a glass of wine, agreeable company and watching the sun set in a blaze of glory.

Trails and Treks

Turkey exceeds expectations when it comes to inspirational walking and hiking trails, ski runs that dare Olympic champions and life-in-the-saddle bridle paths for horse-riding enthusiasts. Taking to the trails and pistes is the ultimate cultural orientation for eco-tourists seeking active and rewarding fun.

Trekkers make their way through a canyon

Twenty years ago, only the most intrepid tourists ventured into Turkey's high mountains, followed ancient trading paths or experienced the heady air of the high plateaus (*yaylas*) where nomadic peoples still migrate seasonally with their animals. More recently, however, walking the pathways and trails and seeing remote hamlets has given outsiders an opportunity to experience timeless village traditions and understand a completely new dimension of Turkish culture. Previously inaccessible (or just unknown) antique sites have gained a new and vibrant audience from a more spirited, adventurous breed of tourist.

Trail riding has made a long-awaited debut and is now another way to understand local history, see lowlands and forest trails or experience Turkish ranch life. The first long-distance horse ride is breaking new ground as a cultural encounter and reviving the country's equestrian tradition.

Few would associate Turkey with skiing, despite its mountains, but far from the common perceptions of Turkey as an exclusively sun-and-sea destination, nine excellent, well-developed ski areas are putting this sport high on tourist agendas.

Much of the appeal of trekking, skiing or riding is in helping to preserve traditions and customs. Trail walking and highland trekking or climbing are part of a strong ecological tradition. A number of local guides speak English and can turn a walk into an amazing natural experience. Enquiring locally or seeking out a professional travel agency can make the difference between a routine stroll and a stimulating quest.

Long-Distance Hiking Trails

Turkey's three best-known long-distance treks are in different regions; each requiring a mixture of abilities but all are cultural conduits that have reshaped tourism in Turkey. **The Lycian Way Walk** (www.lycianway walk.com) was Turkey's first extended trek. It came into being after a competition sponsored by Garanti Bankası to find an environmentally friendly solution that would offer a new dimension to Turkish tourism.

The trek takes you 350km (217 miles) between Fethiye to Antalya over, around and through the Toros Mountain range. Amateurs get under way gently at Fethiye, but by the time they reach Antalya challenging terrain requires serious climbing equipment and a skilled guide. Kaş or Kalkan are good mid-point venues or base camps, and several travel companies, such as **Bougainville Turizm Ltd** (İbrahim Serin Caddesi 10, Kaş; tel: 0242-836 3737; www.bougain ville-turkey.com), arrange day trips on the Lycian Way or longer treks tailored to different abilities. Accommodation on treks other than day trips generally takes the form of camping under the stars in tents, although increasingly local lodgings are being arranged with shepherds in humble surroundings or stables.

The walk was a sporting and cultural first in Turkey because it was the first trek professionally waymarked and conforming to the benchmark French Grande Randonnée system. Many out-of-the-way villages and hamlets had never seen foreigners and suddenly found strangers with backpacks and clumpy boots, speaking funny languages on the threshold. But Turkish hospitality, not to mention curiosity, is a gracious leveller, and now hikers share simple meals en route and snuggle down in a local stable for the night. It is not high-level international diplomacy but the Lycian Way has encouraged a leap forward interculturally for both trekkers and Turkish village dwellers.

The sister trek, and Turkey's second long-distance trail, is the **St Paul's Trail** (www.stpaultrail.com), which actually follows ancient Roman roads much more than St Paul's footsteps.

The trail begins east of Antalya and encompasses Turkey's lovely Lake District to the north of and around Eğirdir. This is 500km (310 miles) of challenging walking from beginning to end but will appeal to seasoned hikers and walkers and requires the kind of specialist kit

The Lycian Way offers some challenging but fascinating terrain

that St Paul would have welcomed on his Christian pilgrimage. Unlike the Lycian Way, there is very little accommodation along the route, so camping is almost obligatory, and the trek involves three separate walks, not one continuous pathway. Trekking through dense forests of cedar, oak and juniper, the descent to the lowland Lake District introduces fertile fields, fruit trees and an amazing diversity of wildlife, migrating birds, and abundant flora, not forgetting classical ruins, like Selge.

Whilst all of the treks and trails are nature-oriented, the **Kaçkar** (www.kackarlar.org) walk is even more fundamentally rooted in the landscapes, culture and ecology that it passes through. The Black Sea region offers lush, deep valleys and mystical peaks for exploration that shelter hidden (and derelict) Armenian and Georgian churches and distinct ethnic groups for whom years of isolation have protected their traditions and cultural autonomy. There are castles to explore, and raging rapids, as well as the Black Sea's distinctive high-altitude architecture and colourful ethnic festivals.

Walking and trekking in this region is the ideal way to wind down, share wholesome local dishes and take part in weddings or festive occasions like Hıdrellez, the annual migration to seasonal pastures. The Kaçkar route snakes in and around the Hemşin Valley, Yusufeli,

The Kaçkar trail takes in stunning mountain and valley scenery

Gümüşhane and the powerful Çoruh River, manna for passionate whitewater rafters.

Bukla Travel Agency (İnebolu Sokak 55/6, Kabataş, Beyoğlu, İstanbul; tel: 0212-245 0635; www.bukla.com/pdfler/eng.pdf) is a leading travel firm highly specialised in eco-trekking, extreme nature and photo safaris in the Black Sea region and Eastern Turkey. They will tailor any trek (or climb) to requirements.

All the way along the three long-distance marked trails, trekkers can take guidance from the excellent maps and comprehensive books loaded with practical information pertaining to history, local customs, essential kit and cautionary advice. All routes have been meticulously researched, trekked and signposted, mostly by volunteers. They have been marked by GPS users and points are generally accurate to within 10m

Taking a rest in the mountains on the Kaçkar trail

(33ft). Good-quality maps, being a particular bugbear in Turkey, have all been designed and produced expressly for the Lycian, St Paul and Kaçkar routes and, cartographically, are the best of their species.

Trekking Tips and Advice

- It is not smart to trek or hike alone, especially in the Black Sea region where mists and fog can quickly disorient you. Try to trek in groups wherever possible.
- Safety on treks and trails is pretty good. But Turkey has its own highly skilled vounteer rapid response team specialising in search and rescue throughout Turkey, called AKUT; it is a member of INSARAG, an advisory group within the United Nations. AKUT Search and Rescue Organisation, Büyükdere Cad. 120, Esentepe, İstanbul; tel: 0212-217 0410; www.akut.org.tr

- Turkey has plenty of snakes and most are venomous. Wear long socks and don't go bare-legged when trekking.
- Ferocious shepherd dogs will often be seen; don't befriend them or come between a dog and its flock. Dogs are there to protect sheep and goats and may be rabid.
- Equine treks usually spell out what to bring and wear (always helmets) and will match your level of skill to a horse. Pay particular attention to insurance and take out your own policy, if necessary.
- For snow bunnies, a global site has up-to-the-minute forecasts on ski conditions (www.snow-forecast.com).

Middle Earth Travel (Göreme, Nevşehir; tel: 0384-271 2559; www.middleearthtravel.com; also at Haşim İşcan Mah., 1297 Sokak 14, Antalya; tel: 0242-243 1148) runs eight- to 15-day trekking tours for all of Turkey's waymarked trails. They are the undisputed local experts in this and will also arrange extreme climbing expeditions to the extinct volcano at **Mount Ararat** in eastern Turkey. The summit is over 5,000m (16,400ft) and crampons, ice picks and ropes are required. Only skilled mountaineers need apply. Permission to climb the mountain is a frustrating exercise that can take two or three months and involves considerable bureaucratic delays.

Short Walks

Independent hikers and free-wheeling nature lovers will love the forest walks and picnic areas found at Kızılcahamam in **Soğuksu National Park** (tel: 0312-736 1115) north of Ankara. There are resorts and healing therapeutic hot springs in the area.

There is also no reason not to join local walking groups, usually comprised of expats spontaneously off for a day's trekking. They'll generally speak English and will regale you with local lore.

For personalised culture and ecotours anywhere in Turkey, **Mr. Özkan Yaşar** (email: ozkankas@hotmail.com) is recommended as a wonderfully knowledgeable and qualified English-speaking guide, with reasonable charges for the professional service he provides.

Horseback Trekking

Turkey's long-distance equestrian trek is known as the **Great Anatolian Ride** (www.thelongridersguild.com). For horse-riding enthusiasts, it is fun, challenging and maintains a cultural, sustainable tourism focus. The beautiful and brave mares used for the treks are Turkish-bred at a farm in Cappadocia and most are an Arabian-Anatolian cross breed; you will see some fine specimens at **Akhal – Teke Horse Riding Center** (Avanos, Cappadocia; tel: 0384-511 5171; www.akhal-tekehorsecenter.com). In antiquity, Cappadocia was known as the 'land of beautiful horses.'

The **Great Anatolian Ride** commemorates a 16th-century prototype

A beautiful Cappadocia horse and its owner

travel writer, Evliya Çelibi, who rambled all over Turkey on horseback and recorded his travels in a colourful and waggish style. Unesco has in fact designated 2011 as the year of Evliya Çelibi. The Ride was started by Turkish and English academics in 2009 to retrace faithfully the route followed by the prominent Ottoman traveller; competent riders who want to be part of establishing cultural routes in Anatolia are welcomed to take part in a trek. Turkey looks entirely different from between the ears of a horse and participants are endorsing sustainable tourism.

The route is about 1,300km (800 miles) long and begins in Sakarya, to skirt İstanbul's notorious traffic. It heads towards Bursa and then follows a circuitous route ending up in Kütahya, Çelibi's home town. The ride invites horse-minded participants to saddle up for one of the three separate treks between September and November, when the weather is temperate for horse and rider.

In 2011, a guidebook detailing two of the routes will be published by Upcountry (Turkey) and can be purchased from www.trekkinginturkey. com. The trails are also suitable for cyclists and keen walkers. Accommodation for the trek is basic camping and living in tents at close quarters with equines.

In 2011, the **Turkey-Syria Friendship Ride** will celebrate the reopening of Ottoman borders and promises cosmopolitan participation and the thunder of hooves in remote regions.

For those who would like to get close to Turkish equine culture

Riding in Cappadocia

Trails and Treks

but be based in one place, a week or more at one of Turkey's horse ranches is a rugged, but congenial, option. Two outstanding ones can be found near Kemer, about 25km (17 miles) from Antalya. **Bagana Ranch** (Yukarıkaraman Köyü, Düzlerçami, Kemer; tel: 0242-425 2270; email: bagana@antnet.net.tr) and **Hotel Berke Ranch** (Akcasaz Mevkii, P.K. 186, Kuzdere Köyü, Çamyuva, Kemer; tel: 0242-818 0333; www.hotel-berke ranch.com) have excellent reputations, gorgeous horses (Berke Ranch has mostly spirited Arabians) and a professional manège where there is jumping and dressage for serious horsemen and women.

Visitors come to muck in (or out); enjoy the home-on-the-range atmosphere, and explore lesser-known parts of Turkey on horseback. Hearty meals are based on the fresh and nutritious

Mediterranean diet. Trekking on a daily basis takes in the lovely lowland trails amidst orange and lemon groves or an extended gallop on the coastal sands.

Skiing

So few people associate Turkey with snow or even cold weather that the well-developed ski scene at first appears unlikely. But skiing is popular, with many areas receiving guaranteed snow dumps for five or six months of the year, while some pistes are for professionals only. Turks themselves love to ski and whole families head for the slopes. In spite of this, no areas are overcrowded at tows or chair-lifts.

In total, Turkey has nine ski areas for downhill or cross-country skiers. Without question, the most spectacular region is **Palandöken**, in the coldest, highest and most easterly part of Turkey. The peaks reach 3,000m (9,840ft) and thick snow is a given from October until May. There are over 40km (25 miles) of powder snow runs, spectacular Alpine terrain and excellent hotels mid-mountain, like the **Dedeman** (Dedeman Palandöken Ski Resort, PK, PO Box, 115, Erzurum, Turkey; tel: 0442-316 2414, call centre: 0444-4336; email: palandoken@dedeman. com; 🔟). This means stepping out the door and onto the slopes – ski-in-ski-out style.

Chair-lifts and T-bars are plentiful and qualified instructors man the ski school. Nearby shops sell and rent ski equipment and accessories. Downhill, cross-country and heli-skiing make the winter scene exhilarating. Palandöken has Turkey's most challenging runs and professionals will revel in the **Ejder Trail**.

A disadvantage to Palandöken is the 1,000km (621-mile) distance from İstanbul that makes flying from there to Erzurum the most economical option. However, it is only a

The best ski conditions can be found at the Palandöken resort

Parascending at Erciyes

short taxi ride (10km/6 miles) from Erzurum to the resort area.

Near **Kayseri** in Cappadocia, an extinct volcano has endowed the region with great ski runs. The **Erciyes Ski Centre** (Erciyes Dağı, Kayseri; tel: 0352-342 2050; www.erciyes-zumrut.com) has snow coverage averaging 170cm (67ins) for about four months of the year. There is mountaineering and climbing on other faces of the mountain and accommodation is nearby or in Kayseri city centre. This is the place to experience the thrill of night-skiing with the pistes all illuminated.

Kiteboarding is also a popular sport here. Four ski lifts, chairs and T-bars access the highest central Anatolian peak (3,900m/12,800ft). Kayseri is a pious city and alcohol is not readily found, but the on-piste hotels have the expected bucolic après-ski agendas.

Skiing at **Saklıkent**, just 45km (27 miles) from Antalya, lets you ski in the morning and descend for a dip in the Mediterranean in the afternoon. A good place to investigate is the **Saklıkent Ski Centre** (Doyran Köyü, Saklıkent Mevkii, Antalya; tel: 0242-446 1138; www.saklikent.com.tr;). The nursery slopes are ideal for beginners and the **Şömine Restaurant** in the ski centre serves warming mulled wine around the fire.

Davraz is another great ski resort, just 25km (15 miles) from Isparta, but with a short season. It accommodates all levels of skiers and has a baby lift. (Ski Centre: tel: 0246-267 2020).

The most convenient and comprehensive ski area for İstanbul is **Uludağ**, near Bursa (www.learningski. com/en/uluda.html). There are 22 lifts and this rates as the best equipped and organised for all abilities of all the Turkish ski resorts.

Trails Calendar – When to Go

Lycian Way: Fethiye to mid-point Kaş, most months of the year but the most pleasant time is Mar–June or Sept–Nov

St Paul's Way: any season but a high level of fitness and hiking and climbing skills are required

Kaçkar: May–Sept

Great Anatolian ride: Sept–Nov only

Horse-riding centres and ranches: Mediterranean ranches can accommodate visitors almost 12 months of the year. In Cappadocia, winter is harsh and riding is best enjoyed May–Oct.

Forest Trails: May–Oct

Skiing: generally Nov–Mar but varies considerably with the altitude of the resort and snow thickness

Bazaars and Shopping

From chic boutiques to Ottoman-era labyrinthine bazaars, most visitors get sucked into the irresistible Turkish shopping experience. Even if you had no intention of buying, the charming salesmen will doubtless lure you in, and attempting to get the best bargains for carpets, coriander or a coffeepot is half the fun.

With its historic link to the Silk Road, Turkey has been a nation of bartering and trading for centuries. Traditional covered bazaars in historic cities like İstanbul, Bursa and Antakya have hardly altered: domed-roofed stone alleys centred around several *bedestens* (domed warehouses), with traders grouped in specific areas and a good-natured babble of business ringing through the air.

Even with the huge growth in tourism, and therefore consumerism adapting to their needs, the traditional ambience remains. Market areas are usually comprised of a covered bazaar, several *hans*, a hamam and mosque – an entire centre of commerce and living. Many places have their specialist products, like Bursa's beloved silks in Koza Han, built in 1491 by Beyazit II, Kayseri's carpets in the 18th-century Vezirhani, and Antakya's rambling streets leading to its metal workshops and plethora of *künefe* (pudding) shops. İstanbul is actually an exception – it sells everything.

In markets such as these, the better bargains are often found in the surrounding streets, taking advantage of lower rents yet governed by the same strict set of regulations by the local *belediye* (council). İstanbul's Egyptian, or Spice, Market (Mısır Çarşısı) is a fantastic example, where outside its L-shaped walls and souvenir stalls, the outside streets retain more of the traditional essence, with plant seeds, medicinal remedies (leeches!) and luscious dried fruits.

Intricate metalware for sale at the Grand Bazaar

Finding Your Perfect Carpet

Turks – or more precisely the Turkic nomads from Central Asia – claim to be the creators of the original *hali* (woven carpet); the *kilim* (flat-weave rug) arrived even earlier, brought by nomads settling in Anatolia who used thickly woven goat's hair to make tents, from around 8,000 years ago. Marco Polo adored them when he crossed Anatolia in the 13th century, and they have lost little of their charm today. Turkish carpets can be the most beautiful and intricate in the world, such as the silk Hareke ones, or a woven village *kilim* in bold designs, sold for a fraction of the price of a carpet, and still a memorable souvenir.

If you've made the decision to buy, there are practical ways to ensure that your carpet is a genuine silk/wool/antique and uses natural dyes. You might research to the hilt so that you'll snap up the best bargain, or inspect the warp and weave on the back of the

A carpet seller in Milas

Most towns have daily street markets, where food and household goods pile high on outdoor stalls. In smaller towns and villages, all the locals stock up their larders at the weekly farmers' market, where neighbouring traders bring their local seasonal produce to sell on makeshift stalls, or perhaps laying it on the ground. These are the places to search for locally produced village cheeses and honey, as well as mouth-watering fresh fruit and vegetables – the Friday market in coastal Kaş is a perfect example.

In tourist towns, especially on the coast, produce is unsurprisingly geared to the foreign visitor. Local handicrafts sit among suncreams, jewellery and souvenirs, and prices are usually higher.

39

Bazaars and Shopping

Buying Antiques?

Before you start looking out for your favourite carpet or Ottoman silverware, it's important to note that it is forbidden to export antiquities more than a century old. If a carpet is genuinely (or looks) old, the dealer should make out a certificate authenticating its age and, therefore, it is OK to take home. If an item 'looks old', it is worth having that certificate to hand when going through customs to leave Turkey. If a dealer is pushing a valuable antique, don't buy it, as it's either illegal to buy, or a fake! There are also, of course, moral issues in taking genuinely old and valuable items out of the country.

carpet to check out its density of knots. The reality is that you're unlikely to get an unbeatable deal these days – many of the best deals are actually to be found in London or New York.

However, the beauty of shopping for a carpet while on your holiday in Turkey is due to the huge array of styles, colours and price ranges, and its cachet as a cultural experience – especially in İstanbul as the range is the best. All the stories you have heard are pretty much true: most carpet salesmen are charmers, smooth talkers, persuasive and make you feel that they are giving it away at cost price. It's all part of the bargaining procedure that you'll remember every time you step on that woven floor covering.

So where do you start? First off, it might be best to avoid the young guy who loiters outside tourist areas to drag you to his 'cousin's' shop. He'll be on a high commission which gets built into the price (it's not advisable to take a guide or anyone from your hotel to buy for the same reason).

Secondly, if there are choices, shop around (easy in a place like the Grand Bazaar) or start out at a fixed-price store, like **Adnan & Hasan** (Halicilar Caddesi 89–92, Grand Bazaar, İstanbul; tel: 0212-527 9887) or **Dosim Aya-sofya Ciftehamam** (2/4 Bab-i Hum-ayun Caddesi, İstanbul) to get an idea of what your money can buy. Some stores are run by foreign residents who know that visitors don't always like the hard sell; a great example is **Tribal Collections** (24C Muze Yolu, Göreme).

Otherwise, feast your eyes on dozens being unfurled while you are proffered glasses of tea, and you'll get an idea of styles, colours and prices. (Don't start

Don't be surprised to be offered tea while shopping

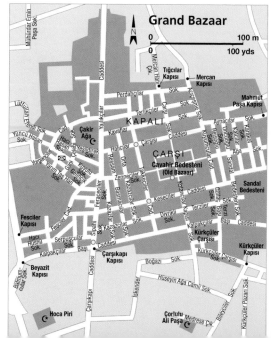

bargaining unless it's something that you're interested in; *see p.44*. Traditionally, different regions of the country meant different styles and patterns; in practice, major trading centres like İstanbul mean that every style is available as their dealers travel countrywide and, in some cases, source cheaper items made in China and India.

You'll soon get a feel of different fabrics, like 100 percent wool, or a mix with cotton or silk. Patterns vary wildly, from bold geometric designs in reds and yellow, to the 'prayer design' indicating the direction of Mecca, and the tree of life motif. A lovely variation of *kilims* is a *sumac*, with an overlay of additional figurative stitching, a specialist design from the areas around the borders of Iran and Iraq.

The Grandest Bazaar

A highlight for most visitors to İstanbul, the interconnecting mazes

Inside the maze-like Grand Bazaar

of **Grand Bazaar** (**Kapali Çarsi**) have been a thriving centre of trade for over five centuries, ever since Mehmet II began to design his new city shortly after the 1453 Ottoman conquest of Constantinople.

Bazaars and Shopping

Turkey's Top Markets and Bazaars

Gaziantep: Just below the impressive Citadel, *usta* (craftsmen) produce hand-beaten copperware, saddles and leather shoes. Fresh produce includes its famous pistachios.

Grand Bazaar, İstanbul: The mother of all markets: thousands of stalls sell leather, ceramics, gold and carpets, plus cheap jeans and T-shirts on its surrounding lanes. Mosques, cafés and a police station make it a living market.

Egyptian (Spice) Market, İstanbul: Piles of cardamom, green peppercorns, henna and tea, plus sun-dried tomatoes, crumbly cheese and lashings of *lokum*. In recent years souvenirs and gold have

become more common. Surrounding lanes sell pots, pans and wooden utensils, plus birds and leeches for medicinal purposes.

Kaş Farmers' Market: The archetypal village weekly market, with farmers travelling from surrounding villages to sell their produce. Everything is fresh, seasonal and, by default, usually organic, including fruits, cheese, honey and vegetables. A multicultural ambience.

Antakya: Near the Syrian border and with an Arabic flavour (of its language and cuisine) this old city market has fresh produce like cheeses and *künefe*, a syrupy sweet made from fine vermicelli.

Markets have always played a crucial role in the formation of cities, and this was a significant example. Its location was vital, formed as a strategic triangle with Topkapi Palace *(see p.69)* to house the sultans, Fatih Mosque as an education and community centre, and the bazaar as a centre of industry and trade – with profits contributed towards the mosque's upkeep. Originally known as the Central Fabric Market, this grew organically over the decades. First opening its doors to traders in 1461, its alleyways were filled with fabrics, weaponry, quilt-makers and fez makers, fountain-filled courtyards, two warehouses *(bedestens)* and stables for travelling salesmen. On the site were also mosques and a hamam, and manufacturing centres filled with workshops where raw materials were transformed into the finished item. Its 65 streets were later covered and vaulted, with small windows on the sides of the roofs for natural light to illuminate the lanes.

Typical of markets in Asia and the Middle East, each street was devoted to one particular trade, and named to reflect that. As eastern practice dictated, no ornaments, signs or adverts promoted any shop or craftsman, representing a noble, unambitious attitude; for an individual to sing his own praises or to signpost shoppers to his own goods was seen as shameful and degrading. Rather than being lured in by sweet-talking and savvy sales chat, people would join the owner who sat on the bench outside his shop, and carry out business leisurely.

How times have changed! Fluorescent lights now attract the passing shopper into a store; signs glare over doorways and a multilingual sales pitch rings out to lure in the foreign tourists. The produce has adapted over time: Gone are the fez-makers, but there are still specific areas for gold, antiques, carpets, ceramics and leather. Sunlight still streams through the windows, but cafés serving lattes and paninis now cluster around the old *Bedesten*, perfect to rest weary feet. The gold dealers still do a roaring trade, as do the sellers of souvenir fez and T-shirts emblazoned with 'I ♥ İstanbul.' And while cash is still king, most stores take credit cards. Housing around 4,000 shops, an infirmary, banks and post office, the bazaar is still a fabulous magnet for thousands of shoppers daily, and for good reason it's a highlight of any visit to Turkey.

Fabrics piled up in the Grand Bazaar

The curvaceously designed Kanyon mall

More than Markets

The flip side of Ottoman-era winding lanes and outdoor fruit markets is Turkey's growing love for malls. These air-conditioned temples of consumerism house an upscale selection of top designers and often (especially in İstanbul), a large proportion of international brands. While most visitors prefer a more traditional experience, this is where middle-class Turks flock at weekends, ending their day out with a film at the in-house multiplex or dinner at stylish restaurants.

In İstanbul, look out for the superbly designed **Kanyon** (Buyukdere Caddesi 185, Levant; tel: 0212-353 5300; www.kanyon.com.tr), with sweeping curves and sheltered walkways housing the likes of Harvey Nichols and Samsonite; an admirable piece of contemporary architecture as well as a top shopping experience. **Cevahir** (Buyukdere Caddesi 22, Sisli; tel: 0212-368 6900; www.istanbulcevahir.com) is one of Europe's largest, with an astonishing 343 shops over ten floors. İstanbul alone has over 40 malls with new ones springing up every year, with an unquenchable local thirst for smart shopping. Not

Key Phrases for Shoppers		
English	Turkish	Pronunciation
Have you got...?	... var mı?	... var muh?
I don't have ...	... yok	... yok
I would like...	... istiyorum	... istiyorum
How much does it cost?	O ne kadar?	O ne kadar?
Is this your best price?	Son fiyatınız bu mu?	Son fiyatuhnuhz bumu?
Very expensive!	Çok pahalı!	Chok pahaluh!
I'll give you...	... vereceğim	... verejeyim
I'm just looking	Sadece bakıyorum	sadeje bakuhyorum
That's my final offer	Bu benim son teklifim	Bu benim son teklifim
Can you wrap it please?	Lütfen paket eder misiniz?	Lütfen paket eder misiniz?
Can I have a receipt please?	Fatura alabilir miyim?	Fatura alabilir miyim?
Have you got a smaller/ larger size?	Daha küçüğü/ büyüğü var mı?	Daha kuchu-u/ buyu-u var mu?
Where are the changing rooms?	Soyunma odaları nerede?	Soyunma odalaruh nerede?

to be outdone, Ankara's **CEPA** mall is the largest in the capital. Locals and visitors flock to the huge **Migros** mall in Antalya (Meltem Mahalessi, 100 Yil Bulvari 155; tel: 0242-230 1110; www. antalyamigros.com), marking a new hub of the city's upmarket shops.

Savvy high-street styles and home-grown stores cluster in towns and cities. Turkey is a hub of cheap fashion production – exporting designer labels in addition to its home-grown brands. Most cities have outlets of **Mavi** (www.mavi.com), loved by teenagers for its wide array of casual urbanwear, jeans and jackets. **Collezione** (www. collezione.com.tr) has plenty of outlets with casual streetwear, jackets and T-shirts. Also found from Adana to Zonguldak, **Koton** (www.koton.com. tr) has fresh, sharp, cotton-based clothing for men and women, and **Beymen** (www.beymen.com.tr) has its own-label stylish clothing, mainly for men.

Beta (www.betashoes.com.tr) fulfils Turkey's love for home-designed shoes with chunky, quirky styles for men and women, and the renowned leather **Desa** (www.desa.com.tr), hailed for its superbly designed leather bags and accessories, has over 70 stores Turkey-wide (plus in the UK and Saudi Arabia).

The Art of Haggling

Although haggling really is half the fun of making a purchase, you'll find it hard to get the better of the salesmen working the market. Turks have been trading since before Ottoman times and are razor sharp, charming and persuasive, so it helps to hone your haggling skills.

Some of the best Turkish purchases can be found at the Grand Bazaar

You might find it easy to bypass the sweet-talking salesman trying to force a piece of kitsch tourist tat onto you – the fez hats, Blue Mosque in the snowstorm or miniature camels may not be your scene. But if you're keen and your potential purchase is a major one – such as a carpet or a fine piece of ceramic – it does pay to shop around and, if possible, try to get an idea of average prices from fixed-price stores.

The key is to decide in your head what is a reasonable price, and then counter-offer whatever the seller is asking (try halving his original price). Take your time. It's likely that he proffers glasses of tea to ease the bargaining process, but even if after drinking you don't come to an agreement, don't feel obliged to buy. It's likely that he makes an offer, you come back with your price, and eventually you agree to meet somewhere in the middle.

Don't start talking money unless you're sure you want to buy – it's bad form to agree on a price only for you to change your mind. If in the end you politely decline and leave, be prepared for the persistent salesman to holler (or chase) after you with a better offer.

Top Turkish Treats and Where to Buy Them

- **Silks and cotton towels: Bursa, Harbiye**
  Bursa is Turkey's prime silk-producing region. Koza Hani ('Silk Cocoon Hall'), once the final stop on the Silk Route, is filled with silks and brocade merchants, plus pure cotton towels and bathrobes.
- **Karagöz shadow puppets: Bursa**
  These flat figures are made from leather and used in shadow puppet theatre. Stalls at Bursa market sell them in characters of humans and animals.
- **Traditional musical instruments: İstanbul (Galip Dede Sokak)**
  The continuation of Istiklal Caddesi is filled with tiny music shops for new and second-hand accordions, *davul* (drums) and *baglama* (stringed instruments).
- **Carved alabaster: İstanbul, Avanos**
  This pale, translucent stone is carved into chess sets, ashtrays and vases, available in İstanbul's Grand Bazaar but originates from Avanos.
- **Antiques (esp.20th-century): İstanbul**
  The best city for 20th-century pieces *(see warning, p.39)*; old European households cleared out their belongings which ended up at Çukurcuma's antique shops. Try Hor Hor Bit Pazari (Aksaray) for 200 tiny stores with Ottoman and French furnishings.
- **Carved meerschaum** *(lületasi)*: **Eskisehir, İstanbul (Grand Bazaar)**
  Soft white stone mined near Eskişehir carved into jewellery and tobacco pipes. Available widely at the Grand Bazaar.

- **Leather and suede: İstanbul (Grand Bazaar)**
  Inside the Grand Bazaar and surrounding streets are the best choices of clothing and accessories, often handmade. They vary greatly in quality so take a close look!
- **Filigree wire silver** *(telkari)*: **Mardin, Diyarbakir, Trabzon**
  Specific style of handmade silver jewellery in delicate styles, using thin wires, woven into shape.
- **Copperware: Eastern Anatolia**
  Rare, antique copperware from the early 20th century is expensive; modern examples are cheaper and still attractive.
- **Inlaid wooden backgammon sets** *(tavla)*: **İstanbul**
  Master the game, then buy a wooden board, either plain or inlaid with mother-of-pearl mosaic (streets surrounding Misir Çarşisi or Grand Bazaar).
- ***Nazar bonjuk* (evil eye beads): throughout Turkey**
  These traditional deep blue 'eyes' ward off evil spirits. In the form of key rings, fridge magnets, jewellery or purely decorative from hand-blown glass.
- **Ceramics: Kütahya, Çanakkale**
  Traditional centre of the ceramics trade. Master potters have been hand-painting Kütahya tiles and bowls, some with the famous tulip motif, since the 16th century. There are also delicate ceramic bowls in İstanbul's Grand Bazaar.

Hamams and Spas

A Turkish bath, or hamam, is an essential ingredient of local culture. The routine involves cleansing, scrubbing with copious bubbles, as much steam as you can stand, then a stiff massage and, finally, cooling off. Pumicing and waxing are fabulous accompaniments. The squeaky-clean afterglow puts this at the top of any Turkish break agenda.

Hamams, effectively saunas with water, are a direct descendant of the boisterous Roman bath, although the orgiastic rowdiness that characterised the Roman experience was somewhat more introverted in the Ottoman era, with an onus on personal hygiene and clean water characterising Islamic bathing routines. The Ottomans were exceedingly superstitious: going to a hamam supposedly brought good luck and it was thought that *djinns* (evil genies) lurked in dank corners. Hamams were originally built as annexes to mosques but later became separate social institutions.

An Ottoman hamam was clandestine in nature and latent sexuality was an integral part of the culture throughout Ottoman times. Despite the segregation of men and women in society, taboos melted away inside the steamy hamam and it is still easy to imagine the hottest gossip ebbing around hamam subcultures. Until the advent of home plumbing and private bathrooms, a visit to the baths was a communal activity that could last for hours, as entire families would spend the day bathing, talking, eating and even dancing.

If communal bathing is not your scene, most mid-priced and upmarket hotels all over Turkey offer spa treatments, massages and Turkish baths in more clincial surroundings. It won't make a difference to the feeling of being revitalised and pampered to perfection. Most hotels open spas and hamams to non-guests, but a treatment or massage may be included in the daily rate if you are a guest. Expect a spa treatment anywhere to start at around 75TL, rising depending on

Chatting in the baths at Bursa

what additional treatments you add to the basic scrub. The scrub-massage routine is especially energising.

Besides traditional hamams and the more luxurious hotels that incorporate spas and Turkish baths, Turkey also has about 1,500 natural hot springs, thanks to a position on tectonic fault lines. The scalding, mineral-laden waters bubble up from the depths of the earth. They soothed Romans, were noted by ancient travellers and nurtured Turkey's founder, Atatürk. Turks went to hamams to get clean but they frequented spas and hot springs for remedial hydrotherapy. All the natural springs contain minerals like calcium, magnesium and potassium that are ingested through the skin by soaking and drinking the waters. Realising the potential of the country's many healing spas is in its infancy. A comprehensive book, *Spas and Hot Springs of Turkey* is available from Boyut Publishing Group in İstanbul.

Only a few notable hotels are endowed with geothermal waters and most Turkish baths use city, or tap, water. Some, but not many, hamams boast thermal waters. Many thermal resorts are clustered near Pamukkale. For a healing mineral spa, you go to a spring, or *kaplıca*. Almost all spas will incorporate the hamam ritual.

Turkish Baths

İstanbul has about 100 hamams still in use, but the two most historic ones, that make the bath experience positively regal, are the 16th-century **Çemberlitaş Baths** (Vezirhanı Caddesi 8, Çemberlitaş, İstanbul; tel: 0212-522 7974; www.cemberlitashamami.com.

In the renowned Çağaloğlu Baths

tr), with its amazing marble architecture, and the even more sumptuous one, **Çağaloğlu Baths** (Çağaloğlu, İstanbul; tel: 0212-522 2424; www.cagalogluhamami.com.tr), built in the 18th century. Much of the former's fame derived from its high-profile builder, the imperial architect, Mimar Sinan.

Hamam Lingo	
camekan	vestibule or entrance hall
göbek taşı	hexagonal marble plinth for massages
sıcaklık	caldarium or steam room
soğukluk	cool room
peştemal	personal wrap of silk or linen
nalın	wooden clogs, often with mother-of-pearl inlay
havlu	towel
sabun	soap

A traditional massage and lathering in a Bursa hamam; the city is known for its spas

Both hamams welcome tourists and are a grand place for novices to take the plunge. Basic cleansing and steaming aside, there are numerous other treatments on offer. Indulge in as many as you can afford to fully appreciate the experience of the bath.

Outside İstanbul, the **Bodrum Hamam** (Cevak Şakir Sokak, Fabrika Sokak, Bodrum; tel: 0252-313 4129; www.bodrumhamami.com.tr) is authentic and professional and will pick you up and deliver you to your hotel or pension. It is related to the Çemberlitaş Hamam in İstanbul.

Built with tourists in mind at Kemer, near Antalya, is a brilliant modern bath complex, **Ottoman Turkish Bath and Spa Centre** (Yeni Mahalle, Kemer II entrance, next to Shell Petrol Station, Kemer, Antalya; tel: 0242-814 5858; www.ottomanhamam.net), which stirs all of the senses with spas, Turkish baths and a sauna as well as some clever beauty treatments.

Bursa is a dignified spa city with numerous thermal sources that feed 15th- and 16th-century spas. **Yeni and Eski Kaplıca** (Old and New Spa; Yeni Kaplıca-Karamustafa and Kaynarca Thermal Hotel and Baths, Kükürtlü Mahallesi, Yenikaplıca Caddesi 6, Osmangazi, Bursa; tel: 0224-236 6968) are impressivly Ottoman. Alternatively, **Çakir Ağa Hamam** (Atatürk Caddesi 101, Osmangazi, Bursa; tel: 0224-221 2580) in the city centre is friendly and relaxed and also benefits from the hot thermal waters.

At Yalova, north of Bursa in the idyllic mountain village, of Termal is **Yalova Thermal Hot Springs** (Yalova Termal, Termal, Yalova; tel: 0226-675 7400; www.yalovatermal.com), a calming nature retreat built around gushing waters and steamy mineral baths.

- Enter the hamam via the *camekan* (vestibule), taking your personal wrap, or *peştemel*, and the slippers (*terlik*) or wooden clogs (*nalın*) that you have been given.
- Sweat it out in the hot room for as long as you can endure.
- Go for the ritual scrub and exfoliating rub down between steams.
- Opt for a full body massage on a marble podium. It may feel like being Exhibit A but is worth it for the blissful aftermath.

- Wind down gently in the adjoining cool room.
- Enjoy a Turkish tea or herbal tea back at the *camekan*.
- Towels and soap are provided but bring your own if you prefer.
- None of this is exactly merciful. Dirt and toxins are stubborn customers that respond to pummelling. Masseurs can be overenthusiastic.
- Don't pennypinch on this extraordinary experience. Splurge if you can.

Therapies are invigorating and the complex is like a health village, Turkish style. As a foreigner, you will be cosseted and indulged.

Hotel Spas

If the bathhouse seems too boisterous or public, upscale hotels all have spas fit for royalty and offer a full range of scrubs, massages, facials and beauty treatments. It is not usually necessary to be an hotel guest. In İstanbul, the **Laveda Spa** at the **Ritz Carlton Hotel** (Süzer Plaza, Elmadağ, Şişli, İstanbul; tel: 0212-334 4444; www.ritzcarlton. com) is a hallmark of sophisticated luxury. Take tea with the urban upper crust in the salon afterwards.

Les Ottomans Hôtel (Muallim Naci Caddesi 168, Kuruçeşme, İstanbul; tel: 0212-359 1500; www.lesottomans.com) and the **Çırağan Palace Kempinski** (Çırağan Caddesi, Beşiktaş, İstanbul; tel: 0212-326 4646; www.ciragan-pal ace.com) both have spas in exquisitely refurbished Bosphorus mansions and prove that there is nothing quite like luxuriating in Ottoman opulence.

Hot Thermal Springs

The limestone cascades at Pamukkale are one of the poster images of Turkish tourism. The majestic travertine and descending pools calcified over 14,000 years and the water temperature is a healthy 37°C (98.6°F). To preserve their beauty, visitors are not allowed to bathe in what is a

The atmospheric spa at Les Ottomans Hôtel

spectacular natural geothermal spa centre, but to experience the healing waters, stay nearby at the thermal village of Karahayıt. **Pam Thermal Hotel** (Beytur Turizm İşletmeleri A.Ş., Karahayıt, Pamukkale, tel: 0258-271 4140; www.pamthermal.com) is a good choice. Pamukkale became a Unesco World Heritage Site in 1988.

Turkey's geology has the country practically floating on geothermal hot springs. Hotels and treatment centres for almost every chronic disease have sprung up around these and welcome tourists. Natural spa waters have been 'on tap' for centuries and going for a hypothermal bathing 'cure' for arthritis or rheumatism has always been part of Turkish culture.

Near İzmir, the **Sheraton Çeşme Hotel, Resort and Spa** (Şifne Caddesi 35, Ilıca, Çeşme, İzmir; tel: 0232-723 1240; www.sheratoncesme.com) sits on its own thermal source at Ilıca. Waters are top-heavy with minerals; soaking in them can make you feel more like a god than a mortal. The panorama is breathtaking, with views of İzmir Bay from the rooms.

The **Balçova Thermal Hotel** (Vali Hüseyin Öğütcen Caddesi 2, Balçova, İzmir; tel: 0232-259 0102; www.balcovatermal.com), also known as Agamemnon's Spring, has heavily sulphuric natural waters at 70°C (158°F) that relieve rheumatic and joint diseases. Even if you are healthy, mud treatments, wraps and remedial therapies are a treat.

Specialising in mostly visiting foreigners with chronic health problems, **Natur-Med Thermal Springs and Health Resort** (Davutlar, Kuşadası; tel: 0256-657 2280; www.naturmed.biz) is close to İzmir with

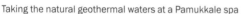

Taking the natural geothermal waters at a Pamukkale spa

The quality of the hamam can often be seen in the smoothness of the *göbek taşi*

a well-qualified German doctor, and emphasises a clinical, disciplined regime for patients. But downtime is for fun and enjoying tasty and nutritious Turkish fare.

The most remarkable thermal spa in Turkey is about 75km (46 miles) from Sivas in Kangal and is a prominent psoriasis healing centre. **Kangal Fish Springs** (Psoriasis Healing Centre; Kangal, Sivas; tel: 0346-469 1151; www.balikli.org) offers 21-day treatments involving extended soaking in the hot waters and pools while fish nibble away excess skin. There is a wholesome, fresh-cooked dietary regime and patients must also drink copious quantities of the mineral waters. They have recently upgraded

to accommodate about 1,200 people, including those who stay here because they just want a retreat in a less familiar area of Turkey.

In the Black Sea region, thermal waters rise in the mountains above Rize at Ayder. These are rehabilitating waters and many pensions with altitude and charm are in the vicinity. A good resource for finding a place to stay is **Ayder Turizm A.Ş.** (tel: 0464-657 2102).

For those seeking a souvenir of their hamam or spa experience that lasts beyond the effects of a soaking or massage session, you can find attractive soaps, towels, and spa and hamam accessories in İstanbul's Grand Bazaar from **Derviş** (Kesiciler Caddesi 33-35, Kapalıçarşı (Covered Bazaar), İstanbul, tel: 0212-514 4525; www.dervis.com).

Did You Know?

- The sign of a high quality-hamam is the *göbek taşı*, or marble massaging stone. The smoother and shinier, the more superior the hamam.
- A cockroach is known in Turkish as a *hamam böceği*, or a hamam beetle.
- İstanbul had over 4,000 hamams in the 16th century. Today, just around 100 survive.
- The high platform sandals worn in a hamam keep feet dry but their real function was to make sure that no *djinns* (evil genies) came into contact with the wearer.
- Hamams provided the ultimate environment for women to scrutinise the in-the-buff suitability of a prospective bride for their sons.

Culinary Experiences

Turkey is a nation that takes its food seriously. And why not? As well as cultivating everything from plump pomegranates to the sweetest tomatoes, its cuisine is simple: use the freshness of ingredients to speak for themselves without disguise, a philosophy utilised for every dish from a street snack to a feast fit for a sultan.

Turks will proudly tell you that their cuisine is one of the best three in the world (together with French and Chinese). To be more accurate, it is Ottoman cuisine that made such a lasting legacy, drawing influences from all corners of the Empire during its rule for almost five centuries, from the Balkans to southern Russia and North Africa, plus the Persians' huge influence. No wonder Ottoman cuisine was considered a hybrid of the very best in the surrounding region.

From their opulent headquarters in İstanbul's Topkapi Palace *(see p.69)*, and as instigated by Mehmet the Conqueror, hundreds of great chefs in huge kitchens created the most sumptuous dishes in the land, using the best ingredients like fresh pomegranates, dried fruits, plump grapes and nuts.

Ingredients had, and still do have, a huge part to play: the Spice Route ran through the Empire, in full control of the Sultans, where only the finest ingredients were permitted to pass. Today, Turkey remains a massive land with abundant climates and so cultivates a huge amount and variety of fresh fruit, vegetables, fish and fowl.

Modern-day Turkey might not have the luxury of culinary grandeur of dishes like cabbage stuffed with chestnuts or casserole of lamb with dried apricots, honey and almonds, but today's Turks (and probably you) adore the ripeness of fruit and flavour of vegetables, relying on the taste of the ingredients alone, use of subtle spices and herbs, and the finest olive oil.

While home cooking is still king, it's inevitable that fast-food culture is making inroads into the cities. But the good news is that chains like **Simit Sarayı** and **Simit Dunyası** (using the good old Turkish *simit* as its base) are more widespread than a certain 'Golden Arches'.

Strings of dried vegetables, used in cooking

Regional Specialities

With such a vast nation, from coast-line to harsh plains, mountains and lush forests, it's not surprising that each region of Turkey has its own specialist dishes and flavours *(see also Kebaps, p.54)*.

Surrounded by four seas, Turkey is a piscatorial paradise. Along the Aegean, octopus and calamari make popular *meze*, and İstanbul winters see oily fish like mackerel and blue-fish, best sampled simply grilled. The Black Sea region makes good use of its anchovies with the hearty rice dish *hamsi pilavi*, *mihlama* corn bread and custard-filled pastry *laz boreği*. Olive trees grow in abundance in Western Turkey, so dishes like *zeytinyağlı* (veg-etables cooked and served cold in olive oil) grace most tables. Travelling further southeast towards the Syria

Turkey is a great place to eat fresh fish

and Iraq borders, things hot up and visitors to Sanliurfa and Adana will have their fill of spicy Adana kebaps, and the adventurous can try *çiğ köfte*, raw minced meat with bulgar. Down

Culinary Courses

Learn to make the best *börek*, perfect pilau or succulent stuffed vine leaves to bring a taste of Turkey back home. Advance booking is required for all cooking courses.

İstanbul Culinary Institute (59 Mesrutiyet Caddesi, Tepebasi; tel: 0212-252 9161; www.istanbulculinary.com) is part of a restaurant, where several weekly workshops might include savoury Turkish pasties or a five-day Turkish cuisine menu.

İstanbul-based TV chef **Engin Akin** (tel: 0532-241 7163; www.enginakin.com) runs three-day residency courses in the coastal village of Ula, where students can try their hand at *meze*, herb flatbreads and a plethora of aubergine dishes.

The 'Cooking with chefs in Turkish Kitchens' course at **Turkish Flavours** (Ugur Apt 14/3, Vali Konagi Caddesi, Nisantasi, İstanbul; tel: 0532-218 0653; www.turkishflavours.com) looks at the influences on İstanbul's cuisine, including Greek, Armenian and Jewish, plus tailor-made culinary tours for individuals and small groups.

At **İstanbul Food Workshop** (111 Yildirim Caddesi, Fener; tel: 0212-534 4788; www.Istanbulfoodworkshop. com) students learn to make Ottoman recipes, including the finest lamb stew with dried fruits. A gourmet's walking tour including buying seasonal produce at the huge market is followed by an Ottoman cooking workshop.

in Antakya, try the *ferik pilav* with a distinctive burnt flavour, followed by the ubiquitous local speciality *kadayıf*, a sweet pastry with fine strands of crunchy wheat, whereas Gaziantep's plethora of pistachio trees results in their nut-filled *baklava*.

You'll be spoilt for choice with seasonal fresh fruit. Countrywide and year-round, you can sample oranges in Antalya (December), delicious apricots from Malatya (June), and huge watermelons from Diyarbakir (September).

Myriad Meze

A traditional Turkish dinner typically kicks off with a vast array of hot and cold *meze*, or appetisers, comprising dips, salads and marinated vegetables. Whether dining in a large group or for two, the waiter will come to your table carrying a huge tray laden with small dishes for you to choose from, where diners should try and select a variety for everyone to share.

Try hot *sigara börek* (deep-fried long pastries stuffed with cheese) and

marinated *hamsi* (anchovies); *patlican salatasi* (smoked aubergine purée) and *ezme* (spicy dip with tomato and chilli) are best when scooped up with crusty bread. *Zeytinyağli* (vegetables in olive oil) are popular dishes to grace any meze table, like *enginar* (artichoke) or *fasulye* (green beans), and a creamy garlicky yoghurty dip like *haydari* rounds things off nicely.

Vegetarians can easily make an entire meal of *meze* alone – although carnivores should ensure they save room for their meaty mains.

Meze are made to eat with the hands, but as with all Muslim nations, only the right hand should be used to touch food directly, as the left hand is considered unclean.

For the best spread of *meze*, you'll probably have to step up to somewhere slightly upmarket – any decent fish restaurant on the coast like **Meğri Lokantası** (Eski Cami Gecidi 8-9, within the Bazaar, Fethiye; tel: 0-252-614 4046), **Antalya Balık Evi** (Eski Lara Yolu 349, Sokak 1, Lara, Antalya; tel: 0-242 323 1823; www.antalyabalikevi.com.tr) or **Harbour Restaurant and Café Bar** (Rıhtım Caddesi, İskele Meydanı (beside the Red Tower), Alanya; tel: 0-242 512 1019) will have the best selection. In İstanbul, *meyhanes* along **Nevizade Sokak** are a good bet for choice.

Kebaps

Forget your experiences back home of the greasy *döner kebap* after a night out – the good news is that, while they do exist throughout Turkey, there are far better examples of this staple, with many regional specialities.

A *meze* plate of cheese, salad and dips

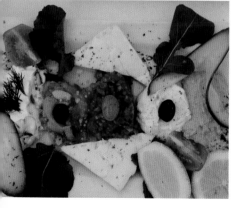

Dönor kebaps are easily found, but make sure to try the different varieties

whole lamb is baked in a brick kiln to produce the succulent *tandır kebap*. Balls of spicy minced lamb, wrapped around the broad skewer, make the popular *Adana kebap*, and a less spicy version of that is *şiş köfte*. *Iskender* or *Bursa kebap* see thinly sliced grilled lamb basted with tomato sauce, served over *pide* bread and drenched in yoghurt, similar to the Beyti variety. Over in Gaziantep, try the *Alinazik kebap* with sautéed lamb on a bed of aubergine puree. For those with a fondness for offal, try *ciğer* (skewered liver), *böbrek* (lamb liver) or even *koç* (lamb's testicle) kebaps.

Şiş kebap is the basic, where small chunks of meat (usually chicken or lamb) spiked on a short skewer are grilled over hot coals. In Konya,

If there are many kebap venues in town, a good way to choose the best (not necessarily the most expensive) is to see which is crowded with locals. Tourist areas are not always the best for food – head instead to busy shopping areas or dining enclaves like Bursa's **Sakarya Caddesi**, and

Culinary Experiences

Top 5 Turkish Foodstuffs to Take Home

As you will be at risk of incurring the wrath of customs officers on arrival back home, it's better to avoid any fresh produce (it's probably illegal to import), and instead stick to dried or preserved food, which is easier to carry and longer-lasting anyway.

- **Turkish Delight (lokum):** Known locally as *lokum*, there's a huge variety to these sweet delicacies. Look out for *kaymakli lokum* from Afyon, made with clotted cream, and *cezerye* made from carrots, chewy and not as sweet.
- **Pistachios (fıstık):** Buy them loose from reputable market stalls – follow the locals to find the busiest. You can get them *tuzlu* (with salt) or *tuzsuz* (without

salt), plump ones from **Siirt** or small and intensely flavoured from Gaziantep.
- **Dried fruits:** Organic sun-dried apricots from Malatya are the best – dark orangey-brown, chewy and full of flavour. Figs are plump and sweet.
- *Pekmez:* This molasses-like syrup is made from condensed fruit, mainly grapes. Locals love it stirred into yoghurt or tahini for breakfast, dipped with fresh bread.
- **Hibiscus:** These deep red, almost black, dried leaves from the hibiscus plant make a warm or cold infusion, known to lower blood pressure, and are often sweetened with sugar.

Eski Sebzeciler İçi Sokak precinct in Antalya. Even in small towns, outdoor tables will spring up in the evenings with an outdoor grill – just follow the crowds and the aroma. Look out for the word *'ocakbaşı'* (barbecue house), an informal restaurant and usually a good middle ground, with a roaring grill and good selection of *kebapler*.

Your meaty feast will probably be accompanied with mounds of salad and warm flatbread, and best washed down with *ayran* (salty yoghurt drink).

Unmissable Turkish Dishes

Some dishes might be regional specialities, but these are available pretty much everywhere in Turkey:

- **Imam Bayıldi**: Literally 'the Imam fainted', as might you if it's a good one. Aubergine is baked whole, stuffed with tomatoes, onion, pepper and garlic.
- **Pilav**: It might only be rice, but Turks make it so well. Often using cracked wheat, cooked with butter, salt and usually chicken stock, accompanying all dishes in a *lokanta*.
- **Aşure**: a traditional pudding, but not as sweet as most. A mix of dried beans, chickpeas, rosewater and dried fruit, sprinkled with pistachios and pomegranate seeds, and served cold.
- **Mercimek Çorbasi**: unmissable because it's ubiquitous, filling and tasty. Lentil soup makes a great breakfast when at a service station on a long journey, or a filling lunch with hunks of bread.
- **Lahmacun**: large circle of flatbread scattered with ground lamb, usually rolled up and eaten as a snack.

Rakı Ritual

Although Turkey is not renowned for a boozy culture, its favourite liquor *rakı* (pronounced rak-uh) is a clear brandy made from grapes and raisins, flavoured with aniseed and similar to French *pastis* or Greek *ouzo*.

Usually, a long straight glass is one-third filled, then an equal amount of water and perhaps some ice-cubes is poured on top, or it is served with a separate glass of water. When diluted, the drink becomes milky white, prompting its nickname Lion's milk (*aslan sütü*).

Most locals – mostly men, of course – would agree that *rakı* comes into its own when accompanied by food, especially cold melon and

Try a glass of Turkey's local liquor, *rakı*

crumbly white cheese, and ideally a *rakı sofrası* (*rakı* table) is laden with *meze* (see p.54). The *rakı* continues slowly through the main course of meat or fish with regular clinking of glasses around the table with a cheerful '*serefe*' (cheers) or '*afyet olsen*' (good health). Care should be taken not to prolong the drink too long after dessert – a *rakı* hangover can be intense for the uninitiated.

The best time and place for *rakı* is undoubtedly in a *meyhane*, with a meal. Although bars of all varieties will sell 'lion's milk', it's not particularly common to drink it on its own. Not surprisingly, it's not a drink favoured by local women, although in tourist areas, the locals are quite used to seeing foreign women develop a taste for it.

Beyaz peynir is one of many distinct Turkish cheeses, often eaten at breakfast

Culinary Experiences

Turkish Cheeses

Centrepiece to a typical Turkish breakfast is usually *beyaz peynir*, a slightly salty crumbly white cheese. And you might presume that that's the lot. But throughout the country an astonishing array of around 160 cheeses vary from soft to creamy, tangy to mature yellow. Some are still handmade by nomads during summer when they take their flocks up to the high plateaux (*yayla*) – keep a lookout at local food markets.

Kaşar is made from the milk of highland cattle, a hard cheese with a pale yellow colour and a strong flavour – it improves with maturity. Crumbly *tulum* cheese is more a description of the method of production, salted and packed tightly into goatskin and aged for up to two

years, often used as a filling in *börek* or *mantı*. The rich ewes-milk cheese *Niğde*, named for its home town south of Cappadocia, can be eaten for up to two years, is used in cooking, and its rare blue-veined variation is smooth and creamy. The creamy *Edirne* white cheese that originates from the northwestern city improves with age and is favoured to accompany *rakı*. At the opposite end of the country, things heat up southeast in Antakya, with *Sürk*, a spicy crumbly cheese enhanced with red pepper and herbs, not for the faint-hearted.

From tourist towns to small villages, most will have a food market, whether it is a weekly street market or a covered bazaar, and it is bound to include a cheese and dairy section. Ask to have a taste; the stallholder will be happy to oblige.

Meat-free Feasts

Although there isn't a huge range of dishes available for the strict vegetarian in local restaurants, certain staples are widespread and always guaranteed meat-free: *mercimek çorbası* (lentil soup) is usually on the menu, and most street snacks like cheese or spinach *börek* are mouthwatering fillers. If you're accompanying your carnivorous friends for dinner, the fantastic array of *meze (see p.54)* is a meal in itself. It's easy to share the Turk's affinity for the humble aubergine, with delicious dishes like *imam bayıldı*, stuffed with tomatoes, onions and peppers, and the smoky dip *patlican salatasi*.

Fresh vegetables in abundance at a market

Çay and Kahve Culture

You'll realise quickly from the piercing calls of '*çay!*' from the lad in the market carrying a tray of steaming glasses that, more than just a beverage, this is the drink that fuels Turkey. Tea bonds business deals, welcomes guests, and keeps the negotiation wheels in motion.

Served black, usually in tiny tulip-shaped glasses, the tea grown in the verdant Black Sea hills is strong and bitter, usually drunk with oodles of sugar (a couple of cubes will be on the saucer). Teabags make the odd appearance in upmarket cafés, although a request for milk is usually greeted with bemusement. If you're offered tea in a private house, most likely it will be brewed samovar-style, poured from the small pot kept warm atop the hot-water urn.

A traditional *çayhane* (teahouse) is usually a male-only affair – not to say that women won't be welcome – and usually smoky, unless and until the smoking ban kicks in. Locals play cards or *tavla* (backgammon), or watch a football match on TV at weekends.

In summer months you'll probably prefer a *çaybahçe* (tea garden), or a venue with outdoor tables. In some cosmopolitan cities, especially İstanbul, smoking fruity tobacco through a *nargile* (sheesha, or waterpipe) has enjoyed a revival, especially with students. The *çaybahçe* is also a favourite with families and courting couples.

If coffee is more your brew, sip a strong, sweet *Türk kahvesi* (Turkish coffee), ideally after a meal. The waiter will usually ask '*Nasil?*'

('how?') referring to how much sugar to prepare it with. Answer *'sade'* (plain/none), *'as'* (little), *'orta'* (medium) or *'çok'* (lots). He may bring the *cezve* to pour at your table, the special tiny pot with a long handle. Don't try to drain the cup unless you want a mouthful of coffee grains!

There's nothing much to distinguish between a good glass of Turkish tea and a bad one, likewise for coffee. But location is everything. Some will relish stumbling across a traditional *çayhane* in the old market in Şanlıurfa, where elderly men play backgammon and sip their beverage slowly. Others will prefer staggering views, like the *çaybahçe* in İstanbul's Gülhane Park overlooking the Marmara.

Sipping strong Turkish coffee; contrary to foreign opinion, it is not as widely drunk as the omnipresent *çay* (tea)

Culinary Experiences

Herbs and Spices

Inhale the enticing aroma at any street market from colourful piles of spices. They look gorgeous, are a reminder of your holiday, and make perfect presents (lightweight and travel well). Try to avoid buying ground spices: it is much better to buy the seeds and grind them yourself back home or, while you're there, you can also buy a mortar and pestle.

Once you use a pack of **pul biber**, you'll wonder how you lived without it. These coarse, dried pepper flakes are a fabulous cooking ingredient, or just to sprinkle on white cheese or salads, and come in various degrees, from sweetness to fiery chilli-like heat. **Aci biber** is similar and sold as a paste, which you can buy in vacuum-packed plastic for practicality, and stir into stews and soups to give them a kick.

The deep purple flakes **sumac** are made from the berries of a sumac bush, with a slightly sour flavour. They are wonderfully versatile and can be rubbed onto meat or fish before grilling, sprinkled onto rice or over a salad in place of lemon juice.

Don't think that **peppercorns** stop with black pepper: in any spice market you will see mounds of green and red peppercorns, which are much sweeter than their black or white cousins. Dried sage leaves make the deliciously refreshing drink **adachai**.

Markets are always the best places to buy spices – especially the traditional street markets at Gaziantep and the weekly one at Kaş, where you'll find the best selection.

PLACES

Getting Your Bearings

Turkey is a vast, varied nation stretching from Europe in the west to Asia in the east, with a coastline of over 7,000km (4,350 miles) along three seas. For easy reference when using this guide, each region has a whole chapter dedicated to its exploration, colour-coded for quick navigation.

İSTANBUL
Pages 64 – 91

BLACK SEA REG
Pages 212 – 229

THRACE AND MARMARA
Pages 92 – 109

AEGEAN REGION
Pages 110 – 143

ANKARA AND CENTRAL ANATOLIA
Pages 176 – 195

CAPPADO
Pages 196 –

MEDITERRANEAN REGION
Pages 144 – 175

Turkey

0   50 km

0   50 miles

BULGARIA

GREECE

UKRAINE

B L A C

CYPRUS

MEDITERRANEAN SEA

The country is divided into five main regions. Thrace and Marmara, in Turkey's far northwest, is the point of division between Europe and Asia, with İstanbul straddling the two continents. South of here is the coastal Aegean region with its capital Izmir, while the Mediterranean region is home to the sands of the south coast with Antalya the major city. Inland you find Turkey's heartland Anatolia, incorporating the capital city of Ankara, Cappadocia and distinctive eastern Turkey, while the north is centred around the Black Sea. Detailed regional maps can be found at the beginning of each chapter.

EASTERN ANATOLIA
Pages 230 – 247

The country veers from golden beaches in the south to plantations in the north, arid highlands in the remote east to irrigated valleys in the southeast. A network of highways and passenger buses provide the best way to crisscross the country.

Every chapter provides in-depth information on what to expect in each place. A listings index is located at the end of each chapter, featuring the best hotels, restaurants and activities that the region has to offer. The listings cater to all budgets, from those on a shoestring through to those who like to travel with no expense spared.

İstanbul

Summon up the traveller's image of Turkey and quite likely that İstanbul is the result: Ottoman splendour, Byzantine beauty and market mayhem. Add to that one of Europe's most cosmopolitan, contemporary art and music scenes and throw in its superb Bosphorus location, and it's not surprising that Turkey's cultural capital is a world-class destination.

Population: 13 million

Local dialling codes: 0212 (European side); 0216 (Asian side)

Local tourist offices: Atatürk Airport (arrivals); tel: 0212-663 0798. Meydanı (Hippodrome), Sultanahmet; tel: 0212-518 1802. Sirkeci Garı (station); tel: 0212-511 5888. Hilton Hotel, Taksim; tel: 0212-233 0592.

Tourist police station: opposite Yerebatan Sarnici, Sultanahmet; tel: 0212-527 4503

Post office: Büyük Posthanesi Caddesi, Sirkeci (main); Yeniçarşi Caddesi, Galatasaray

Hospitals: American Hospital, Güzelbahçe Sokak 20, Nişantaşı; tel: 0212-444 3777; **www.american hospitallstanbul.com**. German Hospital, Sıraselviler Caddesi 119, Cihangir, Taksim; tel: 0212-293 2150; **www.almanhastanesi.com. tr**. Taksim State Emergency Hospital (Taksim Ilk Yardim Hastanesi), Sıraselviler Caddesi 1, Taksim; tel: 0212-249 7804.

Media (English language): Daily newspapers: *Today's Zaman*, **www.todayszaman.com**; *Turkish Daily News*, **www.turkeydailynews.com**. Magazines: *Time Out* (monthly); **www.timeout.com/Istanbul**.

İstanbul's stunning location, split famously over two continents and bisecting waterways, straddles not just Europe and Asia, but also the ancient and modern, secular and religious, traditional and forward-thinking. One moment you're gazing at the Old City's minaret-studded skyline and hearing the call to prayer echoing across the water, a little later you're browsing bijoux galleries, before an evening of sipping cocktails with fashionistas at a terrace bar. Although İstanbul is a frenetic, buzzing city with a population of over 13 million, traffic jams and crowded markets, don't be surprised to find unexpected historic treasures in out-of-the-way neighbourhoods.

The city has seen an incredible development in the last decade with booming property prices. İstanbul is now seen as one of the most happening and energetic cities in Europe, where locals respect its heritage but are just as proud of its modern developments. The city might well be divided between two continents, but most eyes seem firmly on Europe – whether or not Turkey joins the EU.

Most first-time visitors begin their sightseeing in the Old City, where most of the historical sights are within walking distance, and then cross the Golden Horn over Galata Bridge into Beyoğlu and the modern city. It's a journey not just of a few kilometres, but also several centuries.

İstanbul – Old City

For centuries, people throughout the world referred to this area simply as 'the city', a fascinating metropolis known successively as Byzantium, Constantinople and finally İstanbul. It has witnessed the passing of Greeks, Persians and Romans, flourishing in the 6th century under Emperor Justinian, and rising from ruin in the 16th century when the Ottoman Sultan Mehmet II built mosques, monuments and markets. The highlight for today's visitors is still the Old City, centred on

The ornate ceiling in the Blue Mosque

Sultanahmet, home to a staggering wealth of sights in close proximity.

Sultanahmet

The famous city landmark of the **Blue Mosque ❶** (Sultan Ahmet Camii; daily 9am–7pm, except prayer time; free) was built for Sultan Ahmet I, between 1609 and 1616, its location opposite Hagia Sophia intended to demonstrate that Islam surpassed Christianity.

Walk from the Hippodrome for the cascading domes' full effect, to the cavernous interior bathed in the light through 260 stained-glass windows and aglow with 20,000 blue İznik tiles It's usually busy with tourists (non-Muslims must stay at the back); find solace early morning, late afternoon or in the huge marble courtyard. Summer months see the **Sound and Light Show ▥** projected onto the mosque's walls.

Opposite the Blue Mosque, the dusky red Byzantine beauty of the **Hagia Sophia ❷** (Aya Sofya; Tue–Sun 9am–4.30pm, until 7pm in summer; charge) was completed under Emperor Justinian in AD537,

The Arabic medallions beneath the Hagia Sophia's dome are a later Islamic detail

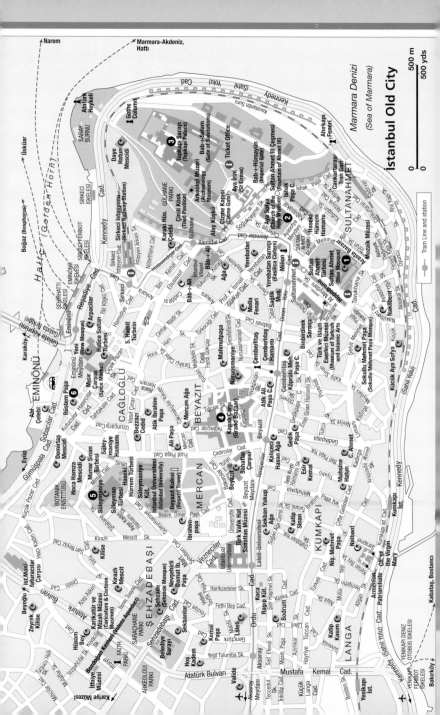

Istanbul Old City

Marmara Denizi (Sea of Marmara)

0   500 m
0   500 yds

→ Tram Line and station

the largest and most important church in the Christian world. Its name means 'Church of the Holy Wisdom'. Ottoman sultans converted it into a mosque, adding four minarets, after their conquest of the city.

Its immense 56m (183ft) -high dome seems to float over the interior thanks to the canny use of hollow bricks. Its interior is best known for its decorative mosaics, whitewashed over by Süleyman the Magnificent as Islamic law forbids the representation of man or animal. This meant that the mosaics were perfectly preserved when uncovered after the Republic was formed.

İstanbul Transport

 Airports: Atatürk Hava Limanı Yolu (Atatürk International Airport), Yeşilköy; tel: 0212-465 5555; www.ataturkairport.com. Sabiha Gökçen International Airport, Pendik; tel: 0216-585 5000; www.sgairport.com. To and from Atatürk airport: Havaş airport express bus service (www.havas.net) departs every 30 mins 4am–1am; ticket 10TL (buy on board); journey time approx 30 mins, terminating at Taksim via Tepebaşı and Aksaray (for Sultanahmet). To the airport, bus leaves from outside Turkish Airlines office, Taksim.

 Metro and Tram: IETT; free tel: 0800-211 6068; www.iett.gov.tr. Tram and metro services run every few minutes from 6am–midnight. Individual tickets can be purchased at kiosks near the bus stop, or jetons at tram and metro stations. If your stay is for several days, it is slightly cheaper to buy an akbil, an electronic top-up token. These are valid on all public transport.

 Taxis: Yellow cabs ply the streets; avoid those outside hotels and major sites. All should use the meter; 50 percent extra for night rate. From Atatürk airport, a metered taxi to the city centre takes from 30 mins, about 25TL. To and from Sabiha Gökçen airport, a metered taxi costs about 70TL, taking 60–90 mins.

 Buses: Most buses are run by the municipality (red and white, or green), IETT (see left) from 6am–11pm. Purchase tickets before boarding. Alternative buses are private (halk otobusi), with similar routes (pale blue and green), and tickets can be purchased on board; major bus terminals include Taksim Square, Eminönü, Mecidiyeköy and Beyazit. The yellow dolmuses are like a shared taxi, departing when full, with no standing. The route is fixed, but passengers can get on and off anywhere (call 'inecek var' to the driver). Pay the driver the fixed fare. Useful night services include Taksim to Akwaray. Minibuses (blue and white) have fixed routes and stops.

 Ferries and sea buses: Passenger boats run year-round between the European and Asian shores, run by IDO (tel: 0212-444 4436; www.ido.com.tr). Pay by jeton or akbil. There are regular services between Kabatas, Besiktas, Beykoz and Sariyer, plus daily Bosphorus cruises (15TL for 2-hour, or 25TL for half-day). Fast ferries also sail from Kabatas to Princes Islands (see p.80).

 Car Hire: These companies are also at Atatürk Airport. Avis; Abdulhakhamit Caddesi 72/A, off Cumhuriyet Caddesi, Taksim; tel: 0212-297 9610; www.avis.com.tr. Budget; Abdulhakhamit Caddesi, Inal Apt 72A, Taksim; tel: 0212-297 4393; www.budget.com. Europcar; Topcu Caddesi 1, Taksim; tel: 0212-465 6284.

istanbul

Mimar Sinan: Architect Extraordinaire

Some of İstanbul's most famous landmarks are thanks to a 16th-century architect, favourite of the Ottoman sultans and creator (or supervisor) of over 300 major structures around the world. Most of his skills were gained as a Janissary, with military campaigns including building bridges and fortifications. Today he's best known and celebrated for elegant creations like the landmark Süleymaniye Mosque, commissioned by Süleyman the Magnificent, the bijoux Rüstem Paşa Mosque, and the lesser-known Şehzade Mosque in Fatih. His tomb lies in the western corner of Süleymaniye Mosque, just outside the high walls.

These well-restored works, mainly in gold, portray saints and angels, including the Madonna and Child, and Christ flanked by the Virgin Mary and John the Baptist. The south gallery has the mosaic of Empress Zöe, and her husband Constantine XI, whose face was superimposed over that of her previous husband.

The **Hippodrome** (At Meydanı) was once Emperor Constantine's chariot-racing track. Little remains of its original structure, but its monuments include the **Serpentine Column** (Yılanlı Sütun), taken from the Temple of Apollo at Delphi, the **Column of Constantine VII Porphyogenitus** (Ormetaş), and the **obelisk** of Pharaoh Thutmose (Dikilitaş), which Byzantine Emperor Theodosius appropriated during his conquest of Egypt. Cool water still

Carving on the column of Theodosius in the Hippodrome

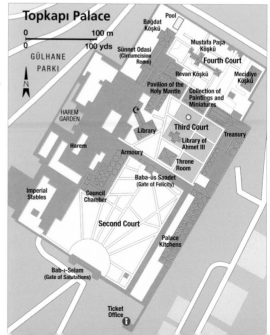

Topkapı Palace

0   100 m
0   100 yds

GÜLHANE PARKI

N

Pool
Bağdat Köşkü
Sünnet Odası (Circumcision Room)
Mustafa Paşa Köşkü
Fourth Court
Revan Köşkü
Mecidiye Köşkü
Pavilion of the Holy Mantle
Collection of Paintings and Miniatures

HAREM GARDEN

Library
Third Court
Harem
Library of Ahmet III
Treasury
Armoury
Throne Room
Baba-üs Saadet (Gate of Felicity)

Imperial Stables
Council Chamber
Second Court
Palace Kitchens

Bab-ı-Selam (Gate of Salutations)

Ticket Office

A fountain in the Topkapi Palace's Harem

The very stones of the **Topkapı Palace** ❸ (Topkapı Sarayı; www.topkapisarayi.gov.tr; Wed–Mon 9am–5pm, closed public hols; charge), the sultans' vast residence and administrative hub, ooze wealth, pleasure and intrigue, in a strategic hilltop location overlooking the Marmara and Bosphorus. This was the seat of Ottoman power after Mehmet II's great grandson, Süleyman the Magnificent, selected this as his royal residence.

From the ticket office in the **Court of the Janissaries** (First Courtyard) enter through the imposing **Gate of Salutations** (Bab-ı Selam) to the **Second Court**. Some of the domed **palace kitchens** have been reconstructed and house a huge collection of porcelain, silver and glassware including Chinese Caledon dinnerware, handy for the suspicious sultans as it reputedly changed colour on contact with poisoned food.

The Baba-üs Saadet (Gate of Felicity) leads to the **Throne Room** and multi-domed **Treasury**, one of several halls housing the famed Topkapı collection of bejewelled treasures, including the 84-carat **Spoonmaker's Diamond** (Kaşıkcı Elması), so called because a peasant allegedly traded it for three spoons. In contrast, the **Pavilion of the Holy Mantle** is a place of great religious significance for Muslims, housing sacred relics of the Prophet Mohammed, including hairs from his beard.

The **Harem** (9am–4pm; extra ticket) is a surprise: rather than a testament to opulence and excess, most concubines were imprisoned in this

flows from the taps of the golden eight-columned **Kaiser Wilhem II's fountain**, his gift to the Empire after his 1898 visit.

One of many vast water tanks built by the Byzantines, the **Basilica Cistern** (Yerebatan Sarnıcı; www.yerebatan.com; daily 9am–6.30pm, winter 9.30am–5.30pm; charge M) today features coloured lights that seem incongruous in an otherwise eerie space. This submerged chamber is supported by 336 9m (30ft)-high columns and wooden walkways over the water, with two huge Medusa heads in the corner, one upside down and one on its side, thought to have been taken from pre-Christian ruins. Scenes from The James Bond film *From Russia With Love* were filmed here.

400-room complex (only a fraction is open to the public), sleeping in dormitories and learning the ways of the palace. Only the lucky few were hand-picked by the sultan's mother *(valide sultan)* and 'trained' to serve the sultan to produce sons. The sultan's brothers and close male relatives were kept inside the prison-like **Gilded Cage** (İftariye) to prevent any dastardly plots of fratricide to gain power.

In the leafy **Fourth Court**, laced with gardens and summer houses, young princes were circumcised inside the **Circumcision Room** (Sünnet Odasi), a richly tiled pavilion, near the elaborate **Bağdat Köşkü** from where the sultans gazed out over the waterways.

The fascinating **Archaeology Museum** (Arkeoloji Müzesi; Tue–Sun 9.30am–4.30pm; charge), officially Turkey's first, contains a collection of around one million antiquities spread over three buildings. Inside the **Museum of the Ancient Orient** (Eski Şark Eserleri Müzesi) the famous Alexander sarcophagus dates back to the 4th century BC, found in the royal necropolis at Sidon (now in Lebanon) in 1887. The museum also houses unique treasures like the world's oldest written peace treaty on cunei-form tablets. Across the courtyard the beautiful **Tiled Pavilion** (Çinili Köskü), covered with Iznik tiles, was built in 1472, displaying Ottoman ceramics inside. The shady **tea garden** is perfect to take a break.

Süleymaniye and Beyazit

The **Grand Bazaar ❹** (Kapalı Çarşı; www.kapalicarsi.org.tr; Mon–Sat 8am–7pm; free; *see also p.41)* is a short walk from Sultanahmet up Divan Yolu. It is one of the world's most famous markets, built under Mehmet II shortly after he conquered the city. Almost destroyed by two recent fires (1954 and 1974), the bazaar retains many of its original Ottoman features, including 18 ornate marble fountains. The size of

İstanbul's Archaeology Museum displays a rich collection of antique artefacts

70

İstanbul

a large city block, its several thousand stalls sell everything from dazzling gold to dusty antiques and myriad carpets. The surrounding lanes outside are filled with cheap clothing stalls favoured by locals and Russian visitors.

On the western side of Grand Bazaar, **Freedom Square** (Beyazıt Meydanı) was a commercial hub for centuries, and site of the forum of Byzantine Emperor Theodosius, built in AD393. The Old City's largest public square is dominated by **Beyazit Mosque** (Beyazit Camii), inspired by Hagia Sophia's domes. Behind it, the charming **Book Bazaar** (Sahaflar Çarşisi), set around a small courtyard, has traded in the written word since early Ottoman times, these days predominantly selling students' textbooks.

İstanbul University's ornate gates (open for visitors) lead to **Beyazit Tower** (Beyazit Kulesi), built by Mahmoud II as a firewatch tower in 1749; the prevalence of wooden buildings meant devastating fires were commonplace. On the square's western side, the former *medrese* building now houses the tiny **Calligraphy Museum** (Türk Vafik Hat Sanatlan Müzesi; Tue–Sat 9am–4pm; charge), with impressive illuminated Korans from the 13–16th centuries, and sultans' *tuğra* (ornate signature).

Considered the greatest achievement of the great architect Mimar Sinan, the **Süleymaniye Mosque ❺** (Süleymaniye Camii; daily 9am–7pm, except prayer time; free) is the largest in İstanbul, located on a hill overlooking the Golden Horn (Haliç). Completed in the 1550s under Süleyman the Magnificent, and therefore a tribute to him,

Carved souvenirs in the Grand Bazaar

its 47m (154ft) -high dome supported by four sturdy columns gives a sense of soaring space and calm on entering. The entire complex was a charitable foundation *(külliye)*, comprising caravanserai for travellers, kitchens *(imaret)* to feed the city's poor, regardless of religion, and school *(medrese)*. The ornate octagonal **Tomb of Süleyman the Magnificent** and more modest **Tomb of Roxelana**, his wife, lie in the peaceful rose gardens.

Eminönü

This workaday neighbourhood is İstanbul at its busiest, with commerce dominated by the **Spice** (or Egyptian) **Market** (Mısır Çarşişi; Mon–Sat 8am–7pm; free). Built in the 17th century,

Immerse yourself in the Baroque excesses of the last Ottoman palace, stretch your legs with a stroll in a picturesque park, and end the day with a relaxing waterside dinner.

From Kabataş, walk north along the main road for a few minutes to **Dolmabahçe Palace** (Dolmabahçe Sarayı), an elaborate palace which led to the Ottoman Empire's bankruptcy in 1875. It's worth taking the guided tour of the palace's *selamlik* and *harem* with the dazzling ornate staircase leading to the Salon of the Ambassadors, and the world's largest chandelier hanging in The Throne Room.

From the palace, it's a five-minute walk along Dolmabahçe Caddesi to the **Depot Museum** (Depo Müzesi), housed in the original palace kitchens. Opened as a museum in 2006, it exhibits

several thousand eclectic items from the palace's daily life, from a dentist's chair to carved wooden cabinets.

Head further along the busy main road with the palace's outer walls on your left, and on the opposite pavement is a permanent exhibition of photographs chronicling the life of Atatürk. After 20 minutes you'll reach **Beşiktaş**, a vibrant local neighbourhood by a bus terminus, ferry docks, and bustling streets, selling everything from fresh fish and cheap clothes to pirated DVDs.

On the western side of the waterside square is the **Maritime Museum** (Deniz Müzesi), filled with Ottoman naval paraphernalia, including artefacts from naval engagements fought by the Turks over the centuries.

Take a detour to just beyond the ferry docks for several Bosphorus-facing cafés and terraces for a relaxing break and people-watching. Continue along Çırağan Caddesi to two prestigious chain hotels on your right: the **Four Seasons Bosphorus** and the **Çırağan Palace**

The ornate Dolmabahçe Palace

Tips

- Distance: 5.25km (3¼ miles)
- Time: A leisurely day
- The starting point, Kabataş, can be reached by tram from Sultanahmet or by funicular from Taksim Square. Bear in mind that Dolmabahçe Palace is closed on Monday and Thursday. Sunday is the best day to visit Ortaköy for the flea market, although it's the day with the busiest traffic so could affect your journey time back into the city.

Kempinski are built upon the grounds of former Bosphorus palaces, worth a look inside for a coffee or cocktail.

Across the road from the Çırağan Palace's main entrance is **Küçük Mecidiye Mosque** (Küçük Mecidiye Camii), built in 1843 for Sultan Abdül Mecit, which marks the entrance to **Yıldız Park** (Yıldız Parkı). Once the sultans' hunting grounds, this is now a bucolic park and popular with locals.

Head up the main path into the park and either turn left uphill towards **Tent Pavilion** (Cadır Köşkü), now a café, or straight on to **Chalet Pavilion** (Şale Köşkü) located at the top of the park, an attractive residence built by Abdül Hamid II in 1882. Slightly southeast is the ornate **Malta Pavilion** (Malta Köşkü), once a hunting lodge and now a pleasant café and restaurant.

The fastest way to descend to Ortaköy from the park is via Palanga Caddesi, downhill from Malta Pavilion. Once on the main road (Muallim Naci Caddesi), cross over and head towards the pier down Vapur Iskelesi Sokak. The once-sleepy fishing village of **Ortaköy**, 3km

In cool Yıldız Park

(2 miles) from Dolmabahçe, is today a vibrant waterside community, filled with quaint shops and restaurants.

You'll first reach **Ortaköy Square** (Ortaköy Meydanı), the neighbourhood's bustling heart, its sea wall lapped by the Bosphorus with bobbing fishing boats. **Büyük Mecidiye Mosque** (Büyük Mecidiye Camii) perches on the waterfront, a neo-Baroque edifice built in 1856, gorgeous in the afternoon sun or lit at night.

During weekends, locals flock to its cluster of *nargile* cafés and craft market stretching along the waterfront and surrounding lanes. Not surprisingly, it's packed during summer. In addition to the restaurants, you can also dine on a budget from stalls on the square behind the mosque, on overfilled jacket potatoes *(kumpir)* and fruity waffles.

Walking Tour of Ortaköy

it specialised in oriental spices along the trade route. Although spices are still piled high at stalls, produce now ranges from souvenirs to gold and the surrounding streets throng with local shoppers. Its income generated revenue for the adjacent **New Mosque** (Yeni Valide Camii; daily 9am–6pm; free), accessed via a cascading staircase, with blue tiles lining its external walls. The **Tomb of Turhan Hatice Sultan** (Hatice Sultan Türbesi), together with the graves of other sultans, lies in the opposite walled-in cemetery.

The hidden-away, tiny **Rüstem Paşa Mosque 6** (Rüstem Paşa Camii; daily 9am–6pm, except prayer times; free) is accessed up a flight of stairs above a row of shops (whose rent pays for its upkeep). Built by Sinan, commissioned by grand vizier Rüstem Paşa, son-in-law of Süleyman the Magnificent, it is one of the city's most beautiful with its facade and interior covered with Iznik tiles in a distinctive circular pattern.

A view from the Galata Bridge

Spanning the **Golden Horn** (Haliç) from Eminönü to Karaköy, the **Galata Bridge** (Galata Köprüsü) is perennially lined with fishermen casting their lines. Underneath the road bridge, fish restaurants and bars line the pedestrian walkway. Sultan Beyazid II was said to have commissioned Leonardo va Vinci to design a bridge in 1503, but it wasn't until 1912 that a pontoon bridge was actually built, destroyed by fire, then replaced in 1992. While walking over, pause to take in views of Topkapı Palace, Hagia Sophia, the Blue Mosque and Süleymaniye Mosque.

Fener and Balat

While slender Ottoman minarets are well known on İstanbul's skyline, Byzantine landmarks form a fascinating contrast. The Old City is dotted

4m (13ft) -high **Patriarchal Throne** in the middle of the nave is the most valuable artefact, with inscriptions beneath the eaves of its gables.

The eye-catching waterfront white church of **St Stephen of the Bulgars** (Sveti Stefan; daily 8am–5pm; free) was built from prefabricated iron sections and sailed down the Danube on 100 barges in 1871. The interior – including its sturdy pillars – is also iron. This was the only church for the city's vast Bulgarian community; today it is used by the Macedonian Christian populace.

Golden Horn

Eyüp is one of the holiest neighbourhoods of İstanbul; only Mecca, Medina and Jerusalem are visited more than **Eyüp Mosque** (Eyüp Camii; daily dawn–nightfall; free)

In the holy Eyüp Mosque

with such beauties, including the **Chora Church,** or **Kariye Museum** (Kariye Müzesi; May–Sept Thur–Tue 9am–7pm, winter 9am–5pm; charge), which is the former monastery of St Saviour in Chora and has renowned Byzantine frescoes, created in 1315–21, depicting a detailed account of the life of Christ and the Virgin Mary. They were whitewashed over when converted to a mosque in 1511, but this actually protected their superb colours.

The golden Iconostasis dazzles inside **St George's Church** (Rum Ortodoks Patrikhanesi; www.patriarchate.org; daily 9am–4.30pm; free), the headquarters of the Greek Orthodox Patriarchate (previously in the nearby **Church of the Pammakaristos,** Fethiye Camii). Located behind high-security walls, with dark wood pews and panels, the

by Muslim pilgrims. The main draw is the adjacent tile-covered **Tomb of Eyüp** (Al-Ansari Eyüp Sultan Turbesi; daily 9.30am–5pm; free), the standard bearer of the Prophet Mohammed. From here, you can walk or take the *teleferik* through the hillside cemetery to **Pierre Loti Café**. It's a 30-minute walk from Eyüp to **Santalİstanbul**, an astounding contemporary art space created from a converted power plant (www.santralIstanbul.org; Tue–Sun 10am–8pm; free).

On the other side of the Golden Horn, accessible over the Old Galata Bridge (Eski Galata Köprüsü), a fantastic venue for children is the **Rahmi M Koç Museum** (Rahmi M Koç Müzesi; www.rmk-museum.org.tr; Tue–Fri 10am–5pm, Sat–Sun

> ### Funiculars Old and New
>
> Hilly İstanbul boasts two systems to ease the journey. French engineer Eugene Henri Gavand built the tiny **Tünel** subway line in 1874 to save the locals from the hike from Galata to Pera, originally with gas lamps and a steam engine. Just 573m (1,880ft) long, this is the world's shortest and second- oldest underground line still operating. Contrast that with the **funicular** from Kabataş up to Taksim, a thoroughly modern railway system opened in 2006, taking under two minutes for the 544m (1,784ft) journey and linking up with the Metro line.

10am–7pm; charge ![icon]). This waterfront museum is housed in an old iron foundry and comprises the private collection of Turkey's famous industrialist ranging from science and technology to transport. Kids can take a ride on a diesel locomotive, take a closer look at an 1898 Malden Steam Car or climb inside the Douglas DC-3 aircraft.

İstanbul – New City

Until the early 20th century, the broad pedestrianised Istiklal Caddesi was known as the Grand Rue de Pera, its smart shops and cafés the place where wealthy European residents felt at home. Their imitation palazzi and chateaux are now foreign consulates. At its northern end, Taksim Square is a busy transport hub, its south leading to Galata, Karaköy and Tünel. This whole area is loosely known today as Beyoğlu, which beats to a very different tune to the Old City.

You can enjoy great city views from the Galata Tower

Karaköy, Galata and Tophane

From the top of the **Galata Tower** ❼ (Galata Külesi; www.galatatower. net; daily 9am–8pm; charge) are panoramic city views. Rebuilt by Genoese settlers in 1348 as part of their defence network (originally built from wood in AD507), it was later used as a dungeon and a fire tower. Visitors can take the elevator to the top floor and walk around the outside perimeter, cameras at the ready.

Opened in 2004 in a former customs warehouse, **İstanbul Modern** (www.Istanbulmodern.org; Tue–Sun 10am–6pm, Thur until 8pm; charge, Thur free) offers a permanent exhibition devoted to the evolution of Turkish art throughout the 20th century. Head to the basement temporary photography exhibitions and an arthouse cinema. The terrace bar-restaurant has fantastic Bosphorus views.

Housed in the former Zulfaris Synagogue and opened in 2001, the **Jewish Museum** (500. Yil Vakfi Türk Musevileri Müzesi; www.muze500. com; Mon–Thur 10am–4pm, Fri and Sun 10am–2pm, closed Sat and Jewish hols; charge) has an extensive display telling the history of Jews in Turkey since the Ottoman conquest of Bursa in 1326. Exhibits include photographs, religious artefacts like silver adornments for the Torah scrolls, plus the printing press introduced by Sephardic Jews in 1492.

In the grounds of the former dervish lodge is the **Galata Mevlevi Dervish Museum** ❽ (due to reopen Dec 2010; Galata Mevlevihane Müzesi; check for opening times; charge). Founded in 1491,

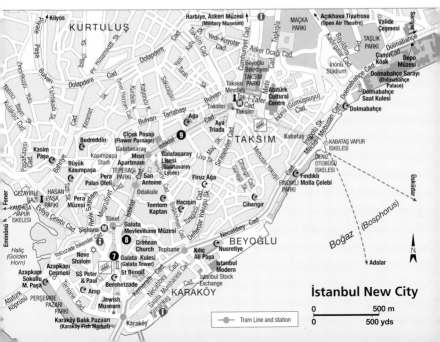

İstanbul New City

this is the venue of the weekly *sema* ceremony, a trance-like 'whirling' meditation for this sect of Islam. Exhibits include illuminated Qurans and Sufi costumes, plus its graveyard where many of its great members are buried.

Taksim and Beyoğlu

İstiklal Caddesi , a broad pedestrianised street, is the artery of 'New İstanbul', a busy hub of fashion shops, cinemas and cafés, dotted with European churches and consulates in 19th-century residential buildings. **Taksim Square** (Taksim Meydanı) is dominated by **Republic Monument** (Cumhuriyet Anıtı), made by Italian sculptor Canonica in 1928 and commemorating Atatürk's founding of the Turkish Republic. Halfway down are the enormous gates to **Galatasary Lycée** (Galatasaray Lisesi), first established in the 15th century and later transformed into a French lycée system. Twentieth-century **Mısır Apartmani** now houses tiny art galleries, plus the fashionable bar-restaurant **360** on its terrace *(see p.89)*. The **historic**

Beşiktaş football team's fans celebrate

tram trundles the 1.6km (1-mile) journey in 15 minutes.

Opened in 2005, the **Pera Museum** (Pera Müzesi, Meşrutiyet Caddesi 65, Tepebasi; www.peramuzesi.org.tr; Tue–Sat 10am–7pm, Sun noon–6pm; charge) is a glorious European building housing permanent exhibitions: Orientalist Painting depicts scenes of 17th- to 20th-century Ottoman life, plus Kütahya tiles and ceramics

Football Mad

Between September and May, İstanbul goes football crazy. Turkey's three top teams – Beşiktaş, Galatasaray and Fenerbahçe – all hail from the city, so after victory in a major match there are often traffic jams with blaring horns and fluttering flags. Sitting above Dolmabahçe Palace is İnönü Stadium 🚇, home to Beşiktaş *(see p.90)*, and on match days (Friday, Saturday or Sunday)

thousands of fans clad in black-and-white scarves and shirts can be seen walking from Taksim Square down meandering Gümüşsuyu street.

Superlig (Turkey's premier league) matches are often screened in tea houses and bars. It's usually easy to get match tickets – İnönü Stadium is the most accessible – attended by a high proportion of women and families.

with stylised floral motifs. Look out for temporary exhibitions usually of European modern artists.

The **Military Museum** (Askeri Müzesi, Harbiye; Wed–Sun 9am–5pm; charge ) is a real favourite for kids. Over 600 years of Turkey's military history comes alive with relics from the Ottoman era to World War II, with military uniforms, woven tents and weapons, plus remains of the chains that Byzantine armies stretched across the Golden Horn. Daily at 3pm and 4pm (outdoors in summer) the famous **Mehter Band** dressed up in janissary finery perform Ottoman military tunes.

The Bosphorus

This famous waterway links the Sea of Marmara (south) to the Black Sea (north), and cuts a broad swathe through İstanbul, dividing it between Europe and Asia. In previous centuries it was a strategic shipping lane; these days it's a way to leave behind the crowded city for waterfront villages, wooden summer houses lining the shore, majestic hill-top fortresses and forested hills. The European side sees villagey Ortaköy, a hub of fashionable nightclubs and waterfront teahouses, and the Ottoman's final home, Dolmabahçe Palace. The Asian side is dominated by large residential suburbs of Üsküdar and Kadıköy, with the Teutonic castle-like Haydarpaşa station in the middle. Linking the two sides is the Bosphorus Bridge.

The European Side

At the western foot of the 1,074m (3,523ft) -long Bosphorus Bridge,

Ortaköy ❿ (*see also Tour, p.72*) is a former fishing village, now a charming waterfront neighbourhood with a string of cafés overlooking the Bosphorus, trendy restaurants and upmarket rooftop nightclubs. Its quaint streets are filled with craft stalls for weekend markets .

The imposing **Fortress of Europe** (Rumeli hisarı Müzesi, Sariyer; Thur–Tue 9am–4.30pm; charge), together with **Anadolu hisarı** on the opposite Asian side, marks the narrowest part of the Bosphorus. Assembled by Mehmet II in 1453, the battlements and watchtowers have soaring views of the waterway. The tiny **amphitheatre** holds occasional summer events.

Housing the Sabanci family's private collection is the **Sabancı Museum** (Sakip Sabancı Müzesi,

Take a ride on Istiklal Caddesi's historic tram to see the length of the street

Emirgan; http://muze.sabanciuniv. edu; Tue–Sun 10am–6pm, Wed until 10pm; charge), housed in an early 20th-century villa (Atlı Köşk), with a modern extension. Its collection of 500 years of calligraphy is astounding, including manuscripts of the Koran. Its modern extension usually holds temporary exhibitions of a more international nature.

The Asian Side

Üsküdar ⓫ is a conservative neighbourhood filled with mosques and lively markets. **Mihrimah Sultan Mosque** (Mihrimah Sultan Camii), a Sinan-built mosque for Süleyman the Magnificent, was built on a raised platform to protect it from the water. A 15-minute uphill walk is the tiny **Tiled Mosque** (Çinili Camii, Çinili Mescit Sokak), adorned with Iznik tiles – hunt down the caretaker to visit inside. A short boat ride travels to

> ## Lady with the Lamp
>
> British nurse Florence Nightingale (1820–1910) is famous for her contribution to the Crimean War, caring for wounded British, Turkish and French soldiers in Selimiye Barracks in Scutari (present-day Üsküdar). She found drastically short supplies of medicine, overworked staff and bad hygiene, which contributed to deaths and disease more than war wounds. It was her subsequent reports to the British government about her findings that led to her far-reaching legacy in health care. Visitors can see her iconic lamp, a Turkish lantern, plus her room and waxworks, in the **Florence Nightingale Museum** (Selimiye Barracks, Harem; open by appointment only; free), providing they fax passport details in advance (fax: 0216-553 1009).

A ferry crossing the Bosphorus from Üsküdar

Maiden's (or **Leander's**) **Tower** (Kiz Kulesi), a Greek watchtower rebuilt as a lighthouse in the 12th century. **Beylerbeyi Palace** (Beylerbeyi Sarayi; www.millisaraylar.gov.tr; daily except Mon and Thur, Oct–Feb 9.30am–4pm, Mar–Sept until 5pm; charge) is 4km (2½ miles) north, a lavish summer palace with terraced gardens overlooking the Bosphorus.

Princes Islands

The **Princes Islands** ⓬ (Adalar) are a group of nine islands 20km (12 miles) off İstanbul's southeast coast and were a place of escape for centuries, including for an exiled Leon Trotsky. It's a popular summer excursion for *İstanbullus*, drawn to the rocky beaches and peaceful forests; no cars are allowed so most explore by bicycle

The Princes Islands are a favoured retreat for locals

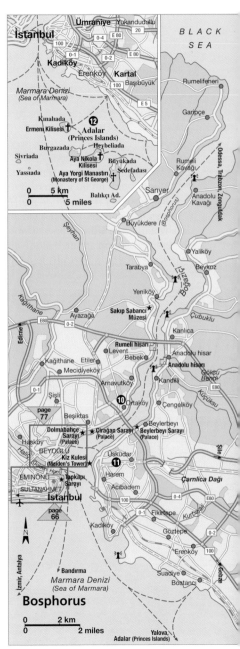

(with a few places to hire) or horse-drawn carriages. **Büyükada** is the largest and most visited island, with wooden mansions surrounded by lush gardens, especially along **Çankaya Caddesi**. Topping one of the island's two hills is the landmark Byzantine **Monastery of St George**, accessed by a steep walk, of great importance to Orthodox Christians and alleged to have healing powers.

The second-largest island, called **Heybeliada** ('saddlebag') because of its shape, is more peaceful, with narrow beaches and pine forests. The hilltop **Hagia Triada Monastery** houses a famous collection of Byzantine manuscripts, but public access is restricted.

🚶 EYÜP

Make your way up the Golden Horn beyond the old city walls to the district of Eyüp, a little way off the tourist track, to one of İstanbul's holiest places and a hugely important centre of pilgrimage in the Islamic world.

Begin from **Eyüp Pier** (Eyüp İskelesi), and walk along Eyüp İskele Sokak into Camii Kebir Sokak, a busy street lined with stalls selling religious souvenirs, prayer beads and Korans. At the top on the left is the **Tomb of the Grand Vizier Sokullu Mehmet Paşa** (Sokullu Mehmet Paşa Türbesi), designed by Sinan.

Outside the tomb, a huge fountain dominates the centre of the square, the other side of which is **Eyüp Mosque** (Eyüp Camii). The mosque was originally commissioned by Mehmet II in 1458, after his *şeyhülislam* (religious governor) dreamt the location of Eyüp Al-Ansari's tomb. Enter through the mosque's Baroque doorway into the first courtyard;

women should enter through the doors to a separate section (modest clothing and headcovering required).

A doorway behind the *şadırvan* (ablutions fountain) leads to the ornate tiled interior of the **Tomb of Eyüp Al-Ansari** (Eyüp Sultan Türbesi), the Prophet Mohammed's standard bearer killed during the first Arab siege of Constantinople in AD674–8. The mausoleum, also a place of pilgrimage, was the site of a special coronation ceremony of all new sultans, from Mehmet II onwards.

Walk straight through the second courtyard into the peaceful Sultan Reşat Caddesi to the **Tomb of Mihrişah Valide Sultan** (Mihrişah Valide Sultan Türbesi), mother of Selim II, who died in 1805. The adjacent *külliye* (mosque complex), built in 1794, includes a *mektep* (primary school) and an *imaret* (public kitchen).

Retrace your steps along Sultan Reşat Caddesi to the end of the street and turn left along Balaban Yolu Sokak.

Worshippers at Eyüp mosque

The great view from the open terrace of Pierre Loti Café

From here take the small path leading up the hill into the main **cemetery** on the right. You can climb to the top of the hill from here (a moderate 15-minute ascent) past Ottoman and more recent gravestones, or walk the other way on Balaban Yolu Sokak and take the cable car (small charge) to save your legs.

At the top of the hill, most head to the gorgeous open terrace of **Pierre Loti Café** (Pierre Loti Kahvesi), named after its most famous customer, a French writer (1850–1923), author of novels including *Aziyadé*, which chronicled his love affair with a Turkish woman whom he met in İstanbul in 1876. The views from the terrace of the Golden Horn are stunning – no wonder that the tables are always full on summer evenings.

Tips

- Distance: 1km (¾ mile)
- Time: 2–3 hours
- Note that the tombs open Tue–Sun until 4.30pm.
- Start this walk at Eyüp Pier. Buses 399B, C or D run to here from Eminönü. The 55T from Taksim Square stops a short walk away. Hourly ferries sail here from Üsküdar, Karaköy and Eminönü. Finish the walk at Pierre Loti Café.
- Eyüp can get crowded at weekends and Fridays, the main day of worship. On Sundays you are likely to see families parading their young sons, lavishly dressed in white princely suits, fur-lined capes and plumed hats, who are visiting the mosque prior to the ritual ceremony of their *sünnet* (circumcision).

ACCOMMODATION

İstanbul's accommodation ranges from palatial five-star hotels to simple *pansiyons* in charming century-old buildings. Unfortunately it's the most expensive place in Turkey and difficult to find anything under 100TL – rooms with shared bathrooms can help bring the cost down. Places to stay are split predominantly into two sharply contrasting areas: the Old City, especially Sultanahmet, has a huge concentration of small hotels and guesthouses, perfect if you want to wake up in sight (or walking distance) of the Blue Mosque – although the dawn *azan* (call to prayer) might mean an earlier start than expected. Over the Golden Horn, Beyoğlu might be short on sights but is the best area for restaurants, shopping and nightlife.

Accommodation Price Categories

Price categories are per night in high season (May–Oct), for a double room, including taxes.

$ = below 30TL
$$ = 30–50TL
$$$ = 50–100TL
$$$$ = 100–200TL
$$$$$ = Over 200TL

İstanbul – Old City

Antique Hostel and Guesthouse
51 Kutlugun Caddesi, Sultanahmet
Tel: 0212-638 1637
www.antiquehostel.com
Very simple rooms in this cosy hostel, which boasts fantastic views from some rooms and the rooftop restaurant. The dorm beds are in the basement – but at least they're cheap! Free internet access. **$**

Four Seasons İstanbul at Sultanahmet
Tevkifhane Sokak 1, Sultanahmet
Tel: 0212-402 3000
www.fourseasons.com
Occupying a century-old former prison, superbly renovated, this luxury hotel has 65 rooms around an open courtyard, immersed in a serene atmosphere. Top facilities include the spa, with massages fit for a sultan. **$$$$$**

Comfortable hotels abound in İstanbul

Hanedan Hotel
Akbiyik Caddesi, Adliye Sokak 3, Sultanahmet
Tel: 0212-516 4869
www.hanedanhotel.com
With just 10 rooms in this converted house, the simple, small rooms are very good value, with good-sized family rooms. For a little extra you can have a Marmara view. Friendly, clean and an unbeatable location, with breakfast served on the terrace. 🏨 **$$$**

Hotel Empress Zoe
Akbiyik Caddesi 4/1, Sultanahmet
Tel: 0212-518 2504
www.emzoe.com
Converted from three townhouses with clever use of wood and stone, all 25 rooms and suites are different, with top terrace suites enjoying views of the Marmara Seat. Peaceful, with a gorgeous central garden. **$$$$**

Hotel Niles
19 Ordu Caddesi, Dibekli Cami Sokak, Beyazit
Tel: 0212-517 3239
www.hotelniles.com
This simple and good-value guesthouse is on a quiet residential street near the Grand Bazaar. Its 29 air-conditioned rooms are simply furnished and the brand-new suites are spacious with traditional touches.

Friendly and helpful staff, and an attractive roof terrace for breakfast. **M** **$$$**

Mavi Ev
Dalbasti Sokak 14, Sultanahmet
Tel: 0212-638 9010
www.bluehouse.com.tr
In a charming restored Ottoman house, rooms are simple with contemporary comforts, just steps away from the Blue Mosque and with perfect views from its rooftop restaurant. **$$$$**

Sirkeci Konak Hotel
Taya Hatun Sokak 5, Sirkeci, Eminönü
Tel: 0212-528 4344
www.sirkecikonak.com
With excellent service, this boutique hotel, once an Ottoman mansion, pays great attention to detail. Extras include a traditional hamam, bijoux swimming pool and jacuzzi in many rooms, luxuries for a hotel of this size. **$$$$**

Tan Hotel
Sokak 20, Çatalçeşme Meydanı, Doktor Emin Paşa, Sultanahmet
Tel: 0212-520 9130
www.tanhotel.com
This affordable boutique hotel down a quiet side street has lovely touches like jacuzzis in each bathroom and LCD screens. The rooftop terrace for breakfast has Bosphorus views and is open 24 hours a day. **$$$$**

Tulip Guesthouse
Akbayik Caddesi, Sultanahmet
Tel: 0212-517 6509
www.tulipguesthouse.com
Situated on a cosy cobbled street, the clean rooms here are small, simple and good value – rooms with a shared bathroom are even cheaper. Friendly and hospitable service, with Bosphorus views accompanying your breakfast. **$$–$$$**

Turing Ayasofya Konaklari
Soğukçeşme Sokağı, Sultanahmet
Tel: 0212-513 3660
www.ayasofyapensions.com

The characterful Büyük Londra hotel

On a charming cobbled street with restored houses behind Hagia Sophia, rooms here have period furniture and bags of atmosphere. 64 rooms including seven suites are spread over 10 buildings, some with courtyard café. **$$$$**

İstanbul – New City
Ansen 130
Mesrutiyet Caddesi 70, Tepebaşı
Tel: 0212-245 8808
www.ansensuites.com
Just 10 luxury suites with huge bedrooms are spread over five floors, each one stylishly decorated. Light, spacious and with fully equipped kitchens and work desk, this is one for a lengthy stay or working holiday. **$$$$$**

Büyük Londra (Grand Hotel de Londres)
Mesrutiyet Caddesi 53, Tepebaşı
Tel: 0212-245 0670
www.londrahotel.net
Faded decadence in one of the cheapest places in town, this has oodles of character even if its historic furnishings have seen better days. Renovated rooms are more comfortable. **$$$**

Galata Residence
Felek Sokak 2, Bankalar Caddesi, Galata
Tel: 0212-292 4841
www.galataresidence.com
A good choice for a longer stay, these

one- and two-bedroom apartments all have simple kitchens and living rooms. Located at the bottom of a cobbled hill near Galata Tower, this was once an old Jewish house. 🏨 $$$

Lush Hotel
Siraselviler Caddesi 12, Taksim
Tel: 0212-243 9595
www.lushhotel.com
From a century-old apartment building, this sleek boutique hotel has oversized artworks in the rooms, all decked out in bold colours. Many of its 35 rooms are small but use the space cleverly – and it's worth the little extra for the larger size. **$$$$**

Pera Palace
Mesrutiyet Caddesi 52, Tepebaşı
Tel: 0212-222 8090
www.perapalace.com
Reopened in June 2010 after huge renovations, this historic landmark was a favourite of Orient Express passengers– including Agatha Christie. Original architectural character has been preserved, including paintings and antique furniture. **$$$$$**

Pera Tulip Hotel
Mesrutiyet Caddesi 103, Tepebaşı
Tel: 0212-243 8500
www.peratulip.com
The standard rooms might be small, but the furnishings are simple and stylish, and the hotel has the added luxury of a small pool and spa. Executive suites have Golden Horn views, DVD players and jacuzzi. **$$$**

W Hotel
Süleyman Seba Caddesi 22, Akaretler, Besiktas
Tel: 0212-381 2121
www.wlstanbul.com.tr
Gorgeous Turkish-contemporary decor and über-chic glamour in a newly restored residential building. Its 136 rooms mix traditional marble bathrooms, goose down pillows and iPod docking station, and some have balconies overlooking a courtyard. **$$$$$**

Smart and stylish: the W Hotel

Witt İstanbul
Defterdar Yokusu 26, Cihangir
Tel: 0212-293 1500
www.wittlstanbul.com
Superbly designed boutique hotel and a big hit since opening in 2008, its open-plan style and arty decor are pure understated elegance, with extras like kitchenette and leather sofa in the living room. Good value, great service, and a well-located residential area. **$$$$$**

World House Hostel
85 Galipdede Caddesi, Beyoğlu
Tel: 0212-293 5520
www.worldhouselstanbul.com
A great backpacker hang-out yet away from the travellers' hub, a room in a 4-bed dorm is a bargain – although there are decent doubles and triples. Simple, clean and friendly, near Beyoğlu's dining and nightlife centre. **$–$$**

The Bosphorus
Sumahan On The Water
Kuleli Caddesi 51, Çengelköy
Tel: 0216-422 8000
www.sumahan.com
Converted from a *rakı* distillery on the Asian side, the 18 huge rooms here have been sensitively designed with super space and light. Each room is unique, some are split-level with huge windows, and most have a real fire. A romantic getaway. **$$$$$**

RESTAURANTS

The Old City might win hands down for sightseeing, but its restaurants lack the variety, quality and value to match. The street Divan Yolu has little in the way of decent eateries; Eminönü is slightly better. The best area for dining is Beyoğlu, where the lively Nevizade Sokak, tucked away off Istiklal Caddesi, is cheek-by-jowl *meyhanes* (traditional taverns) specialising in fresh fish and meat and plenty of *meze*, of course.

Restaurant Price Categories

Price categories are based on a three-course meal for one (including *meze*, grilled meat, bread, salad and fruit) and non-alcoholic drinks.

$ = under 20TL
$$ = 20–40TL
$$$ = 40–60TL
$$$$ = 60–100TL

Istanbul – Old City

Asitane
6 Kariye Camii Sokak, Edirnekapi
Tel: 0212-635 7997
www.asitanerestaurant.com
Off the beaten track, this is the place to splash out and dine like a sultan – literally. Recipes from Topkapi Palace have been revived, with dishes like *mutananjene* (diced lamb with dried apricots) and saffron *pilaf*. **$$$–$$$$**

Bab-i Hayat
Misir Carsisi, Sultan Hamam Girisi, Yeni Cami Caddesi 39
Tel: 0212-520 7878
www.babihayat.com
Located inside the Spice Market (a good choice for lunch), this was converted from a warehouse and opened in 2007, with many features intact. A vast range of kebaps and a salad buffet at lunch on offer.  **$$**

Balıkçı Sabahattin
1 Cankurtaran Caddesi, Sultanahmet
Tel: 0212-458 1824
www.balikcisabahattin.com
Top-quality fish restaurant in the old quarter of Sultanahmet, set on the cobbles with outdoor tables in summer. Fish is simply grilled or fried – ask for the catch of the day. **$$$**

Dubb
10 Incili Cavus Sokak, Sultanahmet
Tel: 0212-513 7308
www.dubbindian.com
One of the few decent restaurants in the area, Indian cuisine here is best loved for its mixed kebaps, cooked freshly in the tandoor oven, with good set meals to sample a range of curries and breads. The open terrace is popular in summer. **$$**

Hamdi Et Lokantası
Kalcin Sokak 17, Tahimis Caddesi, Eminönü
Tel: 0212-528 0390
www.hamdi.com.tr
With staggering views over the Golden Horn, it's not surprising that the roof terrace gets packed with locals and tour groups. Come for succulent kebaps from southeast Turkey. Home-made baklava rounds meals off. **$$$**

Zeyrekhane Restaurant
Ibadethane Arkasi Sokak 10, Zeyrek
Tel: 0212-532 2778
www.zeyrekhane.com
Converted from a Byzantine-era monastery with original sturdy stone walls, most venture here for the huge terrace and Golden Horn views, making the steep prices worthwhile. The kebaps and pastries are excellent. **$$$**

Meyhanes line Sofyali Sokak in Beyoğlu

Listings

İstanbul – New City

Boncuk
Nevizade Sokak 19, off Istiklal Caddesi
Tel: 0212-243 1219
One of many lively *meyhanes* on this street, try its Armenian-influenced *mezes* with fresh fish in season. Outdoor tables can be noisy; reserve at weekends. **$$–$$$**

Canim Cigerim
1 Minare Sokak, off Asmalımescit, Beyoğlu
Tel: 0212-252 6060
A must for liver lovers, this simple but great-value restaurant only serves skewers of roasted liver, served with piles of fresh salad and herbs, and flatbread to make a wrap. Best accompanied with a glass of *ayran*. **$**

Cezayir
Hayriye Caddesi 12, Galatasaray
Tel: 0212-245 9980
www.cezayir-Istanbul.com
This century-old mansion now houses a fashionable restaurant with a huge leafy courtyard. Inventive modern Turkish dishes range from smoked salmon with dried rose petals to broad-bean purée with *rakı* and dill. **$$–$$$**

Hacı Baba
49 Istiklal Caddesi, Beyoglu
Tel: 0212-244 1886
www.hacibabarest.com
Originally the priests' house for the adjacent Greek church, this has been serving up Turkish dishes for the earthly and spiritual alike since 1921. Try Ottoman specialities like lamb shank and stuffed cabbage. **$$**

Hala
26 Cukurlu Çeşme Sokak, off Büyük Parmakkapi Sokak, Beyoğlu
Tel: 0212-293 7531
Specialising in handmade *manti* (a type of filled ravioli in yoghurt sauce) and *gözleme* (filled pancake). An informal restaurant with tasty good-value food. 🍴 **$**

The House Café
Salhane Sokak 1, Ortaköy
Tel: 0212-227 2699

The House Café is a good place to take kids

www.thehousecafe.com.tr
With a huge deck overlooking the waterfront, this specialises in comfort food and brunches like Eggs Benedict, home-made pizzas and grilled chicken, plus a kids' menu. A popular late-night venue for cocktails. 🍴 **$$–$$$**

Kafe Ara
8 Tosbağa Sokak, off Yeniçarşi Caddesi, Galatasaray
Tel: 0212-245 4105
Owned by photographer Ara Guler (his photos adorn the walls), this informal bistro serves pasta, *köfte* and great coffee, popular with students, writers and locals at lunch time. **$$**

Leb-i Derya
Kumbaraci Yokusu 57/6, Tünel
Tel: 0212-293 4989
www.lebiderya.com
One of the city's hippest hang-outs, night views over the Bosphorus almost outdo the contemporary Turkish and international cuisine. Best known for its 40-spiced beef. **$$$**

Sofyalı 9
Sofyali Sokak 9, off Asmalimescit Caddesi, Beyoğlu
Tel: 0212-245 0362
www.sofyali.com.tr
A huge range of hot and cold *meze* starts a meal at this *meyhane*, with cheerful yellow walls and a few outdoor tables away from the crowds. Mains include fresh fish in season, and lamb dishes. **$$**

NIGHTLIFE AND ENTERTAINMENT

Once again it's Beyoğlu that boasts the best selection of bijoux bars and clubs, especially around Tünel and Asmalımescit. In addition to the venues listed below, the café-bars running off Istiklal Caddesi, at the Taksim Square end, often have live *fasil* (folk music) where locals sit at outdoor tables with a beer and a hookah *(nargile)*. Rooftop bars are all the rage in summer, as are the super-clubs on Ortaköy's waterfront where dressing up is key to keeping up with the wannabe celebs. For the classical music and jazz fan, a number of decent venues have year-round concerts from Turkish and visiting orchestras (see also *Festivals*).

5 Kat
5/F 7 Soğanci Sokak, Cihangir
Tel: 0212-293 3774
www.5kat.com
The rooftop terrace is packed in summer for sweeping views, with purple sofas and beaded curtains inside when the nights get cold. Lounge music, snacks and wines from this long-standing favourite.

360 İstanbul
8/F Misir Apartmen, 311 Istiklal Caddesi, Beyoğlu
Tel: 0212-251 1042
www.360Istanbul.com
This top-floor restaurant and bar has a terrace for those jaw-dropping views and is a hub for the city's fashionistas. Late-night weekends see the dancefloor fill up courtesy of music from the resident DJs.

Akbank Sanat
8 Istiklal Caddesi
Tel: 0212-252 3500
www.akbanksanat.com
This small but amazingly diverse cultural venue manages to cram in a theatre, concert hall, cinema and dance venue to its small stages. One of several venues sponsored by a bank.

Anjelique
5 Salhane Sokak, Mualim Naci Caddesi, Ortaköy
Tel: 0212-327 2844
www.Istanbuldoors.com
This three-storey club on the Bosphorus is a much-loved summer venue. Weekends are members only, but call ahead midweek for the guest list to dance on the terrace or nibble on sushi on the sofa.

Atatürk Cultural Centre (Atatürk Kültür Merkezi)
Taksim Meydani
Box office: 0212-251 5600
Although an eyesore, this 1970s building looms large over Taksim Square, and hosts ballet, opera, and concerts, and is a major venue for İstanbul's myriad festivals. Major renovations are set to be completed in 2011.

Babylon
3 Şehbender Sokak, Asmalimescit, Beyoğlu
Tel: 0212-292 7368
www.babylon.com.tr
Nighly live music and DJs mean an eclectic music line-up at this vibrant little club, playing anything from jazz to Balkan punk to Turkish fusion to a packed house. Buy tickets in advance for popular events.

Badehane
General Yazgan Sokak 5, Tünel
Tel: 0212-249 0550
This one-room bar, spilling onto the tucked-away cobbled street, is a favourite of bohemian *İstanbullus*, especially its live Balkan music every Wednesday evening.

Cemal Reşit Rey Konser Salonu
1 Darülbedayi Caddesi, Harbiye
Tel: 0212-232 9830
www.crrks.org
The resident orchestra puts on a diverse programme of concerts, including Turkish and religious music, and is the venue for several festivals (closed in winter).

Dersaadet
20 Bogaz Tarafi, Galata Bridge
Tel: 0212-292 7001
Located at the Karaköy end of the bridge, this
is a simple café-bar where an outside table is
the perfect place for sipping a cold beer, puff-
ing on a *nargile* (waterpipe) and playing backgammon, while watching the boats sail by.

Nardis Jazz Club
14 Galata Kulesi Sokak
Tel: 0212-244 6327
www.nardisjazz.com

Live acts from Turkey and overseas bring the
jazz fans flocking. This is informal, cosy and
friendly, but taking its music seriously.

Pano Şarap Evi
Hamal Basi Caddesi, 12/B, Galatasaray
Tel: 0212-292 6664
www.panosarapevi.com
This traditional Greek wine house has decent
house wine, even better accompanied with
platters of meats and cheeses, or good old
Turkish *meze*. Perch on tall bar stools or join
friends for dinner, with a few tables outside.

SPORTS AND ACTIVITIES

Sporting culture in İstanbul is dominated by football *(see p.78)*, with basketball
coming a close second. For participation, the bowling alley makes for great
entertainment for all ages.

Babb Bowling
Tum Haklaki Saklidir, off Istiklal Caddesi
Tel: 0212-251 1595
www.babbowling.com.tr
Go for a strike at this popular bowling alley,
also with a restaurant, café and billiard
tables. Booking advised for weekends. 🏃

Beşiktaş Football Club
Inönü Stadium, Gümüşsuyu
Tel: 0212-310 1000
www.bjk.com.tr
The most accessible ground in İstanbul,
the 'Black Eagles' play at this picturesque

location, with the Yeni Açik stand overlooking
Dolmabahçe Palace. Tickets available from
any Biletix outlet; avoid local derbies (against
Galatasaray or Fenerbahçe) where tensions
can run high. Season runs Aug–May.

Efes Pilsen
Abdi Ipekci Arena, Zeytinburnu
Tel: 0212-665 8647
www.efesbasket.org
One of the best basketball teams in Europe,
the Efes Pilsen team has won the Turkish
title many times since founded in 1975. The
season runs from Oct–May.

TOURS

If you'd rather the comfort and convenience of an organised tour, there is a huge
range of full-day sightseeing trips, ranging from the famous venues to the more
quirky neighbourhood walking tours. Bear in mind that when arranging a tour, if you
book it through your hotel it's likely that they will add on their own commission.

İstanbul Tours
Return Tourism Travel
2-8/A Dr Eminpaşa Sokak, off divan Yolu
Caddesi, Sultanahmet

Tel: 0212-511 7410
www.Istanbultoursguide.com
This licensed travel agency offers a huge
range of trips including Imperial tours,

Bosphorus Cruise, İstanbul By Night and Ottoman Wonders, plus out of the city to Bursa.

Caddesi and Fatih Mosque to Edirnekapi.
Small groups are led by qualified guides.

İstanbul Walks
5/F, Daire 9, 53 Istiklal Caddesi
Tel: 0212-292 2874
www.Istanbulwalks.net
Specialising in cultural tourism, their range
of daily walking tours include the Jewish
district of Galata, Bohemian walks on Istiklal

Les Arts Turcs
3/F Incili Cavus Sokak 37, Sultanahmet
Tel: 0212-527 6859
www.lesartsturcs.com
This group offers themed cultural and historic tours of İstanbul. Weekly trips to an
evening whirling dervish ceremony.

FESTIVALS AND EVENTS

Most of İstanbul's festivals are
organised by İstanbul Kültür ve
Sanat Vakfı (İstanbul Foundation for
Culture and Arts) and the success and
popularity of their events continue to
soar, especially the music festival. For
most events, tickets are available from
Biletix outlets (tel: 0216-556 9800;
www.biletix.com), including a ticket
counter at 55 Istiklal Caddesi.

Performing at the International Jazz Festival

April
International İstanbul Film Festival
Various venues
www.iksv.org
Screened mainly in venues around Beyoğlu,
this fortnight-long festival profiles old, new,
Turkish and international films, all with
subtitles.

May
İstanbul Grand Prix
İstanbul Park, Tuzla
www.İstanbulparkcircuit.com
On the Formula 1 circuit since 2005,
located on the Asian side, petrolheads
pour into the city for the race. Hotel prices
soar and availability sinks during this
weekend.

Akbank Jazz Festival
Various venues
www.akbank.com

An extensive programme of nu-jazz, ethnic
and classical, and fusion bands, stretching
the traditional concept of jazz to the limit.

June
International İstanbul Music Festival
Various venues
www.iksv.org/muzik
A vast range of performers, from young solo
classical artists to international orchestras,
the beauty here is the rare chance to see
concerts in venues like Hagia Eirene Museum
and İstanbul Archaeological Museum.

July
International İstanbul Jazz Festival
Various venues
www.iksv.org/caz
This three-week festival brings Turkish and
international acts to open-air theatres, parks
and concert halls, including acts such as Joe
Jackson, George Benson and *fasıl* (folk) acts.

Thrace and Marmara

Close to İstanbul but substantially different in character, this is a region of land borders and seas, a historical site of ancient, Ottoman and recent battles. The Sea of Marmara nestles in the middle of land which loops around Europe and Asia. To its north, Thrace is European Turkey, the land of the Dardanelles and windswept hills. South is Marmara, the point where Asia begins.

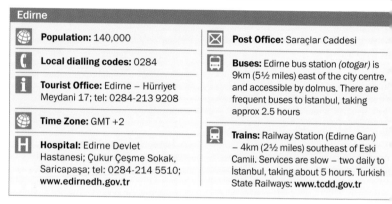

Edirne

Population: 140,000

Local dialling codes: 0284

Tourist Office: Edirne – Hürriyet Meydani 17; tel: 0284-213 9208

Time Zone: GMT +2

Hospital: Edirne Devlet Hastanesi; Çukur Çeşme Sokak, Saricapaşa; tel: 0284-214 5510; www.edirnedh.gov.tr

Post Office: Saraçlar Caddesi

Buses: Edirne bus station (otogar) is 9km (5½ miles) east of the city centre, and accessible by dolmus. There are frequent buses to İstanbul, taking approx 2.5 hours

Trains: Railway Station (Edirne Garı) – 4km (2½ miles) southeast of Eski Camii. Services are slow – two daily to İstanbul, taking about 5 hours. Turkish State Railways: www.tcdd.gov.tr

This northeastern corner of Turkey forms a passage between the Balkan peninsula and Anatolia. It encircles the Sea of Marmara, a small sea that stretches from the Black Sea to the Aegean, and an area often neglected by tourists. On the one hand, its desolate scenery, proximity to international borders and lack of developed coastal resorts seem a hindrance. But on the other, these could be seen as the region's charms. The two jewels in the province, Edirne and Bursa, are immersed in Ottoman history. Both were capital of the Empire, in the 14th and 15th centuries respectively, with superb architectural reminders. Two other contrasting landmarks of history mark the area; the warriors of ancient Troy, and the more modern-day soldiers who died on the Gallipoli battlefield.

Thrace (Trakya) is Turkey's only area that is part of Europe, a province which stretches over the borders into Greece and Bulgaria, with tracts of fertile farmland and vine-covered hills. This was once Turkey's main route into Roman Europe, although these days its successor is a multi-lane highway crowded with lorries transporting cargo, and buses laden with passengers journeying to Sofia. Its provincial capital Edirne is the last major city before heading over the border into Bulgaria or Greece.

Marmara comprises a range of terrain, from the soft hills around İznik to the snowy peaks of Uludağ, tumbling mineral waters in Yalova and the bucolic wonder of Kuşcenneti.

Thrace

The fertile land and lucrative crops in this region mean that the province is relatively comfortable, its locals renowned for their liberal spirit and independent outlook. Previously known as Hadrianopolis, Edirne's strategic position on the route linking Asia Minor with southeastern Europe has been highly sought over the centuries. After falling to the Ottomans in 1362, it was capital of the empire, and it was from here that Mehmet II attacked Constantinople. Unsurprisingly, its outstanding monuments are Ottoman landmarks. Although

The striking form of the Selimiye Mosque lit up at night

Memorial at Gallipoli *(see p.95)*

just a two-hour drive from İstanbul, **Edirne ❶** is a world away, with a charming and easy-going atmosphere, almost provincial. Southwest, in the narrow straits of the Dardanelles which slip into the Marmara, the Gelibolu Peninsula is the resting place of many a fallen soldier from the World War I campaign.

Edirne

Commonly believed to be Sinan's greatest creation *(see box, p.68)*, the **Selimiye Mosque** (Selimiye Camii) **Ⓐ** (daily sunrise–sunset except prayer times; free) dominates the city. Completed in 1575 when the architect was 80, it was designed to surpass the mighty Hagia Sophia (Aya Sofya) in size. Eighteen small domes lead the eye to the vast dome, 45m (150ft) in diameter and supported by eight sturdy pillars, which almost appears to float. Inside, the

Thrace and Marmara

Headstones at Gallipoli

Over the Meriç Bridge

It's a lovely walk down Maarif Caddesi south of the city centre, past the dilapidated **Grand Synagogue**, and over the Maritza River on the 263m (862ft) -long arched **Meriç Bridge** (Meriç Köprüsü). Built in 1847, this has 12 pointed arches and drainage ports to prevent flooding – which is still an issue in the city after heavy rains. On the other side of the bridge is a charming house, **Protokol Evi**, now owned and renovated by the local *Belediye* (council). It's a lovely stop for a late breakfast or just a Turkish coffee, with a superb riverside location and well-kept lawns.

exquisite İznik tiles of the *mihrab* and sultan's *loge* (balcony), 999 windows and lacy stonework give the vast space a feeling of light and serenity. Four slender minarets lift the entire dome heavenward.

In addition to the mosque itself, the vast *külliye* (complex) comprises a courtyard and **Selimiye Arasta**, a shopping arcade. With 73 arches, this was built to bring revenue for the mosque, and today it's where religious items, and souvenirs like Edirne's famous fruit-shaped soaps, are traded. Not surprisingly, that this is considered one of Turkey's architectural gems. The adjacent *medrese* (school) now houses the **Selimiye Foundation Museum** (Selimiye Vakif Müzesi; daily 8.30am–5.30pm;

free), displaying Ottoman crafts, especially calligraphy and ornate carved wood pieces.

Eski Mosque ❸ (Eski Camii) is a restored mosque, constructed between 1403 and 1415 under Mehmet I and most striking for its simplicity. Modelled on Bursa's Ulu Mosque *(see p.97)*, the perfect square is divided into nine domed sections, its interior dominated by huge, elaborate calligraphy on the walls. Inside, on the wall, is a small piece of stone from Mecca, encased in glass. The upkeep was paid for by revenues from the Bedesten, built a few years later, which stored and sold valuable goods. Outside the mosque is the city's symbol – a life-size sculpture of two *pehlivans* (wrestlers).

The sturdy red tower of **Makedonya Kulesi**, also known as Saat Kulesi (clock tower), is a local landmark, built in 1894 and the last tower remaining from Edirne's city walls. Although it's not possible to climb it any more, you can wander the excavated site adjacent to it, which has the remains of a 10th-century Byzantine church, plus city walls which date back to Roman times with pottery ovens.

Gallipoli

The **Gallipoli** (Gelibolu) **peninsula** ❷ is a beautiful area of fine beaches, lush bird-filled pine forests and rolling countryside, a startling contrast to its bleak history. This is the starting point for visiting the battlefields and Allied cemeteries of World War I. Although many visitors use Çanakkale as their base, Eceabat is closer and well connected by regular ferry.

The actual battle was fought in 1915, when on the orders of Winston Churchill, a combined Allied force of almost half a million attempted to force a passage through the narrow Dardanelles (Çanakkale Boğazi) to İstanbul, to defeat Turkey. But Churchill did so without envisaging that officer Mustafa Kemal (later Atatürk) would lead Turkish troops to victory.

It takes a day to visit all the major sites spread across the peninsula, which is why an organised tour is advisable *(see p.109)*. The most famous spots are **Lone Pine Cemetery**, where the Australian and New Zealand soldiers now lie, and **Anzac Cove**, where the Turkish Memorial bears a message of reconciliation written by Atatürk. **Kabatepe Military Museum** (daily 8.30am–5pm; charge) has a moving collection of war memorabilia. In the far south are the British obelisk and French cemetery.

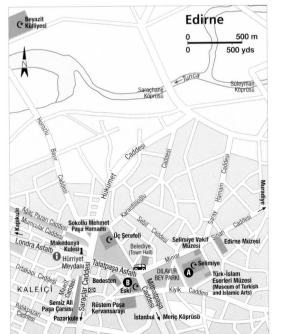

Entering the Selimiye Mosque in Edirne

Contemplation in Bursa's Green Mosque

Marmara

From the shadow-play Karagöz puppets to the dazzling green tiles of the mosques, the city of Bursa still carries its Ottoman treasures. İznik was home to the tilemakers, creating the painted ceramic beauties so adored by the sultans. The region also loves its natural wonders, like the ski slopes of Uludağ National Park, and the hot springs at Termal.

Bursa

The historic city of Bursa ❸ contains some distinctive Ottoman monuments and buildings. As its name suggests, dazzling green and blue tiles adorn the interior of the **Green Mosque**'s (Yeşil Camii) ❹ (dawn–nightfall except prayer times; free) and is considered one of the great Ottoman masterpieces. Built in 1419 under Mehmet I, the decoration is incredible, with circles, stars and geometric motifs, especially around the *mihrab* and the sultan's *loge*. Opposite is the **Green Tomb** (Yeşil Türbe; daily 8.30am– noon, 1–5pm; charge), housing the grandiose sarcophagus of Mehmet I and his large family, its interior dominated by brilliant green tiles.

Along Atatürk Caddesi, the 20 domes – four columns by five – of

Bursa

🌐 **Population:** 2,550,645

📞 **Local dialling code:** 0224

ℹ️ **Tourist Office:** Heykel, Orhangazi Altgecidi 1; tel: 0224-223 8307

🌐 **Time Zone:** GMT +2

🏥 **Hospital:** Özel Bursa, Zubeyde Hanım Caddesi, Çekirge

✉️ **Post Office:** Corner of Atatürk and Maksem Caddesi

✈️ **Airport:** Bursa Yenisehir Airport; tel: 0224-781 8181; www. yenisehir.dhmi.gov.tr. Mainly domestic flights, with some international airlines in the future

⚓ **Ferries:** The quickest way to travel from İstanbul to Bursa is by fast car ferry from İstanbul (Yenikapi) to Yalova, then bus or dolmus to Bursa (www.ido.com.tr/en)

🚕 **Taxis:** minibuses (dolmuş) and taxis are frequent and cheap

🚗 **Car hire companies:** Europcar; 125 Berke Apartmen, Cekirge Caddesi; tel: 0244-235 3270/Bursa Yenisehir Airport; tel: 0224-235 3271; www. europcar.com. Avis; 139 Cekirge Caddesi; tel: 0224-236 5133

the bulky **Grand Mosque** (Ulu Camii) **B** were apparently a compromise to a vow from Sultan Beyazit, made in 1396, that he would build 20 mosques if victorious in battle. It dominates the area like a great fortress, with yellow limestone walls, and doors surrounded by carved marble portals. The huge şadırvan (ablutions fountain) beneath the central dome was made necessary, apparently, when a 14th-century homeowner refused to sell her property to make room for the mosque; the presence of the fountain precludes any possibility of praying on land not donated willingly.

The **Market Bazaar** (Çarşi) **C** was the heart of the old city, founded by Orhan Gazi in the 14th century. In fact it is still the commercial centre

Shadow Play

Bursa is the historic home of the **Karagöz** shadow puppets, popular since the Ottoman period. The puppets are made traditionally from camel hide, then oiled to make them translucent and painted. Manipulated from behind a white muslin cloth, light is shone behind them to cast the bold coloured shadows, and with jointed limbs, the puppetmasters move the characters smoothly across the tiny stage. The ribald stories told usually include Karagöz, traditionally representing the illiterate, simple public, and the cultured, well-spoken Hacivat. Today, the plays are traditionally played out in public squares, coffee shops and inns, and are most likely to be seen during Ramadan in the evenings. The puppets themselves can be bought in the bazaar and make a fantastic souvenir. ⊞

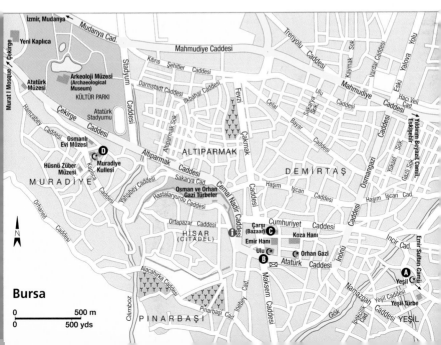

Bursa

0   500 m
0   500 yds

⭐ OIL WRESTLING

Turkey's centuries-old traditional sport of oil wrestling has deep roots in Ottoman history, yet the annual tournament in Edirne – as well as villages around Turkey – is still very much alive, kicking and grappling.

Traditional Legends

Take over a thousand pairs of black leather breeches, several hundred cans of olive oil and a bright green meadow, and you have *yağli güreş* (oil wrestling), one of the world's most ancient sports. Summer tournaments take place in towns and villages around Turkey, its largest event in the celebrated three-day **Kırkpınar festival** (late June or early July), held on the outskirts of Edirne. This sporting encounter dates back centuries, and patriotic Turks, proud of their Ottoman heritage, often feel that *yağli güreş* is in their blood.

Origins

Although its origins are shrouded in legend and theory, the most commonly

Oil wrestling has a long history and remains true to its traditional form

accepted history dates back to 1360 when Süleyman, grandson of Osman Gazi, founder of the Ottoman Empire, returned with 40 of his troops from a successful battle to capture Rumelia. Returning to Constantinople, they rested overnight in a meadow at Samona, now part of Greece. These burly warriors wrestled each other in pairs to pass the time, the winner staying on to fight the next. The final two were clinched in a fight for hours, refusing to give up as this would have been as dishonourable as conceding during war. They continued as night fell, the others drifting off to sleep. When they awoke the next morning, they were shocked to discover that the two men had died in combat, lying in a deathly grip.

Wrestling is deemed to be the ultimate preparation for battle, therefore honouring Allah, so these two soldiers were considered martyrs and buried on the spot. A year later the troops returned to the spot to pay their respects, and were amazed to discover that 40 freshwater springs had appeared in place of their graves. They named the area 'Kırkpınar' (the Turkish for 40 springs), and after Edirne was conquered in 1361, wrestling took place here most years to honour the two wrestlers. In recent decades the festival has been financed by the local *belediye* (council) and prominent businessmen.

Contemporary Oil Wrestling

Today's three-day tournament is held in Kaleiçi, a grassy meadow on the outskirts of Edirne, watched by hundreds of spectators. Almost 2,000 *pehlivans* (wrestlers) participate in 13 weight classes, each round taking place simultaneously, and when each bout is over, the winner stays on. The ultimate winner of the heaviest class is the *başpehlivan*, the head wrestler winning a cash prize and, more importantly, plenty of honour.

True to its roots, each bout begins with the *peşrev*, a prayer to Allah reminding each wrestler of his humble roots. The musicians strike up the *davul* (drum) and *zurna* (reed instrument) and the bouts begin. *Pehlivans* are clad only in *kispet*, hand-made black leather breeches, and drenched in olive oil which makes traditional wrestling grips impossible, so grapples and clever manoeuvres aim to floor their opponent. If there is no decisive throw, the winner is judged on a points system.

In an age when many traditional sports like *kabbadi* and even *sumo* are declining in favour of more profitable international sports like football, *yağli güreş*, ironically, is growing in popularity and funding. In this context, it means that Edirne's hotels and *pansiyons* are booked up weeks in advance.

While the dates of Kırkpınar are well publicised, smaller *yağli güreş* festivals dotted around Turkey's towns and villages are trickier to track down. Check venues such as Karamanmaraş, Elmalı, Isparta, Mentese and Alaplı, which often have wrestling tournaments coinciding with summer harvest celebrations.

Musicians provide an atmospheric backing soundtrack to the spectacle

Oiled-up participants take part in a bout at the Kırkpınar festival

of Bursa, with narrow winding alleys crowded with ironmongers, goldsmiths and cabinet-makers, and with local shoppers inspecting their wares. At the heart of the bazaar is the **Bedesten** (covered market), built by Beyazit I. It is a sturdy structure still used for storing and selling gold and silver, with some of the revenue going to Orhan Gazi's Ulu Camii. At the centre of the marketplace is the two-storey **Silk Cocoon Hall** (Koza Hanı), occupied by silk merchants who have been central to the city's economy for 600 years. It's even more so in June and July, when silk breeders from around the province fill the hall to sell their valuable white feathery torpedoes in the annual silk auction.

South of Çekirge Caddesi, the medieval **Muradiye** district has well-preserved Ottoman houses belonging to the wealthy locals of bygone centuries, including **The Museum of 17th-Century Ottoman Houses** (Osmanlı Evi Müzesi; Tue–Sun 8am–noon, 1–5pm; charge), which is one of the oldest houses in Bursa. It displays decor and artefacts from 17th-century living.

In front of it is the **Muradiye Kullesi** (complex) **D**, completed in 1426 and comprising a mosque, *imaret* (soup kitchen), *medrese* and the tomb of Murat II (summer 8.30am–5.30pm, winter 8am–5pm; charge/tip) and other members of Ottoman royalty.

In the gardens, 12 tombs include that of Murat, on a dome on antique columns, fulfilling his wish to be buried under the rain and stars, in stark contrast to his father's tomb

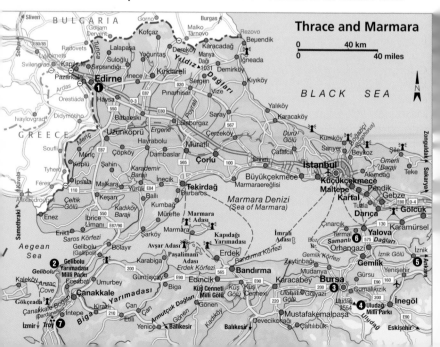

İznik's famous pottery is ideal for a souvenir *(see p.102)*

at Yeşil Turbe. From here it's a steep walk up to the **Citadel** (Hisari) and tombs of Osman and Orhan Gazi, the first Ottoman leaders.

To the west of Bursa's centre, **Cekirge** is an elegant area long known for its hot mineral waters, ever since Emperor Justinian built a bathhouse here in the 6th century, although they have been somewhat depleted since 2009. Many of the upmarket hotels will have their own private mineral bath; one of the most attractive is the beautifully restored **Eski Kaplica** (Old Spa), with plunge pools in the hot rooms. This is also the place to catch a shadow puppet show *(see box, p.97)*.

Uludağ National Park
Thirty km (18 miles) southeast of Bursa, the 2,554m (8,343ft) -high richly forested slopes of **Uludağ National Park** (Uludağ Milli Parki; 🗷 ❹ are the highest point of Marmara and the location of one of Turkey's main ski resorts. A cable car journeys from Bursa up to the Sarilian Plain, and then a dolmuş travels to the hotel area of the park. The season runs from December to March, with reasonable facilities including snowboarding and even heli-skiing. Spring and summer see people flocking to the area for walks in beautiful surroundings of high plains, deep valleys and mountain lakes – or just to grill meat on family picnics. On Uludağ's lower eastern slopes, the picturesque village of **Cumalıkızık** still has Ottoman houses – albeit rather dilapidated – plus a mosque and tiny museum on charming cobbled streets.

The Art of Ceramics

Turkish hand-painted tiles have, through the years, given mosques their hue, dinner tables their decoration and palaces their motifs. In the mid-16th century, Selim I resettled tile-workers in İznik, which coincided with his fascination with Chinese porcelain, and they began to produce utensils. But that soon changed to architectural decoration when Süleyman I ordered the building of countless major mosques, at the time when the Ottoman Empire was at its peak. The tile-workers of İznik were put to work producing glorious hand-painted tiles to adorn the sultan's mosques including Süleymaniye, Sultanahmet and Rüstem Paşa (İstanbul), and Selimiye (Edirne), plus more utilitarian goods like decorated bowls and dishes for display. Stylised motifs soon developed, and the tulips made their appearance together with carnations and roses. Once the Ottoman Empire was in decline, the İznik pottery trade also dwindled because of lack of demand. The ceramics you see today in the markets – albeit beautiful creations and often hand-painted – are more likely to be made in Kütahya, especially for tourists.

İznik

Formerly known as Nicaea, **İznik** ❺ is a small town on the banks of **İznik Lake** (İznik Gölü) 80km (50 miles) northeast of Bursa, and contains some of Turkey's best Byzantine sights. It was also one of two major centres for producing fine, hand-painted glazed tiles through the Ottoman era. After its founding in 310BC and subsequent position at the forefront of empires and battle, the town played a significant role in the history of Christianity, with two ecumenical councils held here in AD325 and AD787. It has since been occupied by Byzantines, Persian, Mongols and Turks over the centuries.

Today, İznik's lakeside location is a huge attraction, along with its ancient walls and four great gates. Inside the ruined basilica of Aya Sofya is the **Aya Sofya Museum** (Aya Sofya Müzesi; Tue–Sun 9am–noon, 1–5pm; charge); look for the sections of a mosaic floor, and fresco of Christ, John the Baptist and Mary, dating back to the times of Justinian.

Also inside the city walls is **Haci Özbek Mosque** (Haci Ozbek Camii), built in 1333, the earliest-known Ottoman mosque in Turkey. **İznik Museum** (İznik Müzesi; Tue–Sun 8.30am–noon, 1.30–5pm; charge) is housed inside the old Nilufer Hatun Imareti, the kitchen, which serves food to the poor, named after Murad I's mother. Inside there's a mix of exhibits, including Greek tombstones, Roman

A classic İznik tile

Byzantine architecture in İznik

Thrace and Marmara

antiquities and, of course, Seljuk and Ottoman tiles.

Yalova

On the southern shore of the Gulf of Izmit, Yalova is a popular holiday spot with middle-class Turks, and used as a base for the spa town of **Termal** , 12km (7½ miles) south-west. Here, the famous hot springs gush mineral-rich waters, loved since the days of the Romans and Byzantines. A selection of pools, hotels and baths make the most of the waters' healing properties today. **Kurşunlu** bath was built by Justinian 1,700 years ago, and later developed by Abdulhamit II to celebrate his 25th anniversary of his reign, in 1900; it is now known for its outdoor pool. Yalova is well connected to İstanbul by regular fast ferry.

Yalova

 Population: 188,440

 Local dialling code: 0226

 Tourist Office: Iskele Meydani 5; tel: 0226-814 2108

 Time Zone: GMT +2

 Hospital: Yalova Devlet Hastanesi; Yalova Merkez; tel: 0226-811 5200

 Buses: Intercity Bus Terminal (Sehirlerarasi Otobus Terminali); Yeni Yalova Yolu. Located 10km (6 miles) north of the city centre, this modern terminal has long-distance buses to most other cities in Turkey

Ferries: Fast Car Ferry from İstanbul (Yenikapi) to Yalova (**www.ido.com.tr**)

Troy

Homer's famous *Iliad* was long believed to be myth, until the 19th-century German businessman Heinrich Schliemann excavated the site of **Troy** (Truva) ❼ and uncovered nine layers of architecture. Gold, daggers, lance heads and silver vases were all prizes that he unearthed, some of which date back to the Bronze Age civilisation. Today, Troy (Hisarlık; daily, summer 8am–7.30pm, winter 8am–5pm; charge), where the 13th-century BC Trojan War was fought, displays ruins dating back to 4000BC until around AD300. It also includes evidence that a battle took place around the time of the *Iliad*.

Still standing are the huge east wall and gate, with a paved chariot ramp leading into the city, and Roman theatre. If you stand on the ramparts and look over towards the sea, this is where thousands of ships of King Agamemnon laid siege to Troy. And of course the infamous wooden horse itself – a reconstruction of the Greek's original Trojan horse – can be entered from underneath, from where you can look out over the ruined city and the plains of Troy.

The site has relatively little to show for its illustrious pedigree, though multiple explanatory panels placed along a circular touring path help make sense of the place. Begin a tour at the massive tower in the great wall of Troy VI and continue through the east gate, passing the carefully constructed houses of Troy VI, to the more careless edifices of Troy VII. From the summit you can look over the plain to Homer's 'wine-dark sea', and see Schliemann's great north–south trench. Northwest of the paved ramp, against the wall of Troy II, was where he found the hoard of treasure.

The wooden replica of the Trojan horse

ACCOMMODATION

There's nothing terribly flashy in the way of accommodation in this region, but hotels are generally down-to-earth and comfortable, with some guesthouses in delightfully converted Ottoman houses, especially in Bursa and Edirne. In Bursa, the elegant suburb of Çekirge has most of the best hotels, which make the most of its mineral waters, and the downtown area Tahtakale is the one with the cheapest hotels. Because Edirne sits close to two borders, there tends to be passing trade in the form of truck drivers, for whom frills and fancies are not a priority.

Accommodation Price Categories

Price categories are per night in high season (May–Oct), for a double room, including taxes.

$ = below 30TL
$$ = 30–50TL
$$$ = 50–100TL
$$$$ = 100–200TL
$$$$$ = Over 200TL

Thrace

Antik Hotel
Maarif Caddesi, Garanti Bankası Sokağı 6, Edirne
Tel: 0284-225 1555
www.edirneantikhotel.com
Previously known as Karam, this is almost a boutique hotel. Its 11 high-ceilinged rooms including 2 suites have cable TV and minibars. Live music at weekends in the courtyard restaurant. **$$$$**

Otel Açikgöz
9 Cilingirler Caddesi, Tahmis Meydani, Edirne
Tel: 0284-213 0313
www.acikgoz.com
It might look a little drab on the outside, but the 28 rooms and 6 suites are spotless, all with TV, and located down a quiet side street. 🍴 **$$$**

Rüstempaşa Kervansaray
57 Iki Kapili Han Caddesi, Edirne
Tel: 0284-212 6119
www.edirnekervansarayhotel.com
Located in a 16th-century *caravanserai* built by Sinan, this has been restored to a simple hotel with a lovely courtyard. **$$$**

Selimiye Taşodalar
Selimiye Camii Arkasi, Edirne
Tel: 0284-212 3529
www.tasodalar.com.tr
There are just nine rooms in this newly restored Ottoman house, right next to the Selimiye mosque. Traditional touches include kilims in the rooms and simple dark-wood furniture, and a large tea garden. **$$$$**

Tuna Hotel
17 Maarif Caddesi, Edirne
Tel: 0284-214 3340
http://edirnetunahotel.net
A pretty new hotel on the main drag, this is well run and has a bright restaurant area and shared living area on the ground floor. The 18 rooms are neat and simple. **$$$**

Marmara

Çelik Palas Hotel
79 Çekirge Caddesi, Bursa
Tel: 0224-233 3800
www.celikpalasotel.com
The original part of the hotel was established in 1935 by Atatürk, and reopened in summer 2010 after major renovation. It has 150 luxury rooms, and the huge outdoor pool and luxury spa with Turkish bath are a huge draw. Bang in the city centre. **$$$$$**

Hisarlik Otel
13/15 Piri Reis Caddesi, Troy
Tel: 0286-283 0026
Although overpriced, this is the only accommodation in the area, just a 10 minute walk to the ruins of Troy. Rooms are clean, with a shared balcony and decent restaurant. **$$**

Listings

Enjoy fantastic views over Bursa while eating breakfast at the Kent Otel

Hotel Çeşmeli
6 Heykel Gümüşçeken Caddesi, Bursa
Tel: 0244-224 1511/2
A small hotel run by women, so good for solo women travellers. Rooms are spotless and breakfast is decent. In a central location on a quiet side street, price seems to be negotiable. **$$$**

Hotel Gonluferah City
20 Birinci Murat Caddesi, Cekirge, Bursa
Tel: 0224-233 9500
www.gonluferahcity.com
This huge 4-star, previously the Dilmen, has 90 rooms and comforts like a garden terrace, sauna and mineral water baths. **$$$$**

Hotel Güneş
75 Inebey Caddesi, Tahtakale, Bursa
Tel: 0224-222 1404
If you don't mind a simple room and shared bathroom, this family-run guesthouse is friendly and clean, in a historic neighbourhood with winding streets. **$**

Kent Otel
69 Atatürk Caddesi, Bursa
Tel: 0224-223 5420
www.kentotel.com
Modern, bright rooms with great city views are close by the major sights in this large hotel, with added facilities like Wi-fi and a huge top-floor restaurant. **$$$$**

Kitap Evi Otel
Kavaklı Mahallesi, Burç Üstü 21, Bursa
Tel: 0224-225 4160
www.kitapevi.com.tr
Once a bookstore in an Ottoman-era house, this delightful boutique hotel has 12 individually designed rooms, plus a Turkish bath and pretty little garden. **$$$$$**

Safran Hotel
Ortapazar Caddesi, 4 Arka Sokak,
Tophane, Bursa
Tel: 0224-224 7216
In a restored wooden Ottoman house, this charming guesthouse has modest amenities in its nine rooms, located in an historic neighbourhood near Osman and Orhan tombs. **$$$$**

The tasty *Iskender kebap* is a local treat

RESTAURANTS

There's little of İstanbul's big-city sophistication in the Marmara and Thrace region – instead, think hearty kebaps, of which the *Iskender Kebap (see p.55)* is king. In Bursa, birthplace of this national delicacy, inexpensive restaurants line Sakarya Caddesi, the old Jewish Quarter. In Edirne, the equivalent street food is the *Edirne ciğeri* (deep-fried liver), although restaurants and cafés along the River Meriç are more atmospheric locations in which to spend an evening.

(see p.55)

Restaurant Price Categories

Price categories are based on a three-course meal for one (including *meze*, grilled meat, bread, salad and fruit) and non-alcoholic drinks.

$ = under 20TL
$$ = 20–40TL
$$$ = 40–60TL
$$$$ = 60–100TL

Thrace

Balkan Pilic Lokantasi
14 Saraçlar Caddesi, Edirne
Tel: 0284-225 2155
This cheap and cheerful *lokanta* (canteen) has spit-roast chicken plus typical hearty dishes with lamb and vegetables. **$**

Melek Anne
18 Maarif Caddesi, Kaleiçi, Edirne
Tel: 0284-213 3263
Cosy home-cooking in this informal eatery in a restored old house, with dishes like *mantı* (ravioli), *börek* and grills. **$**

Villa Restaurant
Karaağaç Yolu Üzeri, Edirne
Tel: 0284-223 4077
www.edirnevilla.com
With a picturesque location on the River Meriç, the menu is grilled meat-focused, with many lamb kebap varieties. There's also a good range of spirits and Turkish wines. **$$**

Marmara

Bursa Hakimevi
10 Cekirge Caddesi, Bursa
Tel: 0224-233 4900
This low-key restaurant is housed in a charming restored Ottoman house on the edge of the Culture Park (Kulturparki). **$$**

Cumurcul
Celik Palas Otel Karsisi 18, Çekirge Caddesi, Bursa
Tel: 0224-235 3707
This popular restaurant, based in a converted old house, has a full range of excellent meze, plus grilled meats and fish and a couple of international dishes. Good views from the terrace. **$$$**

Dârüzziyafe
36 Murat II Caddesi, opposite Muradiye Camii, Bursa
Tel: 0224-224 6439
www.daruzziyafe.com.tr
Set in the mosque's 15th-century kitchens which once fed the poor, the garden here is the real draw. The huge menu has traditional dishes like *börek* (pastries), vegetables cooked in olive oil, and lamb with white beans. **$$**

Deniz Tabaği
6 Sakarya Caddesi, Bursa
Tel: 0224-221 9239
Specialising in fresh fish, this busy and friendly restaurant has a long list of fresh fish which comes directly from their fish shop, served simply cooked with mounds of salad. Traditional music most evenings. **$$–$$$**

Kebapci Iskender
60 Orhan Sokak, Atatürk Caddesi, Bursa
Tel: 0224-221 1076
A real locals' favourite, and run by descendants of the inventor of the Iskender kebap, this no-frills kebap joint has a few tables inside but more people queuing outside for service. **$$**

Listings

NIGHTLIFE AND ENTERTAINMENT

Don't expect İstanbul's standard and selection of nightlife when you head to cities like Bursa and Edirne. Bursa's Kültür Parki is the focus of informal nightlife, with several bars, restaurants and cafés scattered throughout. It comes alive during summer months; look out for special events and concerts.

Karagöz Theatre
Çekirge, Bursa
Tel: 0224-220 5350 (enquiries)
Occasional performances, organised by the folk who run Karagöz Antikaci, 12–13 Eski Aynali Carsi, in Bursa's Covered Bazaar. 🎭

Open Air Theatre
Cultural Park (Kültür Parki), Bursa
Look out for summer performances on posters around the city.

Piccolo Bar
16 Sakarya Caddesi, Bursa

Tel: 0224-223 5658
Signs to prevent male-only groups from entering caused an uproar with regulars, but this is still a popular joint with plenty of live music.

Resimli Bar
Uludağ Universitesi Gorukle Kampusu, Bursa
Tel: 0224-223 1700
www.resimli.com.tr
This pumping student bar and club puts on live bands – usually rock – on most Thursday, Friday and Saturday nights. On other nights it's still a lively place for a drink.

SPORTS AND ACTIVITIES

The Uludağ National Park (Uludağ Milli Parkı; *see p.101*) is the main focus of outdoor activities in the region. The cable car from Bursa reaches the glorious slopes, lush in summer and snowy in winter, for walks or skiing respectively. It reaches the main area of the ski resort, where there is a small collection of hotels, with equipment hire available.

Bursaspor Külübü
Ataturk Stadyumu
Tel: 0224-444 1963.
www.bursaspor.org.tr
The city's football club plays in the Turkish Super Lig (top division) at weekends, at the Atatürk Stadium. Playing in a green strip, the team has fluctuated between the top league and second over the last three decades. However, in the 2010–11 they qualified for the UEFA Champions League for the first time, after finishing the season in second place. ⚽

Skiing at Uludağ
Although the resort isn't quite up to Western European standards, it's very popular with local tourists. At an altitude of between

1,750m (5,740ft) and 2,547m (8,356ft) in the Uludağ National Park, the resort includes ski runs for beginners, intermediates and experts, and cross-country skiing.

Skiing at Uludağ

TOURS

As many visitors prefer to spend just a couple of days in the area, local tour agencies are useful. Especially invaluable are those arranging tours of Gallipoli for the battlefields, which can be in a large group, or as individual trips. Some are based in İstanbul and arrange day trips, or an overnighter to Bursa or Çanakkale.

Commemorating the fallen at Gallipoli

Hassle Free Travel Agency
59 Cumhuriyet Meydani, Çanakkale
Tel: 0286-213 5969
www.anzachouse.com
Specialising in backpacker tours, this popular agency runs trips from Anzac House, including regular battleground tours in Gallipoli.

Karagöz Tourism Travel Agency
4 Eski Aynali Carsi, Kapalicarsi, Bursa
Tel: 0224-220 5350
www.karagoztravel.com
This reputable Bursa-based agency offers day trips, guided tours of the city and hotel reservations, as well as trips out of town.

Sedan Turizm
Talatpaşa Asfalti Adil 2, Sitesi 60, Edirne
Tel: 0284-213 2146/6742
Organising tours of Edirne and around.

TJ's Tours & Hostel
5A Cumhuriyet Caddesi, Kemalpasa Mah., Eceabat
Tel: 0286-814 3121
www.anzacgallipolitours.com
Run by a Turkish-Australian couple specialising in tours to the Gallipoli battlefields and Troy (which can both be done in one day), plus extra services like locating a grave of someone who fell in the Gallipoli campaign.

FESTIVALS AND EVENTS

From traditional wrestling in Edirne to shadow puppets in Bursa, plus the solemnity of remembrance at Gallipoli's battlefields, there is a great variety of events on offer.

April
Anzac Day
25 Apr; ceremonies at Gallipoli
A dawn service starts the day to honour Australian and New Zealand Army Corps (ANZAC) who fell at Gallipoli during World War I. The evening can be boisterous, with many young backpackers from Down Under.

June
Kırkpınar Oil Wrestling Festival
Late June; Saraiçi, Edirne
www.turkishoilwrestling.net
Three-day festival of the traditional sport *yağli güreş*, which takes over the city *(see p.98)*.

November
Bursa International Silk Road Film Festival
Assorted venues
www.ipekyolufilmfest.com
New films from Turkey and around the world, free workshops, documentaries and the International Golden Karagöz Film Competition.

Karagöz Shadow Puppet Festival
Nov/Dec; various venues
www.trtazerbaycan.com
Showcasing this very Turkish traditional puppetry, using flat painted leather pieces with a light shining through.

Aegean Region

From classical theatres and ancient cities to the thump of Turkish nightlife and the delights of sun-soaked beaches, the Aegean coast has attractions that will tantalise the inquisitive and fun-loving traveller. Follow the coastal road to investigate the march of ancient history, eat, drink and be merry in Bodrum or Marmaris, or set sail for a relaxing Blue Cruise on sparkling waters.

İzmir

Population: 1.9 million

Local dialling code: 0232

Tourist Office: 1344 Sokak 2, Pasaport Quay, Alsancak, İzmir; tel: 0232-472 1010

Time Zone: GMT + 2

Police: 155 (call centre), Vilayet Bloklar, F Blok, Konak, İzmir; tel: 0232-489 0500; www.izmirpolis.gov.tr

Hospital: İzmir Ege Sağlık Hastanesi, 1399 Sokak 25, Alsancak, İzmir; tel: 0232-463 7700; www.egesaglik.com.tr

Post Office: Atatürk Caddesi 434, Alsancak, İzmir

Car Hire: Avis, Şair Eşref Bulvarı 18/D, Alsancak, İzmir; tel: 0232-441 4417: www.avis.com.tr

The northern Aegean coast is the beginning of Asia Minor. Over time, this long peninsula has witnessed much thrilling ancient history, including the superimposition of different religions, and even the most seasoned international traveller will be struck by the unparalleled geographical variety and historically significant attractions found along the coast.

Conveniently, most major sights are located along a shoreline road and are easily accessible from either İstanbul or the region's main city, İzmir. But the lush lowlands, more remote mountain villages and pine forests are worthwhile attractions in their own right. İzmir is also well located for visiting the limestone cascades at Pamukkale or touring Ephesus (Efes). Anyone on a cruise to Turkey will come ashore at the seaside resort of Kuşadası. Sights like Priene, Milet (Miletus) and Didyma are only a short trip from here. The nearest town to Ephesus is Selçuk, an attractive town with good accommodation and excellent restaurants.

South of Kuşadası, the coast becomes more rugged with verdant coniferous forests and jagged rocks plunging down to the sand. Winding peninsulas are the gnarled fingers reaching into the sea. Flamboyant Bodrum, with its sombre Crusader castle, has the most vibrant nightlife, and Marmaris, renowned for its pine-scented honey, has delightful restaurants that line the harbour. A loyal disco crowd convenes here, as well as international yachting enthusiasts. Both Marmaris and Bodrum are the ideal starting points for the sailing expeditions around the Gulf of Gökova, the famous Blue Cruise.

North Aegean

Assos and Pergamon are two of the classical sites of greatest interest, but the smaller coastal villages that have retained their fishing-village image will enchant all visitors.

Fortunately there are still areas on the north Aegean coast that have not

A fishing boat in Assos harbour (see p.113)

The white sands of Bozcaada beach

been overrun by tourists, where traditional life adheres to its own rules without a glance at modernity. Shepherds are still herding their wayward flocks, donkeys labour under heavy loads and farming is the way of life for most folk – at least those who are not in the tourist trade.

Bozcaada

The small island of **Bozcaada** ❶ 🏛, only 5km (3 miles) across, lies south of Troy and about 60km (37 miles) southwest of Çanakkale on the Biga Peninsula. Here the Greek fleet moored while waiting to surprise the Trojans inside the legendary wooden horse. The island is blissfully relaxed and pleasant. İstanbulites come here for the unspoilt beaches.

The main sight is an impressive Byzantine **citadel** (Apr–Nov daily 10am–1pm, 2–7pm; charge). The island is known for its outstanding wines, but very little is produced, so it is not easy to find beyond Bozcaada.

Aegean Region

Bozcaada ❶

Sminthion

Babakale

Pétra

Lésvos

GREECE

Mytilini

Polyhnitos

Plomári

Hios

Venezia

Karlóvassi

Ikaría

Agios Kirykós

Fourni

Agathonisi

Arki

Pátmos

Lipsí

Léros

Kinaros

Levítha

Kálymnos

Astypálea

GREECE

Kós

Giali

Nisyros

Tilos

Sými

Taşlıca

Ródos (Rhodes)

Hálki

Alimía

Ródos (Rhodes)

Álinda

İstanbul

Çanakkale Boğazı

Troy

Geyikli

Çanakkale

İntepe

Odunluk

Ezine

550

Bayramıç

Ayvacık ❺ Adatepe

Gülpınar ❷ Assos

Küçükkuyu

Behramkale

Çandar

Şeytan Sofrası

Ayvalık ❸

Sarımsaklı

Altınova

Dikili

Bergama

Pergamon ❹

Çandarlı

Çandarlı Körfezi

Aliağa

Eski Foça

Karaburun

Küçükbahçe

Mordoğan

Yeni Foça ❺

Phocaea

Menemen

İzmir Körfezi

Uzun Adası

Çeşme ❼

Çeşme

Ilıca

Alaçatı

Hios

İzmir ❻

Buca

Urla

Seferihisar

Klaros

Notion

Gümüldür

Doğanbey

Teke Burnu

Sığacık

Kuşadası Körfezi

Efes (Ephesus) ❾

Meryemana

Kuşadası

Söke

Dilek Yarımadası Milli Parkı

Priene

(Miletus), Milet ❿

Akköy

Bafa Gölü

Herakleia ad Latmos

Yenihisar

Akbük

Didyma ⓫

Altınkum

İassos

Selimiye

Güllük

Güllük Körfezi

Yalıkavak

Ortakent

Gümüşlük

Turgutreis

Bitez

Akyarlar

Gümbet

Bodrum ⓮

Ören

Kös

Knidos

Datça

Bozburun

Reşadiye Yarımadası

Şehir Adası (Cleopatra's Island)

Marmaris ⓯

Larymna

Kaunos

İztuzu

Turunç

İçmeler

Datça

Sıralan

Çanakkale

Biga Yarımadası

210

Çan

Etili

Yenice

Hamdibey

Danışment

Kalkım

Balya

Edremit

Havran

Armutova

Madra Dağı 1338

Kazdağı 1774

Akçay

Ören

Kayapa

İvrindi

Ertuğrul

Sarıbeyler

Göçbeyli

Soma

Bakır

Kınık

Kırkağaç

Zeytindağ

Yuntdağ

Palamut

240

Güzelhisar Barajı

Osmancalı

Gediz

Muradiye

Menemen

250

565

Manisa

Spildağı Milli Parkı

Gediz

Kemalpaşa

E96

Turgutlu

0-30

Sart (Sardis) ❽

Salihli

Bozdağ 2137

Alaşehir

Gölcük Gölü

Bayındır

Çırpı

Ödemiş

Kaymakcı

Kiraz

Beydağ

Tire

Gökçen

Ovakent

Küçük Menderes

Aydın Dağları

Selçuk

Şirince

Germencik

Nyssa

Sultanhisar

Aydın

İncirliova

Koşk

Bağarası

Koçarlı

Büyük Menderes

Yenipazar

Nazilli

Babadağ

Hörsünlü

Sarıköy

Karacasu

Aphrodisias ⓬

2308

Bozdoğan

Akdağ 2254

Denizli

Karahisar

Tavas

Alinda

Alabanda

Çine

Madrababa Dağı 1792

Karpuzlu

Doğu Menteşe Dağları

Labranda

Gerga

Kemer Barajı

Kavaklıdere

Göktepe

Kale

Acıpayam

Gölgeli Dağları 2419

Milas

Turgut

Yatağan

Batı Menteşe Dağları

Ören

Peçin Kale

Yeşilyurt

Muğla

Beyağaç

Kelekçi

330

Sakar Geçidi

585

Ula

Akyaka

Çiçekbaba Tepesi 2294

Köyceğiz Gölü

Köyceğiz

Dalaman

Çameli

Gök Tepesi 2254

Üzümlü

Gökova Körfezi

400

Dalyan

Ortaca

Göcek Geçidi 115

Metriş Geçidi 110

Kemer

400

Kurtoğlu Burnu

İbliz Burnu

Göcek

Fethiye Körfezi

Pınara

Eşen

Sidyma

Letoön

Fethiye

Ölüdeniz

Antalya

350

N

0   20 km

0   20 miles

İstanbul

E90

200

Karacabey

Bursa

Eskişehir

Ulubat Gölü

Uludağ 2403

Mustafakemalpaşa

Keles

565

220

Kütahya

Büyükorhan

Harmancık

230

Orhaneli

Çaltıbük

Susurluk

Devecikonağı

Balıkesir

555

Kepsut

Durak

Kireç

Bigadiç

Yağcılar

Gökçedağ

Dursunbey

Eğrigöz Dağları 2181

Emet

Akdağ 2089

Hisarcık

Düvertepe

Caygören Barajı

Demirci

Simav

Yarbasan

240

Pazarlar

Afyon

Akhisar

Gördes

Köprübaşı

Selendi

Gediz

595

Marmara Gölü

Demirköprü Barajı

Güre

Uşak

E96

Kula

300

Afşar Barajı

Sarıgöl

Buldan Barajı

Adıgüzel Barajı

Güney

Çal

Eşme

Ulubey

585

Buldan

Pamukkale ⓭

Hierapolis

Burharkent

Kuyucak

Laodiheia

E87

320

Honaz

Serinhisar

Kunanda

Olive Oil

Olive oil is one of nature's healthiest foods, an elixir *extraordinaire*. It has not been modified, denatured or cloned. Turkey is an olive-growing country and those from the Aegean are particularly prized; the smell of pressed olives wafts in the air around Ayvalık and other Aegean coastal towns. Compared to Spain, Italy or Greece, Turkey produces a small amount of olive oil, but you can buy it in one of the farmers' markets where the oil has been produced locally and where you can sample it. Quality olive oil should be greeny-yellow and quite clear without too much sediment. Decant it into a glass bottle as soon as possible.

Assos to Ayvalık

The ancient site of **Assos** ❷ (daily 9am–dusk; charge) is located on the Bay of Edremit, near the main highway, 100km (60 miles) south of Çanakkale. It is best reached through the picturesque small town of Ayvacık, a popular holiday centre. The 14th- century Ottoman humpbacked bridge, no longer in use, indicates you are on the right road. Rising majestically in the distance is the lofty acropolis of ancient Assos, within which is found the Temple of Athena, dating from 530BC. Athena was Zeus' favourite child and a ruthless battle-goddess. A few Doric columns remain. The view to the Greek island of Lesbos is breathtaking at sunset but dramatic at any time.

From Assos it is a steep and treacherous drop down a winding, single track to the village of **Behramkale** nestled at the bottom. There is a stony beach here, a lovely atmosphere and several small but excellent restaurants and pensions. It is wonderfully romantic and the prevalence of artists and painters has given it a bohemian tinge. The restored buildings were once depots for chestnuts *(kestane)*. There is a creamy local cheese here, impossible to find elsewhere, and restaurants know how to store and serve it perfectly.

Returning to **Ayvacık**, the highway continues southeast along the coast to **Edremit**, a useful transit point. Much of this area is backdropped by the Kazdağı mountain range and nowhere typifies the tranquil lowland life more than the unassuming seaside town of **Akçay**. Only 5km (3 miles) from Edremit off the main coastal road, fishermen still come to the harbour with the day's catch and buying and bargaining on-site ensues. There are beautiful stretches of beach that seem only to have been discovered by Turkish State Railways personnel, who come here for company holidays.

A local craftswoman in Assos

From Ayvacık the modest little resort of **Ören** can be reached via the village of Burhaniye. A local minibus (dolmuş) service runs to the resort. The beach is the best feature of the place and there is no shortage of accommodation along the road heading west towards **Ayvalık** ❸, whose name means quince orchard. But it is the excellent olive oil that will tempt gourmets.

The old part of Ayvalık, with its narrow cobbled streets and overhanging balconies, is very picturesque and has retained its Hellenic ambience after the exodus of Ottoman Greek citizens in 1923. Several Greek Orthodox churches had minarets affixed to become mosques. Ayvalık also supports a healthy colony of flamingos.

Sun and fun lovers will delight in **Sarımsaklı**, 8km (5 miles) to the

south of Ayvalık, with the finest white-grained sandy beaches in all of Turkey and a range of activities including windsurfing and daily group excursions by yacht. The waterfront promenade springs to life at night, with its scores of hotels, cafés, discos, bars and eateries.

Bergama

Leaving Ayvalık, the highway leads you south through ancient Aeolia, weaving through rich agricultural land. Traditional farming methods still apply here and women work the fields while men are often seen in the tea or coffee house chatting and putting the world to rights.

On approaching the town of **Bergama**, along the valley of the Bakır Çayı (the ancient Caicus River), you will see two odd-looking hills or mounds seen just outside the city; these once served to protect Bergama from invasion. Nowadays, foreigners invade Bergama specifically to see the ruins of Pergamon or to shop for kilims or carpets. There are restaurants and cafés here feeding busloads of tourists who have worked up an appetite after viewing the antique site.

Pergamon

Towering 300m (1,000ft) above the city, the ruins at **Pergamon** ❹ command an incredible 360-degree view. The 8th-century BC Hellenistic city was once a thriving centre of culture, commerce and medicine to rival the other centres of Mediterranean Hellenism such as Ephesus, Alexandria and Antioch.

Pergamon possessed a library as celebrated as that of Alexandria; it was here that parchment was invented after

The entrance to the sanctuary and bath houses at Asklepion in Pergamon

A poppy field at Pergamon

the jealous Egyptians cut off the supply of papyrus. In 133BC, Pergamon was the capital of the Roman Empire in Asia Minor. Its fame came into particular prominence when the physician, Galen, was born here in AD129.

Allow a full day to visit the **ruins** (daily 8.30am–5.30pm, until 7pm in summer; separate charges): there are two main areas – the Asklepion and the Acropolis – as well as many minor ruins and several sites within Bergama itself. Visitors without their own transport should consider a tour that includes transport to and from both sites as they are 8km (5 miles) apart.

The ruins of the **Asklepion** are about 1km (½ mile) up the hill from the town centre. This was not your average medical clinic but a complete health spa. The prospective patient could seek out psychotherapy treatment (where dreams were analysed, 2,000 years before Freud), browse through literature in the library, or go for a dip in the sacred healing spring. One could easily spend several days relaxing and recuperating from the strains of stressful Graeco-Roman life.

Back in town, stop at the small but satisfying **Archaeological Museum** (Pergamon Arkeoloji Müzesi; daily 8.30am–noon, 1–5.30pm; charge), on the main street near the tourist office.

Approaching the Bergama Çayı, the **Red Basilica** (Kızıl Avlu; daily 8.30am–5.30pm, Apr–Oct until 7pm; charge) dates from the 2nd or 3rd century AD and was once a vast temple to the Egyptian god Serapis. Two underground tunnels

Aegean Region

Pergamon

Royal Palaces
Monumental Gate
Temple of Trajan
Library
Hellenistic Theatre
Acropolis
Temple of Athena Polias Nikephoros
Temple of Dionysus
Altar of Zeus
Roman Baths
Upper Agora
Sanctuary of Demeter
Gymnasium
Kaikos
City Wall
Lower Agora
Ulu
South Gate
Soma & Rail Station
Bergama Çayı
Selinus
Roman Amphitheatre
Hippodrome
Kızıl Avlu (Red Basilica)
Asklepion
Hamam
Roman Theatre
Cumhuriyet Cad.
Sacred Way
Temple of Asklepios
Pergamon Arkeoloji Müzesi (Archaeological Museum)
İzmir Cad.
Temple of Telesphoros
İzmir
N
0   500 m
0   500 yds

The Temple of Zeus at Pergamon

the only reminder of a glorious altar with stone reliefs, now in the Pergamon Museum in Berlin.

Especially impressive, although a good imagination helps, are the ruins of the famed Library of Pergamon, once filled with over 200,000 volumes written on parchment, so illustrious that it was later presented to Cleopatra by Antony as a wedding gift.

Like most Roman theatres, this amazing auditorium is overpowering with 80 rows or seats for nearly 10,000 theatre-goers. The royal box is distinguished in exquisite marble. Its setting on the edge of the cliff is incomparable and this is the place to experience the quality of ancient acoustics. An actor (or tourist) standing centre-stage and talking in a normal voice can be heard even at the top, a lesson in design often forgotten today.

The Gymnasium is also interesting, for it was here in the ephebeia that the young minds of Pergamon were shaped and guided.

The substantial remains of the baths that can be seen date back to Roman times, and it is still possible to make out the washbasins made of marble.

As you leave Pergamon, take special notice of the 4km (2½- mile) -long enclosure walls of the ancient city, which show clearly the restorations made during the Ottoman period, when rocks, stones and bricks were bonded by mortar instead of the previous 'dry wall' technique.

Eski and Yeni Foca

Continuing down the coast, past industrial towns like Aliağa, a turn-off to the right winds through the hills to

carried water from the Selinus River, beneath the building's foundations. Originally, the red-brick building was covered in marble, but nowadays only the floor paving retains its marble finish.

From the old Turkish quarter, cross the Bergama Çayı, turn left and follow the road up a steep hill until you reach the car park of the fabled **Acropolis**. The natural impulse is to wander around this vast site on your own at random, but it is more rewarding to follow the posted signs with helpful information.

To the left of the royal gate are the foundations of the Temple of Zeus,

emerge along the coast, revealing some dramatic vistas and finally ending at the neighbouring villages of **Eski** (old) **Foça** and **Yeni** (new) **Foça** . The two are about 20km (12 miles) apart. Eski Foça was the site of ancient Phocaea, referred to by Herodotus. There are extensive beaches, and small coves that can be explored by boat, as well as some exclusive resort hotels built over the beach in the new part of town. Eski Foça discourages modernity and has kept its traditional charm and old-style dwellings. The coastal area around

both Foças is one of the few remaining habitats of the endangered Mediterranean monk seal, and the World Wide Fund for Nature scheme protects them. They are shy and emerge only rarely to delight seal watchers.

İzmir to Sardis

Once Turkey's most cosmopolitan, commercial and cultured city, İzmir retains a libertine rhythm and overlooks a stunning half-moon bay on the Aegean coast. The modern world has left ancient Sardis virtually unscathed.

İzmir City Transport

 Airport: Adnan Menderes (ADB) 18km (11 miles) from city centre; tel: 0252-455 0000 (international terminal); 0252-274 2626 (domestic terminal); **www.adnanmenderesairport. com/izmiren**. A shuttle-bus service operated by Havaş runs in both directions every hour from 3am until 11.30pm (tel: 0232-444 0487; **www. havas.net/otobus-ve-otopark/izmir**).

 Trains: Turkish State Railways (TCDD) operates six trains (afternoons only) between Adnan Menderes Airport and Alsancak station downtown. The journey takes about 30 minutes.

 City-centre buses: Two interrelated bus companies, ESHOT and İZULTAŞ, cover the major urban districts. İzmir's transport accepts a prepaid electronic card (Kentkart), which is cheaper than buying a ticket. These are available at kiosks located near bus stops and can be topped up electronically here too.

 Urban Ferries: İzdeniz operates 24 ferries that shuttle commuters between 8 quays on the city-centre side, across the Gulf of İzmir to Karşıyaka, taking about 15–20 mins. Ferries operate 6am–midnight.

 Intercity Buses: The central bus terminal *(otogar)* is on the fringe of İzmir but bus companies operate free shuttle services from here to their central offices. Reliable companies are Pamukkale (tel: 0232-444 3535; **www.pamukkale.com.tr**); or Varan (tel: 0232-444 8999; **www.varan. com.tr**). Reservations are essential and tickets can be booked online.

 Metro/LRS: İzmir is proud of its underground transport, combined in places with an overground Light Rail System. The electronic Kentkart can be used on the Metro. İzmir's metro system will soon stop at the airport.

 Intercity Trains: One express train departs daily from Basmane Station to Bandırma, where passengers can link up with high-speed catamarans to İstanbul. Trains are run by Turkish State Railways: **www.tcdd.gov.tr**.

 Taxis: Taxis are always waiting outside the airport: at 60–70TL to get into town, this is the most expensive option. In the city, taxis are plentiful and can be hailed in the street at any hour. Your hotel or pension will always ring a local firm for you.

Turkey's second-largest port and third-largest city, İzmir (ancient Smyrna) is also one of the country's major commercial centres and is decidedly upbeat with projects like the Space Camp at the Aegean Free Trade Zone, a high tech- industrial park. For international travellers, the city is a good base for excursions to archaeological sites and ruins that lie to the north (Pergamon) and south (Ephesus). It is served by an excellent International Airport (ADB).

İzmir

During the prehistoric period, the tiny initial settlement of Bayraklı, northeast of the centre of **İzmir** ❻, grew in size and importance under the Ionians, who took over the **Smyrna** region in the 9th century BC. In the 1st century BC the Romans ushered in an era of peace and prosperity. Smyrna was one of the seven churches of Asia Minor, and its bishop, Polycarp, was martyred for defending his faith. Throughout the Ottoman period, the city hosted many nationalities; latterly these were predominantly Greek Orthodox, but all adored the glittering soirées, multiculturalism and the trade and commercial opportunities.

Turkish nationalism, however, burned just as fiercely as the mysterious inferno that destroyed İzmir in 1922 and altered the fortunes of the city forever. One of the consequences of these traumatic events was a bizarre population exchange between the Greek and other minority Ottoman populations in İzmir, and the Turks who had long ago settled in Greece. Some areas of the city, like Bornova,

İzmir

The clock tower on Konak Meydanı

An **Agora** (Tue–Sun 8.30am–noon, 1–5pm; charge) dates back to late Hellenistic times, but today the relatively small clearing contains colonnades around a central esplanade, built during the reign of Marcus Aurelius late in the 2nd century AD. Descending from it, take the crowded, narrow streets towards the waterfront at **Konak Meydanı** with its symbolic clock tower dating from 1901. Konak is a central hub, and from here, ferries constantly whisk commuters and serious shoppers across the bay to **Karşıyaka**.

Fronting İzmir Bay, the area known as **Kordon** ⑧ 🏛 was once bustling commercial docklands, but is now a beautifully groomed pedestrian area with benches and a promenade to enjoy the prevailing breeze, the *imbat*. For backdrop, the competitive restaurants and cafés have nouveau food and romantic views over the bay. The calèche ride in a horse-drawn carriage is free to 'commuters' along this 2km (1 mile) stretch of parkway.

The **Culture Park** (Kültür Parkı 🏛) is located east of Basmane train station and its coolness and shade make it a magnet for relaxing, meeting friends, drinking coffee, and family walks or picnics.

İzmir's two museums are within walking distance south of Konak. The **Archaeological Museum** ⓒ (Arkeoloji Müzesi; Halil Paşa Caddesi; Tue–Sun 9am–noon, 1–5.30pm; charge) has a varied collections of finds from the Bayraklı Mound and some attractive glassware. The

Aegean Region

retain a faded elegance from the pre-fire days, minus the gaiety.

The centre of İzmir has a lively atmosphere. The main tourist office is on the renovated quay (Akdeniz Mahallesi, 1344 Sokak 2, Pasaport; tel: 0232-445 7390) that now hosts floating shops, restaurants and a cinema. İzmir is proud of its new underground Metro system, a potent symbol of urban development.

The imposing fortress of **Kadifekale** ⓐ on Mount Pagus rises up majestically behind the city and offers an unparalleled view of the harbour and city below. The grounds of the 'Velvet Castle' contain a wonderful mixture of picnicking folk, well-dressed citizens out for a stroll, and young romantics sipping tea in the shady open-air cafés.

★ BOAT BUILDING

Looking around Turkey's harbours and marinas at the thoroughbred yachts and ocean-going cruisers, most people don't realise that many are made in Turkey as well as being docked there. From traditional wooden yachts to the magnificent mega-clipper *Maltese Falcon* with its futuristic carbon-fibre masts, Turkish boat builders are continuing a heritage that stretches back centuries.

Boat-Building Heritage

If you are lounging on a *gulet* enjoying the Blue Cruise, chances are your wooden boat has been designed and built in the İçmeler district of Bodrum. With 8,340km (5,180 miles) of coastline, mostly along seas, Turkey's maritime heritage is well founded.

The **Bodrum Museum of Underwater Archaeology** *(see p.133)* is filled with salvaged evidence of early maritime trade and ancient boat construction. In the 1st and 2nd centuries AD, villages like Kaş and Finike had abundant timber for planks and tall staves for masts. Towns like Ephesus and Patara were thriving commercial trading ports.

As the Ottoman Empire expanded, it gained territory but also skilled craftsmen, including shipwrights. The first Ottoman shipyard was in Gallipoli in 1390. By 1543, Turkey was a formidable naval power and Barbarossa was Admiral of the Ottoman navy.

Contemporary Industry

Today, Turkey's heritage craft skills have been supplemented by marine

Traditional *gulets* moored in Kalkan

architects and engineers, space-age materials and computer-aided designs. From an artisanal skill, modern boat building in Turkey has developed into a state-of-the-art global industry. But traditional techniques remain important and utilised. Most *gulets* today are still made of wood. The classical technique is ribs attached to a keel. Then planks are fastened to the ribs to form the outer membrane, or skin, of the hull. Laminated hulls have several layers of planks superimposed on each other and are glued together with strong adhesives or resins. The smooth laminations give the hull rigidity and strength.

Whilst Antalya and Tuzla in İstanbul build fibreglass and steel hulls, Bodrum is accredited as the master building area for wooden boats in Turkey.

Gulets

Gulets differ from other wooden boats in the shape of their broad, rounded sterns. This makes it an ideal vessel for lounging, eating and socialising on board. The bow of the *gulet* is exposed for sunning and sea sprays. A typical *gulet* is about 20–25m (65–82ft) long with six or seven cabins below. Upmarket *gulets* are longer with fewer cabins, but still retain their definitive characteristics; they may also be ocean-going. Most *gulets* are outfitted with rigging and sails, but many daily or weekly tours actually chug off under motor.

Although pine wood was the material traditionally used in *gulet* construction, today hardwoods like teak are favoured because they are more durable and withstand the salty seas better.

Gulets cruise around the Turquoise Coast – the Aegean Region's southern shoreline

Boat Building

The time-honed design of a Bodrum *gulet*

Treasury (Hazine) contains exquisite gold coins and jewellery from the 6th to 3rd centuries BC. The exhibits in the next-door **Ethnographic Museum** (Etnografya Müzesi; Tue–Sun 9am–noon, 1–5.30pm; charge) include a reconstructed Ottoman pharmacy, a bridal chamber and a circumcision room.

Çeşme

Under an hour's drive (80km/50 miles) west of İzmir, on the tip of the peninsula, is the strikingly beautiful and popular resort town of **Çeşme** ❼ . It is easily reached by car or bus from İzmir, and from May to October there are also regular ferry services to the Greek island of Híos and the Italian port of Brindisi. The dominant feature of the town is a 14th-century Genoese castle. The small **Archaeological Museum** (Tue–Sun 9am–noon, 1–5.30pm; charge) will not detain you for long. Nearby Ilıca is known for its geothermal healing springs. Wander the backstreets to see the traditional Greek houses and some old windmills. There is also an interesting Ottoman lighthouse here.

The intense winds that blow off the sea have turned **Alaçatı**, just along the coast from Çeşme, into a paradise for international surfers. In this very creative, bohemian town, many entrepreneurial artisans have set up shop.

Sardis

Sardis ❽ (Sart; daily 8am–noon, 1–5pm; charge) is 100km (60 miles) east of İzmir. It has been occupied for over 3,000 years and was the capital of the Kingdom of Lydia. The most intense structure at Sardis is the **Temple of Artemis** (separate charge), located in the Pactalos Valley.

The 14th-century castle at Çeşme is the town's focal feature

Its enormous stature, eight columns at each end and 20 along each side, rivals the three great Ionian temples at Ephesus, Samos and Didyma. Like many temples of Artemis in the Aegean, it faces west.

Behind the city is the **Acropolis**. The ascent requires stamina but the fabulous view from the summit makes it worth the effort.

Crossing to the other side brings you to an impressive Roman **Gymnasium** and bath complex, constructed in the 2nd century AD. The columns are decorated with heads of gods and satyrs.

The remains of a remarkable 3rd-century AD synagogue are in a large hall beside the Gymnasium. South of the bath-gymnasium complex is the **House of Bronzes**, which owes its name to the interesting bronze utensils found inside.

Southern Aegean

The Southern Aegean offers compelling nightlife, shopping and dining, but is also home to a host of spectacular ancient sites that vie for the visitor's attention. The town of Kuşadası, or 'bird island', is set in a superb gulf known for its sparkling water and broad sandy beaches; as Turkey's largest deep-water port, it is a favourite port of call for cruise ships. Dozens of hotels and holiday villages line the shores, and an ever-increasing number of seafood restaurants and discos cater to locals and tourists.

Day trips can be made from Kuşadası to Ephesus, Priene, Miletus and Didyma. Some tours cram a visit to all four sights into one day, but

The Roman Gymnasium at Sardis

classical fatigue can set in and it is better to soak up one place than just get a superficial overview. Any of the sights can be seen by public transport from Kuşadası, changing buses at Söke.

A Fortune In Coffee Grounds

The art of reading one's fortune in coffee grounds is known as *falcı*. It is a delightful tradition that many take pretty seriously. It only works with Turkish coffee because of the thick residue it leaves after drinking. When you have drunk your potent brew, you let it settle and then turn the cup upside down on the saucer and let the grounds settle into their fortuitous patterns. A skilled *falcı* reader will determine your destiny by the patterns on the inside of the cup. It is superstitious and serious at the same time but great fun and extends the coffee drinking ritual into the sphere of the mystical.

Ephesus

Unmatched by any archaeological site anywhere in terms of sheer magnitude, **Ephesus** (Efes) , appeals to every visitor, from the serious archaeologist delighted by the intact visual evidence, to the casual visitor who wants an authentic glimpse of Roman life. *See Walking Tour of Ephesus, p.130.*

Ephesus entered a golden age during the Roman era, when Augustus declared it the capital of the province of Asia Minor. It had a population of 250,000 and was the financial hub of its era for Asia, the only threat to its prosperity being the constant silting up of the harbour by the Cayster River. Despite many battles with nature to deepen the channel, Ephesus eventually became landlocked.

St Paul arrived in AD53 and gained enough followers to challenge Rome's various and complicated deities. St John later spent several years here.

Most of the surviving ruins of Ephesus belong to the Roman imperial period. An outstanding exception is the Hellenistic City Wall, built by Lysimachus. The road leading from the Kuşadası highway to the ruins brings one to the **Gymnasium of Vedius**, combined with its decorative baths. The horseshoe-shaped **Stadium** was built during the Hellenistic period but restored to its present condition during Nero's reign (AD 54–68). Across the road and to the south is the **Church of the Virgin Mary**, the first church in Christian history dedicated to the Virgin.

The city's impressive Harbour Street (**Arcadian Way**) stretches from the harbour to the imposing theatre. The **Harbour Baths** were next to the Gymnasium with its signature colonnades and mosaic courtyard. The magnificent **Theatre** dates from the 3rd century BC and accommodated 24,000 spectators. From the top tiers, there is a splendid view of the entire city.

Below the theatre stands the **Library of Celsus** – what everybody comes here to see and photograph.

Ephesus's Harbour Street

The ornate, symmetrical facade is as magnificent now as it was in the 2nd century AD.

Here you turn right onto Curetes Street, which stretches to the **Hercules Gate**. First on the left are the **Baths of Scholastica**, built in the 1st century AD. The baths were meant for all strata of society but only the rich could afford the time to linger and gossip and indulge in massages.

Next door, a peristyle house was the town's **Brothel** and, nearby, the intact latrines demonstrate that communal bathing was not the only activity that Romans preferred en masse.

One of the most memorable sights in Ephesus is the fascinating **Temple of Hadrian** on Curetes Street. Dating from AD138, it is one of many arches supported by Corinthian columns that Hadrian erected around Asia Minor to commemorate his triumphal visits.

Selçuk

The small town of **Selçuk**, 80km (50 miles) from İzmir, is a half-hour's

A classical wall detail from an Ephesus house at the Ephesus Museum in Selçuk

distance on foot from Ephesus. There is accommodation to suit most budgets and many people stay here to be close to Ephesus and other sites, like the **Ephesus Museum** (Efes Müzesi; Tue–Sun 8.30am–noon, 12.30–5pm, until 7pm in summer; charge). There is an exceptional collection of mosaics and frescoes from the houses at Ephesus. Of particular note are the bronze statuette of Eros on a

125

Aegean Region

Camel Wrestling: Lords of the Ring

Camel wrestling survives from nomadic times, when two alpha males slugged it out regularly in Aegean arenas. Duels take place between December and February when female camels are fertile – otherwise males are meek. Aydın and Selçuk are the best-known venues, but other smaller towns have wrestling pageants. Camels are regally festooned and given names like Rambo. Revelry and socialising are part of the fun and whole towns turn out.

Rivals are matched according to weight and style of fighting. The winner must chase his rival off the field, outmanoeuvre him with cunning leg or neck work, or topple his opponent. Each round is over in about 12 or 15 minutes. There is no shame in retiring to chew your cud. Animals are restrained if they look like injuring each other. Camel wrestling lacks the major sponsors of international sports, but it is chivalrous entertainment, as well as a uniquely Turkish game.

dolphin, and the marble statue of an inexhaustibly fertile Artemis.

The quintessentially Byzantine **Basilica of St John** is located south of the Selçuk fortress on the hill and dates from the 6th century AD. At the foot of the hill are the ruins of the elegant 14th-century **İsa Bey Mosque** (İsa Bey Camii; usually open except prayer times).

It is believed that the Virgin Mary came to Ephesus with St John, and her house, the **Meryemana** (8km/5 miles south of Selçuk; dawn–dusk; charge), is now a chapel and a popular place of pilgrimage for both Christians and Muslims.

Şirince, with its old Greek houses on the hill, is only 8km (5 miles) east of Selçuk and provides a delightfully tranquil interlude after the bustle and crowds of Ephesus.

Priene

The ancient Ionian harbour city of **Priene** (daily 8am–5.30pm, until 7.30pm in summer; charge) is reached by a short but picturesque drive from Kuşadası. The location is spectacular at the foot of a steep cliff on Mount Mycale. The town silted up and was relocated using the Hippodamian grid plan in the 4th century BC. The sites of note here are the 3rd-century BC theatre, a temple to Athena Polias (goddess and protector of the city), a shining example of Ionian architecture in the 4th century BC, and the *bouleterion*, or town hall. Priene is important as one of the most intact Hellenistic sites. The city went in decline under Roman rule.

Miletus

Miletus (Milet; daily 8.30am–5.30pm, until 7.30pm in summer; charge) ❿ was another large and prosperous city in Anatolia and was the birthplace of the astronomer **Thales**, one of the Seven Sages of Antiquity. Like Priene, the post-sedimental 'new' town was purpose-built on a grid system. It was an enterprising city and became an intellectual focal point. The finest surviving building is undoubtedly the 2nd-century BC **Theatre**, capable of seating an audience of 15,000. The **Bouleuterion**, built between 175 and 164 BC during the reign of Seleucid King Antiochus IV Epiphanes, is one of the oldest buildings surviving in Miletus. Opposite, there was a three-storey Nymphaeum with elaborate reliefs. The well-preserved **Baths of Faustina** were dedicated to the extravagant wife of Marcus Aurelius, and predated the Roman thermae, or

The Temple of Apollo in Didyma

A view from Herakleia ad Latmos to the village below

Turkish hamam. The Hellenistic **Stadium** is still impressive.

The site also has a small **museum** (daily 8.30am–12.30pm, 1.30–5.30pm; charge), but the remains of the **İlyas Bey Mosque** (İlyas Bey Camii), built in 1404, are noteworthy for their delicate grillwork and artistry. It combined social, residential and religious functions, and a small 15th-century *caravanserai* would have once formed part of the complex.

Didyma

It is no exaggeration to say that the **Temple of Apollo** (daily, winter 8am–5.30pm, summer 9am–7pm; charge) at **Didyma** ⓫ is about the grandest site on the Aegean coast, effectively conveying the one-time power and influence of prophets and oracles around the 6th century BC. It is not just the colossal stature but the scale of artistic carving, especially on the bases of the Ionic pillars (there were once over 100), which is superb, as are the antechamber to the temple and tunnels

leading to the inner temple *(cella)*. The marble is overwhelming and the iconic scowling **Head of Medusa** with her unruly locks is evocative. Oracles, alas, went out of favour around AD380. Didyma can be reached by public transport from either Söke or Milas going to Yenihisar.

Lake Bafa and Around

For a diversion from the more popular coastal areas, **Bafa Gölü** (Lake Bafa) is wonderfully refreshing and, although some of its sites, like the Carian sanctuary of **Labranda** (15km/9 miles north of Milas), are difficult to access, this amplifies the sense of a trip here as an exploration. Across the lake is **Herakleia ad Latmos**, with brooding fortified towers and a Temple of Athena. It can be approached by land off the main Söke–Milas highway, or by boat from the shore of Lake Bafa.

An excursion to the remote hermitages of **Mount Latmos** is best undertaken with a guide. A sight to

Aegean Region

make time for is the curious shrine to **Endymion**, still shrouded in legends and myths. The surrounding area also includes **Euromos** (daily, summer 8.30am–7pm, winter 8.30am–5.30pm; charge) on the southeast side of the lake. Pagan spirits and legends pervade the area. Intrepid trippers who make it to Labranda will feel a sense of achievement.

Aphrodisias

Named after the goddess Aphrodite and synonymous with the celebration of sensual love, the ancient city of **Aphrodisias** (Afrodisias) ⑫, was renowned throughout Asia Minor as a centre of medicine, philosophy, sculpture and the arts.

Extensive excavation and modern cataloguing revealed an unparalleled cache of sculpture carved from the nearby marble quarries. The most intact remains are a Roman **stadium** seating 30,000 and a **Tetrapylon** (monumental gate) resembling the arch-and-Corinthian-column construction revered by Hadrian to commemorate his triumphant stopovers. The **Temple of Aphrodite** was completed in the 1st century AD and was something of a cult shrine; it later became a place of Christian worship. All the recognisable characteristics of a Roman city in artistic flower, such as baths, agora and theatres, are in evidence at Aphrodisias. Take time to visit the small **museum** (daily 9am–6pm; charge).

The Petrified Falls

The fantastical **Pamukkale** ⑬ (8am–5pm, until 7pm in summer; charge), which translates as 'Cotton Castle', lies 20km (12 miles) north of Denizli, off the main highway from Aydın. It is a shimmering white cascade created by limestone-laden geothermal springs that have calcified into white

The ruins of the Tetrapylon at Aphrodisias

The travertine terraces at Pamukkale

Pamukkale and has a high iron content, which makes the waters anything but pristine white.

Bodrum and Marmaris

Bodrum, with its aura of mythology and history, and spectacular sandy beaches, rocky coves and fjord-like inlets, is a good starting point for a journey along the Carian coast. Bodrum is the home port for local Turkish yachtsmen and women, but it is Marmaris that serves the international nautical community with **Netsel Marina**. Marmaris has few high spots of historical interest, but the restaurants that line the front are attractive and this is the perfect place to relax and watch the world go by.

waterfalls tumbling over descending terraced pools. Hydrotherapy was once part of many religious and cult practices. Bathing and wading are no longer allowed since it became a Unesco World Heritage Site, along with Hierapolis, the ancient city that lies adjacent to the falls.

Hierapolis was founded by Eumenes II of Pergamon and the site today has a necropolis with graves also made from travertine, a Greek-style theatre with exceptional friezes, the 5th-century AD **Martyrium of St Philip** and the great baths, which now house an archaeological museum. Many people just come to see the cascading limestone pools, but Hierapolis reinforces the impression of a classical wellness centre or health farm.

Accommodation is in the nearby village of **Karahayıt**, which has numerous spa hotels. The spring is from a different source than

Turkey's Lighthouses

With 8,334km (5,178 miles) of coastline and many strategic bays and lookout points, lighthouses were once a strategic feature of Turkish coasts. In fact, Turkey still has 415 lighthouses along her shoreline. The antique lighthouse in Alexandria was built on the island of Pharos in 280 BC and gave us the Turkish word for lighthouse, *fener*. One of the loneliest lighthouses is Deveboynu in Knidos. A long and steep path leads up to it, and its tactical position surveying the Aegean and Mediterranean is unmistakable. The insignia is in French and, like most of the coastal lighthouses, it was built under one of the (later to be unpopular) concessions granted to foreign states by the Ottoman Sultan in 1855.

⚐ EPHESUS

Ephesus epitomises a Roman city during the centuries before and after Christ. A walking tour takes several hours and gives a real-life portrait of the Romans' cultural sophistication and the refined everyday life they enjoyed.

If time permits, the nearby Ephesus Museum in Selçuk, 3km (2 miles) away, is worth a visit for its classical artefacts, especially the fruitful and fertile statue of Artemis. Also here, the 14th-century İsa Bey Mosque is exquisite, and the Basilica of St John underlines the region's Christian connections (*see p.125 for Selçuk*). Onsite however, this self-guided tour identifies the main attractions in Ephesus. Committed history buffs can easily spend a whole day soaking up the glories of eastern Rome's most important city.

Tips

- Area: 1.5 sq km (1 sq mile)
- Time: Allow a minimum of two hours to walk the city streets
- Entrepreneurial touts greet you at the entrances, but a well-informed, licensed guide can turn a walkabout into a trip back to the 2nd century
- Getting to Ephesus early in the day is recommended
- Bring a hat, as the summer heat can be sizzling and there is little shade
- *See p.124 for more on Ephesus*

Enter the site by the lower gate which leads you past one of the **gymnasiums**, where Ephesus' 250,000 citizens worked out and kept fit. Just ahead is the magnificent **Theatre** with seating for thousands, an enduring symbol of leisure and pleasure in the 3rd century BC. Turn right down **Marble Avenue** to the **Library of**

The impressive and well-preserved theatre at Ephesus

Celsus, a stunningly gracious icon to ancient learning and literacy. The library once contained 12,000 scrolls and reputedly a book-to-bed tunnel linked it to the opposite peristyle house, the **Brothel**. The **Baths of Scholastica**, named after a classical procuress, are also on the left. This end of town also showcases the very public and intact toilets, or latrines, an intriguing magnet for visitors.

Note the soaring vaulted **Gate of Mazeus and Mithradates**. Turn right down **Curetes Street**, one of the main thoroughfares, lined with statues of notable city fathers. The lovely **hillside houses** located on the right were dwellings for affluent residents of the city, their courtyards and villas adorned with fine mosaics and elegant frescoes. Further down on the left is the **Temple of Hadrian**, one of dozens venerating his 2nd-century AD expedition

The remains of Ephesus' library

with its beautiful marble reliefs mounted on Corinthian columns.

Before you come to **Hercules' Gate** with its lion reliefs and winged victory symbols, look at the ornamental **Trajan Fountain** on your left, still undergoing restoration. Curetes Street was a pedestrian precinct, as Hercules' narrow gate barred vehicular traffic!

Continuing on your right, next to the commercial **Agora** is the **Temple of Domitian**, christened after a brutal and unpopular emperor. The Agora, or marketplace, indicates the scale and importance of Ephesus as a trading centre in the 3rd century BC. Facing the Temple is the **Memmius Monument** on the north side, and opposite is the **Pollio Fountain**, named after a prominent local family.

At the end of Curetes Street is a 3rd-century BC **Prytaneion** where a sacred flame burned eternally. On the left is an **Odeon** and this overlooks the upper entrance to the site. This tour can just as easily start from this entrance, beginning with a promenade along the city boulevards to give a look at life as the Romans lived it.

Walking Tour of Ephesus

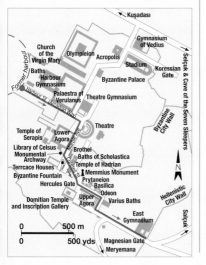

A foam party at Halikarnas nightclub; Bodrum is known for its hedonistic nightlife

Bodrum

Situated on a peninsula facing the Greek island of Kos, **Bodrum** ⑭ 🍴 continues to nurture its reputation as the pleasure and leisure capital of Turkey. More demure are the city's emblematic whitewashed 'birthday cake' square houses with blue shutters. Many historical attractions balance its yachts and contemporary party-time reputation. This is the ideal place to weigh anchor on a one-day or longer cruise, known as the Blue Voyage.

The town also has a serious shopping scene, plus more upmarket, innovative restaurants than the rest of the Aegean coast can muster. Bodrum was once the ancient city of Halicarnassus and one of its grandest monumental sites is the **Mausoleum** (Tue–Sun 8am–noon, 1.30–5pm; charge), containing the remains of an imperious stone tomb commemorating the Carian ruler Mausolus.

Bodrum's gem is the 15th-century **Crusader Castle of St Peter** that,

Bodrum	
🌐 **Population:** 50,000	Caddesi 33-35, Bodrum; tel: 0252-313 6566; www.ozelbodrumhastanesi.com
☎ **Local dialling code:** 0252	
ℹ **Tourist Office:** Barış Meydanı; tel: 0252-316 1091	✉ **Post Office:** Cevat Şakir Street 3, Bodrum
🌐 **Time Zone:** GMT +2	✈ **Airport:** Milas-Bodrum Airport (BJV); tel: 0252-523 0080; www.bodrum-airport.com/en/index.php
🚕 **Police:** Kıbrıs Şehitler Caddesi, Bodrum; tel: 155 (call centre)/0252-316 8079; www.bodrum.pol.tr	
	🚕 **Airport Taxi:** 0252-536 6147
🏥 **Hospital:** Özel Bodrum Hastanesi, Türkkuyusu Mahallesi, Marsmabedi	🚗 **Car Hire:** Sixt Rent-a-Car; Milas-Bodrum Airport; tel: 0252-444 0076

as the **Museum of Underwater Archaeology** (www.bodrum-museum.com; Tue–Sun 9am–noon, 1.30–7pm; charge, additional charge for several exhibitions 🅜), houses the remains of magnificent underwater cargoes and artefacts and showcases meticulous reconstructions of Bronze Age trading ships. This is easily one of Turkey's top five museums for content and layout and should be a highlight of a visit to Bodrum. There are amphora exhibitions, shipwreck halls, and a hall dedicated to a wealthy Carian princess complete with her personal treasury of gold jewellery.

Traditionally, Bodrum has been touched with the bohemian brush. This began in the 1920s when Cevat Şakir Kabaağaçlı, the 'Fisherman of Halikarnassos', was exiled here. His books and stories about Bodrum attracted intellectuals and artists to the (then) tranquil seascape.

Bodrum's nightlife is vibrant and invigorating. After an evening meal, the night is still young and the entertainment and disco scene comes alive. At the eastern end of Cumhuriyet Caddesi is the glittering open-skies **Halikarnas Disco** (summer only; charge). **Marina Yacht Club** is the ultimate muse of sophisticated nightlife and the jazz evenings are world-class.

Just up the street from Halikarnas Disco is the **Zeki Müren Museum**. Müren was one of Turkey's most accomplished and flamboyant musical performers, often referred to as

133

Zeki Müren

One of Turkey's most prolific singers, composers and film actors, Zeki Müren was an immensely beloved national cultural guru and a virtuoso performing artist. Unlike other singers who sang theatrically but not always from the musical score, Müren was a highly trained and skilled musician and composer. He was also a gifted painter and poet and is now a national legend, fondly remembered in Bodrum. Almost 200,000 people have visited his house, which is now a museum with his glittering costumes on display, along with his golden Cadillac in the front garden. These contrast unexpectedly with the modest rooms, unpretentious furniture and an archaic gramophone.

the 'Turkish Liberace'. The museum was his house and is sombre and humble compared to his glitzy lifestyle.

The best beaches are found outside of the city centre. **Gümbet** , 5km (3 miles) from Bodrum, has a long sandy beach dotted with motels and *pansiyons* and is easily reached by bus from Bodrum. Buses from the central terminal will also take you around Bodrum Peninsula to resorts like **Bitez**, **Turgutreis**, or the picture-postcard village of **Gümüşlük**. **Yalıkavak** was a sponge fishing village but has good restaurants fronting onto the water. Much of the Bodrum Peninsula has become a haven for Turkey's elite who have exclusive summer villas here.

Marmaris and the Reşadiye Peninsula

The resort of **Marmaris** 🅱 is reached along a 32km (20-mile) road off the highway between Muğla and Fethiye, which descends through fragrant pine forests to a perfect natural harbour. Not as racy as Bodrum, Marmaris still has its 'Bar Street' that attracts young and lively revellers.

The resort area of Marmaris is at **İçmeler** 8km (5 miles) across the bay, and the package-holiday crowd usually head for this area. The beach curves around the bay and there is a choice of water sports, including windsurfing. This is an ideal venue for a family holiday.

A day trip around the **Reşadiye Peninsula** can be done by car and affords panoramic views eventually bringing you to the little village of **Datça**, divided into Old and New Datça. It is quiet and traditional and is the geographical 'divide' between the Aegean and Mediterranean seas. There is accommodation here; this is also the gateway to the ancient city of **Knidos** (daily 8am–7pm; charge).

Bobbing masts in Marmaris' yachting harbour

A classic Dalyan riverboat trip to the Kaunos rock tombs

Aegean Region

Gentle Giants

The loggerhead turtle, *Caretta*, favours Turkey's sandy south-facing beaches as a habitat for breeding and hatching eggs, especially around Dalyan and İztuzu Beach. The turtles mature to 77-158kg (170-350lbs) and are the world's largest hard-shell turtle. The female nesting period is between June and July and she lays between 100 and 126 leathery eggs which take about 80 days to incubate in the sand.

Attracted by the moon on the water, the hatchlings then head for the sea in a race for survival. It took international pressure to convince local authorities that tourism developments were threatening the turtles' habitat. If you are swimming or snorkelling and feel one nudge your leg, feel privileged to encounter one of the sea's gentle giants.

The road is excruciatingly rough but passes through some quaint villages. The site of Knidos occupies a vast and windswept location at the extreme tip of the peninsula. An Ottoman lighthouse majestically surveys the sea to Greece but requires stamina to reach on foot. A provocative Aphrodite statue by Praxiteles was apparently made for Knidos in the 4th century BC, and controversy about its whereabouts continues.

Lake Köyceğiz and Dalyan

If time permits, take a detour to **Lake Köyceğiz** (Köyceğiz Gölü), a haven for diverse species of birds. The restful town has good accommodation and lakeside restaurants. It has a period manor house that once belonged to a local cotton magnate.

Dalyan is a small and intimate riverside resort whose name means fishing weir. The thing to do here is take a boat trip upriver to the historic Carian ruins at **Kaunos** (daily 8.30am–5.30pm; charge). Imposing Lycian rock tombs gaze down at the passing river boats and their day-trippers. At Ilıca, at the northern end of the lake, is a series of gooey thermal mudbaths, reputed to alleviate many aches and pains.

Dalaman is a small town whose main claim to fame is its airport used mainly for charters from Europe. It helped to open up the Aegean and Mediterranean regions to touristic potential.

ACCOMMODATION

Assos Harbour (Behramkale) has become a hotspot for İstanbul's jet set. It is a good idea to book early if you want to stay in one of the sophisticated boutique hotels. İzmir has hotels for every budget. The cheapest pensions are found in the narrow streets opposite Basmane train station. The Çeşme Peninsula is a racier and more animated place to stay. Kuşadası has over 300 hotels in all categories, but is less charming. Selçuk is smaller and more tranquil, with attractive accommodation options. Bodrum combines seaside appeal with grand hotels and many intimate boutique hotels. Package tourists will usually be based opposite Marmaris at Içmeler.

Accommodation Price Categories

Price categories are per night in high season (May–Oct), for a double room, including taxes.
$ = below 30TL
$$ = 30–50TL
$$$ = 50–100TL
$$$$ = 100–200TL
$$$$$ = Over 200TL

North Aegean

Alakoç Hotel
Akçay
Tel: 0266-384 8071
Fronting onto the beach with a cool, shaded garden, the family-run pension typifies the tranquil and friendly atmosphere of Akçay. **$$**

Assos Hotel
İskele Mevkii, Behramkale
Tel: 0286-721 7017
One of the oldest hotels on the harbour front, with great views across to the Greek island of Lesbos. Open all year round, and fishermen bring in the daily catch for your perusal. **$$$**

Assos Kervansaray
İskele Mevkii, Behramkale
www.assoskervansaray.com
Attractive, stone-built harbour-front hotel with great views and 50 rooms with all mod cons, but who needs them at this romantic place? Super restaurant and café. **$$$$**

Behram Hotel
Behramkale İskele, Behramkale
Tel: 0286-721 7016
www.behram-hotel.com
A venerable 17-room hotel with an outstanding seaside fish restaurant. Open all year. **$$**

Berceste Hotel
Sivrice Feneri Mevkii, Bektaş Köyü, Ayvacık
Tel: 0286-723 4616
www.bercestehotel.com
Overlooking the beach near Assos, this ornate and statuesque hotel scores by being comfortable and close to the beach. Will appeal to those who cherish an out-of-the-way experience with atmosphere and flair. **$$$$**

Çetmihan Hotel
Yeşilyurt Köyü, Küçükkuyu, Ayvacık, Kazdağları
Tel: 0286-752 6169
www.cetmi.com
A gem of a boutique hotel in enchanting surroundings with sincere hosts and friendly service. Highly recommended for discerning guests. **$$$$**

Evim Pansiyon
216 Sokak 40, Foça
Tel: 0232-812 1360
Renovated old house with seven rooms and an enchanting garden. **$$**

Grand Hotel Temizel
Sarımsaklı, Ayvalık
Tel: 0266-324 2000
www.temizel.com.tr
One of the largest and smartest local hotels for package tours. All activities, sports, Turkish bath and swimming pools and a private beach. **$$$**

Hanedan

Sahil Caddesi, Foça
Tel: 0232-812 1515
An economic but comfortable choice on the
harbour, ideal for budget travellers. **$$**

Hotel Kalif

Hürriyet Caddesi 19, Sarımsaklı, Ayvalık
Tel: 0266-324 4914
www.kalifhotel.com
Pleasant resort hotel adjacent to the beach.
Excellent, plentiful food and willing, helpful
service.  **$$$**

Kaptan Hotel

Balıkhane Sokak, Ayvalık
Tel: 0266-312 8834
A converted soap mill, this is an excellent
budget choice, with 13 rooms and two
suites, and balconies with sea views. **$$**

Karaçam

Sahil Caddesi 70, Foça
Tel: 0232-812 3216
A charming period Greek house with 24
rooms, popular with tour groups. It is advis-
able to book in advance. **$$$**

Yalı Pansiyon

Behind the Post Office #25, Ayvalık
Tel: 0266-312 2423
www.yali-pansiyon.com/index.html
An authentic 150-year-old Greek building
restored with love and attitude. Shaded
water-front garden with a private pier. Five
sunny bedrooms filled with nostalgia. **$$**

İzmir and Sardis

Antik Han Hotel

Anafartalar Caddesi 600, Çankaya, İzmir
Tel: 0232-489 2750
www.otelantikhan.com
Charming city-centre hotel in a restored
Ottoman mansion. Convenient to city-
centre sights and located in an energetic
part of the city. **$$**

Balçova Thermal Hotel
(Agamemnon Kaplıca)

Vali Hüseyin Öğütcen Caddesi 2, Balçova,

Many hotels have rooftop views

İzmir
Tel: 0232-259 0102
www.balcovatermal.com
Just on the outskirts of İzmir in a secluded
forest area, this is a fine hotel that excels at
treatments and therapy and is thoroughly
European in outlook and standards. **$$$$**

Çeşme Kervansaray

Çeşme Kalesi Yanı
Tel: 0232-712 7177
Romantically restored 16th-century *caravanserai* round a fountain courtyard, two suites
and 32 rooms, many with sea vistas. **$$$**

Hilton Hotel

Gaziosmanpaşa Bulvarı 7, İzmir
Tel: 0232-497 6060
www.hilton.com
The Hilton is a city landmark that still excels,
and the panorama from the Windows on
the Bay bar on the 31st floor rounds off
the other superb amenities. Open all year.
$$$$$

Sheraton Çeşme Hotel, Resort and Spa

Şifne Caddesi 35, Çeşme, İzmir
Tel: 0232-723 1240
www.sheratoncesme.com
One of the most dazzling hydrotherapy spa
resorts on the Aegean coast with natural
thermal waters, activities and entertainment
for all the family. Great food and marvellous
atmosphere.  **$$$$**

The Imbat hotel in Kuşadası has fantastic leisure facilities

Swissotel Grand Efes
Gaziosmanpaşa Bulvarı 1, Alsancak, İzmir
Tel: 0232-414 0000
www.swissotel.com/izmir
Everything you would expect from a Leading Hotels of the World hotel highlighted by a superb panorama over İzmir Bay and the marvellous Amrita Spa and Wellness Centre. This is İzmir's premier hotel. **$$$$$**

Southern Aegean
Club Caravanserai
Öküz Mehmet Paşa Kervansaray, Atatürk Bulvarı 1, Kuşadası
Tel: 0256-613 1203
www.kusadasihotels.com
A 17th-century hostelry in the city centre with palm trees, ethnic decor and great entertainment, belly-dancing evenings and a grand all-inclusive family experience. Book online for substantial price savings. **$$$**

Hotel Kismet
Gazi Beğendi Bulvarı 1, Kuşadası
Tel: 0256-618 1290
www.kismet.com.tr
You will be starry-eyed at this beautiful hotel with every upmarket service – and the sea right beside you. **$$$**

Imbat
Kadınlar Denizi Mevkii, Kuşadası
Tel: 0256-614 2000
www.imbat.com.tr
One of Kuşadası's big resort hotels with all the trimmings one would expect from a 5-star hotel that glitters with amenities. **$$$$**

Kalehan
On the main street that runs through the town, Selçuk
Tel: 0232-892 6154
www.kalehan.com/uk/index.htm
Long-established family hotel in Ottoman style with every modern comfort. Highly recommended and continuing the trend of excellence. Open all year. **$$$**

Korumar
Gazi Beğendi Bulvarı, Kuşadası
Tel: 0256-618 1530
www.korumar.com.tr
Attractive hotel where everything is big and in high definition but perfect for a family holiday, with almost every activity and extra you can imagine. Open year-round. **$$$$**

Nazhan
Saint Jean Caddesi, 1044 Sokak, Selçuk
Tel: 0232-892 8731
There are many attractive features in this elegant six-room *pansiyon*, including a bar on the rooftop and a tiny courtyard for breakfast in the shade. Open all year. **$$**

Villa Konak
Yıldırım Caddesi 55, Kuşadası
Tel: 0256-614 6318
www.villakonakhotel.com
Attractively restored mansion with a pool and beautiful garden and courtyard away from the razzle of Kuşadası. Children under 10 are not welcome. **$$$$**

Bodrum and Marmaris
Antique Theatre Hotel
Kıbrıs Şehitleri Caddesi 243, Bodrum
Tel: 0252-316 6053
www.antiquetheatrehotel.com
Luxury boutique hotel and gourmet restaurant affiliated to the prestigious Chaîne des Rôtisseurs Association. **$$$$$**

Aqua Hotel
İçmeler, Marmaris
Tel: 0252-455 3633

A landscaped garden leads down to the beach, while indoors there is a fitness centre and a tennis court. Open all year. 🎿 $$$

Colossae Hotel Termal
Pamukkale, Karahayıt
Tel: 0258-271 4156
www.colossaehotel.com.tr
Located in a purpose-built thermal village behind the main travertine falls, with everything that clusters of all-inclusive hotels tend to have to keep guests on site. $$

Green Nature
Siteler Mahallesi Armutalan, Marmaris
Tel: 0252-417 6120
www.clubgreennature.com
Most guests here are on package deals. Adult and children's pools, sauna, fitness centre, tennis court, billiards room and a Turkish bath. Closed in winter. 🎿 $$$$

Hotel Begonya
Hacı Mustafa Sokak 101, Marmaris
Tel: 0252-412 4095
Attractive converted barn with a courtyard garden in the middle of 'Bar street', so particularly suitable for late-night revellers. $$

Karia Princess
Eskiçeşme Mahallesi, Myndos Caddesi 8, Bodrum
Tel: 0252-316 8971
www.kariaprincess.com
Upmarket accommodation within walking

Beachside hotels line Bodrum's coastline

distance of the town centre, but away from the noisy discos and bars. The gardens are a botanical paradise with over 30 different plant varieties. $$$$

Konak Melsa
Atatürk Caddesi 55
Tel: 0252-284 5104
www.konakmelsa.com
Quiet, beautifully appointed attractive 24-room hotel with local stone and palm trees. Great swimming pool and restaurant. $$$

Lavanta Hotel
Papatya Sokak 32, Yalıkavak
Tel: 0252-385 2167
www.lavanta.com
This hotel gets the most rave reviews and praise imaginable but fully lives up to expectations. Highly recommended in every way, including village charm and panoramic vistas. Open 1 May – 14 Oct only. $$$

Majesty Hotel Marina
Neyzen Tevfik Caddesi 226, Bodrum
Tel: 0252-313 0356
Call centre: 0242-441 100
www.majesty.com.tr
Comfortable 4-star hotel opposite the marina, an easy walk down the main thoroughfare to all the action in Bodrum. Restaurant, bar, coffee shop, pool and harbour view. $$$$

Manastır Hotel
Barış Mevkii, Kumbahçe, Bodrum
Tel: 0252-316 2854
www.manastirbodrum.com
Luxury whitewashed Mediterranean-style hotel on the site of a former monastery. All rooms have balconies and the hotel has a pool, sauna and two restaurants. $$$$

Sevin Pension
Türkkuyusu Cad. 5, Bodrum
Tel: 0252-316 7682
www.sevinpansiyon.com
A short walk from the bus terminal, this pension is clean and neat, and the owner is on site. Highly recommended at the cheap and cheerful end for budget travellers. $

Listings

RESTAURANTS

Turks eat when they are hungry and restaurants are open from morning until evening. Along the coast, everybody tries to find the best fish restaurants by the shore. İzmir has restaurants for all tastes and wallets with many innovative and international restaurants to choose from, while most of the upmarket hotels have excellent dining facilities. Kuşadası has many seafood restaurants and you will be spoilt for eating choices. Choose the freshest fish you can find and check prices before ordering. Food and restaurants in Bodrum are outstandingly good, creative and typical of Turkish culinary ingenuity.

North Aegean

Öz Canlı Balık
Gazinolar Caddesi, Ayvalık
Excellent meze and fish, near the seafront. No credit cards. **$$**

Sağlam
Cumhuriyet Meydanı 29, Bergama
Tel: 0232-667 2003
www.saglamrestaurant.com
Great regional specialities served with flair at this busy venue, convenient for tour buses.
$$$

İzmir and Sardis

Deniz
Yalı Caddesi 396, Karşıyaka, İzmir
Tel: 0232-364 7261
www.denizrestaurant.com
Handy for the shopping district across İzmir Bay and highly regarded for the freshest sea food and speciality dishes. Open all year. **$$$**

Körfez
İskele (harbour), Çeşme
Tel: 0232-712 6718
Popular spot with a tempting range of *meze* and fish. Keep to the Turkish choices and you won't be disappointed. Open all year. **$$**

Lamia Dinner Cruise
Bostanlı Feribot İskele, Bostanlı, İzmir
Tel: 0232-336 5686
www.lamia.com.tr
For a romantic cruise on the luxury catamaran Lamia, nobody does this better. Sophisticated dinner cruises, brunches and private parties. Reservations essential. **$$$**

Seçkin
M. Kemalettin Caddesi 16/A, Konak, İzmir
Tel: 0232-489 2404
No-frills reliable restaurant offering traditional Turkish dishes and desserts. **$**

Southern Aegean

Ali Baba
Belediye Turistik Çarşısı 5, Kuşadası
Tel: 0256-614 1551
The most tempting displays of fresh seafood

Many cafés are set up for alfresco dining

and everything is as good as it looks. Try to get a table beside the water. **$$$**

Ferah Balık
İskele Yanı, Kuşadası, within Güverçin Park
Tel: 0256-614 1281
A friendly neighbourhood restaurant on the seafront with passable fare. 🍴 **$$**

Kalehan
Kalehan Hotel, Selçuk
Tel: 0232-892 6154
Turkish dishes served as set meals or à la carte in Ottoman style. Open all year. **$$$**

Şelçuk Köftecisi
Vergi Dairesi altı 37/J, Şelçuk
Tel: 0232-892 6696
This café specialises in meatballs, though the kebaps are good as well, and it is often overlooked by visitors (partly due to its unassuming decor). Worth a visit. 🍴 **$$**

Bodrum and Marmaris
Gemibaşı Restaurant
Neyzen Tevfik Cad 17A, Bodrum
Tel: 0252-316 1220
Comprehensive menu of typical Turkish fare,

freshly prepared. The kind of place you can take the whole family or just yourself. 🍴 **$$**

La Jolla Wine Bar and Bistro
Neyzen Tevfik Caddesi 174, Bodrum
Tel: 0252-313 7660
www.lajollabodrum.com
Small chic bistro close to the marina open all day and serving breakfast. Meals combine Mediterranean with Tex-Mex and more. Great selection of wines. Open 9am–11pm. **$$$**

Kocadon
Saray Sokak 1, Bodrum
Tel: 0252-316 3705
www.kocadon.com
Fabulous gourmet dining in an elegant restored ancestral dwelling. Dinner only served. Summer garden is a dream. **$$$$**

Secret Garden
Eskiçeşme Mahallesi, Danacı Sokak 20, Bodrum
Tel: 0252-313 1641
It is no secret that this is the most brilliant and typically Mediterranean restaurant with outstanding gourmet creations. Open in summer for dinner only. **$$$$**

NIGHTLIFE

Being beside the sea is not just focused on sailing, swimming and sunning. Coastal Turkey is known for its uninhibited nightlife and nowhere does it better than Bodrum and Marmaris. Bars and restaurants may transform into discos after midnight, and music, dancing and laser shows preside over the night until around 3am, while more upmarket venues feature live entertainers and jazz.

Crazy Daisy Bar
Bar Street 121, Marmaris
Tel: 0252-412 4856
www.crazydaisybar.com
The wildest, loudest and unrivalled disco in Marmaris. Events change constantly and the shows and DJs are legendary.

Ecstasy
Kaleiçi Sakarya Sokak 10, Kuşadası
Tel: 0256-612 2208

Spread out over two floors, this popular club attracts a young crowd from all over the area.

Halikarnas Disco
Cumhuriyet Caddesi, Bodrum
Tel: 0252-316 8000
www.halikarnas.com.tr
Celebrating 30 years in song, dance, music and knock-out laser shows, the music rocks on for dedicated party-goers and celebrities. Open May–Oct.

Hilton Hotel
Gaziosmanpaşa Bulvarı 7, İzmir
Tel: 0232-497 6060
www.hilton.com
The panorama from the 31st floor is magical and the music is soothing and moody. This is İzmir's place of choice for late-night birds.

Küba
Neyzen Tevfik Caddesi 62, Bodrum
Tel: 0252-313 4450
www.kubabar.com
Open-air upmarket and upbeat bar with rhythm and atmosphere. There is a great restaurant attached.

Marina Yacht Club
Bodrum Marina, Neyzen Tevfik Caddesi 5, Bodrum
Tel: 0252-316 1228
www.marinayachtclub.com
Bars, restaurants and the coolest of cool

Enjoying a *nargile* in Marmaris

coastal jazz. Attracts the cream of the yachting brigade and even paparazzi.

SPORTS AND TOURS

Most activities and tours involve water-based activities and sports. A *gulet* tour is the best of these, and Bodrum and Marmaris are the main places to join a Blue Cruise *(see Coastal Activities, p.22)*. Many charter and travel agents can also arrange other activities, rent cars or arrange diving excursions.

Akustik Travel & Yachting
Neyzen Tevfik Street, Nr. 200 (near the marina), Bodrum
Tel: 0252-313 8964
Sightseeing tours and daily boat trips.

Alternatif Turizm
Çamlik Sokak 1, Marmaris
Tel: 0252-417 2720
www.alternatifoutdoor.com
Adventure specialists since 1991, they arrange hiking, canyoning and all water activities. Well qualified and recommended.

Anker Travel
İnönü Bulvarı 14, Kuşadası
Tel: 0256-612 4598
www.ankertravel.com

Offers a wide range of local excursions, rental cars, boat charter and tours further afield in Turkey, from skiing to spas, plus a full-service travel agency. Well recommended.

Arya Yachting
Caferpaşa Caddesi 25/1, Bodrum
Tel: 0252-316 1580
www.aryatours.com/en/start_e.php
Yachting excursions for both day trips and extended holiday periods.

Aşkın Dive Centre
Bodrum
Tel: 0252-316 4247
www.askindiving.com
Specialised in diving but will arrange archaeological and Blue Cruise holidays.

Blue Point Yachting
Bodrum
Tel: 0252-316 9556
www.mspapajoe.com
www.bluepointyachting.com
Hard to find a more heavenly yacht for charter than the 34m (111ft) *Papa Joe*, an ocean-
going schooner with first-class everything.

Costa Turca Yachting
Şirinyer Mahallesi, Durmazlar Sokak 20,
Marmaris
Tel: 0252-417 6420
www.costaturca.com
Specialists in boat charter with the largest
choice of yachts, schooners and sailing
boats for low budget to high.

Kaya Güneri Yachting
Atatürk Bulvarı 107, Konacık, Bodrum
Tel: 0252-319 0485/1667
www.kayaguneriyachting.com
An excellent choice for Blue Cruise *gulet*
rental: great food and plenty of sailing time.

Netsel Marina
Netsel Tourism Investments Co. Inc,
Günnücek, PO Box 231, Marmaris
Tel: 0252-412 2708
www.netselmarina.com/index_eng.htm
One of Turkey's largest (720 boats) and
most proficient, professionally run marinas.

Pupa Yachting
Neyzen Tevfik Caddesi 242/7, Bodrum
Tel: 0252-316 7715
www.pupa.com.tr
They have a grand selection of yachts whether
you want to travel as a prince or prefer budget
options. Also bareback charters.

**Yeşil Marmaris Turizm Yat
İşletmeleri.A.S**
Barbaros Caddesi 1, Marmaris
Tel: 0252-412 1033
www.yesilmarmarislines.com
This company has a virtual monopoly on
hydrofoil services to and from Rhodes, but
winter schedules are unreliable.

FESTIVALS AND EVENTS

Being beside the sea means that local events are more partial to boating activities
or water sports. But, inland, camel wrestling is a colourful pageant that should
not be missed. Local village fairs are often staged on an impromptu or traditional
basis: small villages may still celebrate annual migration rituals. Ask for the latest
news from the local tourist information office.

January–February
Camel Wrestling Pageant
İzmir and Selçuk
Heats are held in small towns, with champion-
ship competitions staged in İzmir and Selçuk.
Final bouts are well publicised one month in
advance in local media.

May
International Marmaris Yacht Festival
9–13 May
www.miyc.org/_en/index_en.asp
Any type of boat can qualify according to
weight and class. Charter boats put their best
innovations in front of a global audience.

August
İzmir International Fair
22–31 Aug
www.izfas.com.tr
The oldest trade show in Turkey showcasing local export products. Festivals and
other social events are planned around it.

October
**International Bodrum Yacht
Regatta**
21–26 Oct
www.bodrumcup.com
A festive nautical rally for wooden boats
only. Held annually.

Mediterranean Region

Rugged landscapes, antique cities, castles and classical theatres contrast with the sun-kissed beaches and a gentle sea in this picture-postcard holiday region. The Turks call the Mediterranean *'Akdeniz'*, or white sea. Others prefer to call this land of spectacular vistas the 'Turquoise Coast', in honour of its translucent waters – it is indeed this colour imprint that will stay in your mind's eye.

Antalya

Population: 850,000

Local dialling code: 0242

Tourist Office: Cumhuriyet Caddesi, Özel İdare Altı 2, Antalya; tel: 0242-241 1774

Time Zone: GMT +2

Police: 155 (call centre) Güvenlik Mahallesi, Vatan Bulvarı, Çallı, Antalya; tel: 0242-345 4100

Hospital: Medical Park Antalya; Fener Mahallesi, Tekelioğlu Caddesi 7, Lara, Antalya; tel: 0242-314 3434; **www.medicalpark.com.tr**

Post Office: Antalya PTT; Güllük Caddesi 9, Antalya

Airport: Bayındır International Airport; tel: 0242-330 3600, ext. 1433

Car Hire: Avis; Fevzi Çakmak Caddesi, Talya Hotel 30; tel: 0242-248 1772; **www.avis.com.tr**

Once a neglected area where a trip from Antalya to Kaş was a four-day journey by donkey, the quaint fishing-village appeal of much of the Mediterranean region has largely faded. But many towns retain evidence of their Greek origins with a central village square, whitewashed houses and wooden shutters. Many have typical Byzantine churches with a minaret attached that turns it into a mosque. An airport in Antalya has encouraged charter groups and opened up new tourism avenues that local Turks would once barely have dreamt of. Additionally, many foreigners love the area and lifestyle so much when on holiday that they return to buy houses and live or retire here permanently.

The coast has been conveniently divided into four sections, based roughly on the ancient kingdoms. Lycia, in the west, is undoubtedly the most scenically beautiful, with the wild Taurus Mountains plummeting to a coastline of cliffs and coves. Resorts are in every budget category from backpackers roughing it in tree houses at Olympos to the all-inclusive glittering resorts around Kemer.

Pamphylia is bounded by cities, stretching from sophisticated Antalya in the west to Alanya in the east. In between is fertile agricultural land that inclines to golden beaches trimming the coasts. Fabulous archaeological sites such as Perge, Aspendos and Side balance the ancient and the contemporary.

Western Cilicia (roughly Alanya to Adana) has spectacular crags and cliffs and a hair-raising road to navigate. Alanya is the banana capital of Turkey, and the many medieval castles and battlements are evidence of a more bellicose past.

Turn south into the Hatay and the region is quite distinct from the rest of Turkey, with a more diverse and Arabic-influenced cultural mixture.

Fethiye promenade and harbour

Lycia

Lycia was home to a proud, autonomous community who depended on the sea for trade and food. The harsh landscape afforded them sanctuary and independence to hold out against Roman rule until the brutal end.

The independent-minded Lycians settled the wide peninsula between present-day Fethiye and Antalya from around 1400BC. They had their own unique language and an early form of proportional representation government but are best known today for their elaborate burial tombs.

From the 6th century BC, 20 cities in this urbane region banded together in a loose federation. Lycians fell under Persian rule by 546BC but, in 170BC, the Lycian League, with Patara as its capital, was formed, a democratic political alliance of city-states. The degree of autonomy was well in advance of its time and studied by James Madison as a keystone for the US Constitution.

By the 1st century AD, Roman Emperor Vespasian had brought Lycia back under Roman control and it eventually faded into obscurity in Byzantine times. It lay undisturbed until 1839, when Charles Fellows made the first of three journeys to ancient Lycia and discovered Xanthos. He was later knighted for bringing much of Lycia's antiquities back to Britain.

Fethiye

At the western edge of Lycia, **Fethiye** is a small, attractive port town tucked between a broad bay and the sheer cliff face of Mount Cragos, the western endstop of the Taurus Mountains. The town was almost completely rebuilt after an earthquake in 1957. A Lycian sarcophagus and some rock tombs remain, the most prominent being the **Tomb of Amyntas** (up the steps from

The stunning white sands of Ölüdeniz

Kaya Caddesi; daily 8.30am–sunset; charge). The town's small **museum** (off Atatürk Caddesi; Tue–Sun 8.30am–5pm; charge) contains finds from various local archaeological sites, including Xanthos and Kaunos.

Fethiye is dignified and quiet as charter tourists tend to head 19km (12 miles) south to Ölüdeniz and Hisarönü. The town has a restful promenade with waterfront restaurants and a lovely marina. Visitors also come for the excellent market in the city centre. The nearest beach resort to Fethiye is **Çalış** 🏖️, 4km (2 miles) west where a cluster of resort hotel holds sway.

Ölüdeniz

Splashed on the front cover of many tourist brochures, **Ölüdeniz** ❶ 🏖️ was the most beautiful beach on the Mediterranean, a turquoise and cobalt lagoon encircled by platinum sand, with pine trees inclining over the water. Development has deprived it of pristine beauty but not of its popularity as a bathing paradise. Above the beach, **Mt Babadağ** provides liftoff for paragliders.

Kayaköy

The deserted Greek town of **Kayaköy** provides a fascinating historical excursion, reached off the main road between Fethiye and Ölüdeniz. A poignant relic of the Muslims and Christians who once existed harmoniously in the town, it was emptied of its multiethnic Ottoman residents when they were forcibly relocated to Greece in 1922. Take time to walk the steep and narrow, overgrown streets and marvel at the frescoes in the churches.

Tlos and Saklıkent

Head out of Fethiye towards the coastal road. Keep on the N-350 signed to Korkuteli after 22km (13 miles) and follow signs to Yakaköy. You are also signposted to **Tlos** (open access; charge), known to the Hittites in the 14th century BC. The site has many Lycian house tombs and it can be seen along with nearby Saklıkent.

Forty-four km (26 miles) southeast of Fethiye (3km/2 miles from the main road), **Saklıkent** is a lofty,

Admiring the rock tombs at Tlos

verdant haven, a sanctuary from the coastal summer heat. A constricted gorge is impassable to all but the technically equipped after about 2km (1 mile) in; for everyone else a wooden suspension bridge leads over the river to excellent trout restaurants beside icy fresh springs.

147

Mediterranean

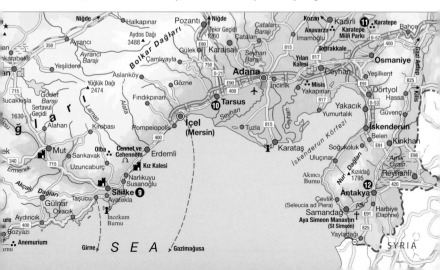

The Coastal Cities

Back on the coast, serious (and sturdy) students of ancient cities will delight in the immense 4th-century BC settlement of **Pınara** (daily 8.30am–6pm; charge), 40km (24 miles) southeast of Fethiye. Turn south to the village of Minare, then fork left to the car park, 3km (2 miles) further along. This is a regal site and comprises a Lycian acropolis, a hillside honeycombed with tombs, a theatre, agora, scant remains of baths and a spectacularly ornate King's Tomb. Access is steep and difficult but worth it.

Three km (2 miles) southeast, just west of Kınık, a signposted side road leads 4km (2 miles) down to the extremely worthwhile ruins of **Letoön** (daily, May–Sept 7.30am–7pm, Oct–Apr 8.30am–5pm; charge). Partly submerged by the rising watertable, and now clad in reeds and inhabited by frogs, terrapins and waterbirds, this is the site of three adjacent cult temples dedicated to Leto, Artemis and Apollo, reigning deities of Lycia. As with all deities, legends proliferate and this adds to the charisma of the site.

Xanthos

Xanthos is reached from the town centre of Kınık, 1km (½ mile) off the N-400 coastal road (daily, May–Oct 8am–7pm, Nov–Apr 8am–6.30pm;

Investigating the day's catch at Patara beach

charge). The city was besieged by Brutus in 42BC, and its fiercely proud residents fought to the death rather than surrender.

Xanthos was gloriously rebuilt by Mark Antony after he defeated Brutus, and it became the most important capital of the Lycian League. Today's ruins are extensive and brilliantly superimpose Lycian, Persian and Greek civilisation upon each other. Hieroglyphics on the Inscribed Pillar enabled scholars to decipher the Lycian language. There is a city gate, an impressive Lion Tomb, and market-place (agora), as well as the ruins of a Byzantine basilica to detain you for at least several hours here. Don't over-look the 5th-century BC Harpy Tomb.

By the 7th century BC the city had declined and lay intact for 400 years until its discovery by Charles Fellows in 1839.

Patara

Patara ❷ 🏛 was another powerful Lycian city that prospered from com-mercial sea trade. Today it is known for its 18km (11 mile) white-sand beach, the longest and widest in Turkey. There is little shade and only one café, so go prepared. Turn off the N-400 9km (5 miles) west of Kalkan; the site is 8km (5 miles) further along through the village. The ruins and nearby beach are open daily May–Sept 7.30am–7pm, Oct–Apr 8.30am–5pm; entrance and parking fee.

This giant sandpit is protected for the breeding loggerhead turtle, so no hotels front onto the beach. The area behind the dunes is a stunning archaeological site. The town was also

Bustling Kalkan at night

the birthplace of St Nicholas in the 4th century AD (see box, left). Today's ruins are scattered over a wide area among the fields and dunes.

The triple monumental arch from the 1st century BC greeting you at the entrance to the site also doubled as an aqueduct. The theatre is awe-inspiring and extremely well restored. It is easy to imagine yourself as a Roman window-shopper when strolling along the remains of the fashionable colon-naded street. An important discovery was the Stadiasmus, a Roman mile-stone of great historical significance. Even more important is a 2,000-year-old lighthouse, now well inland and being reconstructed. Like other coastal towns, Patara's fortunes dried up with the receding sea.

Kalkan

If anything typifies the transformation from fishing village to villa-land, it is

Mediterranean Region

Kalkan. The central area retains its lovely houses and sentimentality but villas and unsightly building obliterate every centimetre of the surrounding hillsides. A new coastal road at the western end of Kalkan now bypasses several of the smaller inland towns and some dangerous hairpin bends. Home to droves of British residents, Kalkan has delightful pensions, enchanting harbourside dining and some fascinating shops. Kalkan has a small stony beach; so those in search of sand head 6km (3 miles) east along the dramatic cliff-hugging route to **Kaputaş** Beach.

Kaş

Kaş ❸ (120km/75 miles southeast of Fethiye) once nestled by a pretty little harbour and was accessible only by boat. It now sprawls up and over the surrounding heights. A long peninsula stabs into the sea and is now covered with hotels and houses but with superb southerly views over the Greek island of **Meis** (Kastellorizo), 4km (2 miles) offshore.

Known as Antiphellos in Roman times and an important port, Kaş' central area today has shady lanes and quintessentially Mediterranean Turkish houses that were inhabited by Greeks until the 1920s. There is a **Hellenistic Theatre** (open access) that is still used for performances, and a temple with a few basalt blocks survives from the 1st centuries BC and AD. The symbol of Kaş is a Lycian Lion Tomb that looks down on the main shopping street, Uzun Çarşısı. The mountainside is dotted with majestic 4th-century BC rock tombs.

Kaş is the scuba-diving capital of Turkey but also has excellent shops whether you want knock-offs or the designer original. It is the centre for day trips by *gulet* to Meis and Kekova *(see below)*, adventure activities like canyoning and paragliding, and there is a notable residential art camp in the village of **Çükürbağ** 12km (8 miles) in the plateau above. The town overflows with restaurants and disco bars, retaining its reputation as the hippest spot on the coast. A new yacht marina is changing the face and tone of the town and is due to open in 2011.

Üçağız, Kekova and Simena

The best activity by far is a daily boat tour to **Kekova Island** to cruise around a Sunken City (Batı Kent) 🅼, poke the bow into a chilling bat cave or go ashore to miniature Simena

---

Oya: Symbolic Language of Anatolia

Oya is a type of crocheting, also known as Turkish lace and it dates back to the 8th-century BC Phrygians. If a Turkish woman has time to spare, she will bring out her needle or crochet hook and begin to intricately edge a scarf, headdress, towels or serviettes. Various needles or hooks can be used, but the delicate designs, flower motifs and colours all symbolise an event, an emotion, or feelings towards a lover or even a suitor a girl does not fancy. Beads are added for decorative effect. The art of *oya* conveys a message through its shape and colour; a girl in love wears purple hyacinths. *Oya* has no equivalent in other languages and no bride's trousseau, or *çeyiz*, would be complete without it.

The ruins of the castle at Kekova loom over the island

(Kale) and trek up to Turkey's tiniest theatre with only 300 seats – situated in a lofty 15th-century castle with crenellated ramparts. Excursions leave from Kaş or from Andriake, just west of Demre (*see below*). Local boats also ferry you from the seaside town of **Üçağız,** about 30km (18 miles) east of Kaş, off the N-400. This diminutive fishing village has several good seafood restaurants.

Adjacent to **Üçağız** lies the Lycian necropolis of Teimiussa, its chest-type tombs spread along the shore. Be sure to see **Aperlai** with its submerged ridge-backed Lycian tombs. Both sites are best seen by boat and most boat tours will drift past here.

Demre and Myra

Demre is also called Kale and you are here to see the ancient city of **Myra,** 3km (2 miles) from the town centre (daily, May–Sept 7.30am–7pm, Oct–Apr 8am–5.30pm; charge). Founded in the 5th century BC, this was another stellar city in the Lycian Federation. The rock tombs are the most pleasing visual feature but have lost the vibrant painted decorations that Charles Fellows noted in 1839. There is an impressive classical theatre and, although the site has a rough and tumble overview, its grandeur is hard to deny. Like many of Turkey's classical ruins, a good imagination helps to re-create the splendour of the era.

The other reason for visiting Demre-Kale is the **Church of St Nicholas** or Noel Baba Kilesi (daily 8.30am–4.30pm; charge). This is the most evocative Byzantine church in Turkey, tiny, intimate and sacred all at once. Born in Patara, St Nicholas was bishop here in the 4th century AD. The splendid Byzantine frescoes have been a bit luridly retouched, but flocks of pilgrims in tour buses descend on the church almost constantly. Try to arrive early to appreciate the serenity and divinity of this biblical treasure.

Three km (1½ miles) west of Demre the road leads to Çayağzı (ancient Andriake). Try to imagine the thriving port in historical terms, the bustle, commerce, trade, and the 2nd-century Roman granary. The area is marshy and reedy and has many scattered ruins, and legends tell of an oracle at Sura, inaccessible up the meandering, marshy delta. The most tangible remains are on the main road, an icy-cold natural spring with a pungent sulphur content. Most of Turkey's natural springs are steamy hot; so this one is unusual. Many stop here, although only the brave take the waters.

Finike

Set amidst lush citrus orchards, **Finike** is primarily an agricultural town. Its oranges are recognised as second only to California's in export quality. The town is the best run along the coast but mostly 'golden years' tourists come here for the peace and quiet. The marina is a beacon for professional yachters and crews. The two nearby sites that are worth a trip are **Limyra** and **Arykanda**. Leaving Finike on the north highway, the N-635, after 7km (4 miles) turn right to Limyra upon reaching Turunçova. The ruins comprise the 4th-century BC Tomb of Pericles, a theatre, and the freestanding Catabara sarcophagus with reliefs of a funeral banquet. The lofty necropolis (it is a 40-minute climb) affords astounding vistas. On the ground the cenotaph to Gaius Caesar tops off the Roman remains.

Return to the main road and continue towards Elmalı for 21km (13 miles), to the mountain hamlet of Arif and the stunningly beautiful settlement of Arykanda (open access; charge), a Lycian city dating from the 2nd century BC. It is remote and the

Travelling in a traditional way in Demre

lower area centres on a bathhouse. Sheds cover the mosaic floors of a large Byzantine basilica, while further up the hill are the odeon, theatre, stadium and agora of the Roman city. There is a theatre in excellent condition.

The Olympic Coast

The view from the mountain road above **Olympos** ❹ 🅼 is enthralling enough to make you believe all the legends of the Greek divinities. The ancient city of Olympos (open access) is down a steep roller-coaster road of narrow hairpin bends. Once there, the visitor can see the remains of a monumental gateway, an acropolis, a river port, a small theatre and two sets of baths. The area is inhabited mostly by water birds that nest in the reeds.

An extended pebble beach leads to a seasonal ford over the river and across to **Çıralı**, a favourite haunt of wilderness campers, backpackers, tree dwellers and those who revel in the magnificent natural setting. Çıralı can also be reached from the 'high' road via a minibus service that departs from the roadside pit stop, Olympos Dinlenme Tesisleri. Everyone marvels at the eternal flame, **Yanartaş**, and its link to the Greek myth of the fire-breathing Chimera. Olympos is the centre for many climbing and adventure tours, and there is superb scuba diving.

The surrounding mountains all belong to the **Bey Mountains Olympos National Park** (Beydağları Olympos Milli Parkı). **Phaselis** (daily, May–Oct 7.30am–7pm, Nov–Apr 8am–5.30pm; charge) is the most idyllic of the ancient Lycian cities with its tranquil beach and pine trees. It lies 16km (9 miles) south of Kemer, set on a wooded peninsula between three curved bays, once serving as harbours for this busy (and swashbuckling) trading port. Remains are scattered haphazardly but include an agora, aqueduct, Roman baths and a fine paved street.

Just before Antalya, you come to the city of **Kemer** 🅼, which now engulfs the satellite towns of Tekirova, Çamyuva and Göynük. This is the undisputed holiday-club and package-tour belt. Despite the sheer size and grandeur of everything here, hotels enjoy high occupancy rates year-round.

Between Tekirova and Çamyuva, a well-signposted road leads to the

Mediterranean Region

Olympos beach is pebbly but still good for swimming (see p.153)

base station for the aerial-cable car ride to the 2,365m (7,760ft) summit of **Mt Tahta** (www.tahtali.com/english; daily, summer 9am–7pm, winter 10am–5pm; charge) **M**. The journey takes 10 minutes and the views are incredible.

Pamphylia

Less proud and more pragmatic than Lycia, Pamphylia (meaning 'all tribes') was a Roman Province in Asia Minor. It was happy to cooperate with Alexander and share the largesse of victory. In more recent times, Antalya has had a head start on tourism as the first Mediterranean coastal city to build an international airport. The city has been one of the fastest-growing in Turkey and is blanketed with houses and hotels. But with the azure-blue bay spreading out below the mountain peaks, the view remains mesmerising. Large shopping complexes on the periphery have hollowed out the city centre and irreversibly altered the centre of gravity.

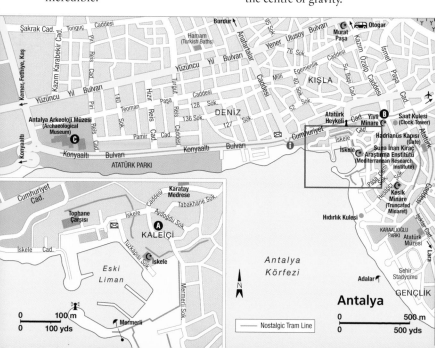

Antalya

Antalya is the jewel of Turkey's Mediterranean coast, naturally endowed with stunning beauty and a temperate climate for almost the entire year. The usual succession of Romans, Byzantines, Arabs, Seljuks and then Ottomans have left their various signatures on the town and these are the main antique attractions. Your first port of call, or if time is short, is the Archaeological Museum, one of Turkey's most beautifully laid-out showcases.

The heart of the city and inner citadel is known as **Kaleiçi** . The quayside and the citadel walls above are lined with outdoor seafood restaurants and cafés, but boats bob in the harbour and fishermen still mend their nets. The area is the oldest part of Antalya and has narrow, winding streets that ooze with atmosphere. Restoration has been spectacular in some blocks but improbable in others. But the atmosphere is musty and historic. You will never know quite where you are; so don't be afraid of getting lost.

Above the harbour, marking the boundary of the 'old' town and up a steep incline, is the **Clock Tower** (Saat Kulesi) 'built in 1244' and, just opposite, the artistic **Seljuk Fluted Minaret** (Yivli Minare) pierces the sky. Antalya's most photographed building, it provides a magnificent foreground for the panorama across

Mediterranean Region

Antalya City Transport

 Airport: Bayındır International Airport (AYT; tel: 0242-444 7423; www.aytport.com) is 12km (7 miles) from the city centre. A shuttle-bus service operated by Havaş (tel: 0242-444 0487; www.havas.net/otobus-ve-otopark/antalya) travels from 2am–10pm hourly to and from the airport and Akdeniz University and to a stop near the main Post Office. The journey takes about 40mins and costs 10TL.

Taxis: Taxis are always waiting outside the airport terminals. They take 20mins to the city centre and cost about 50TL, double this between midnight and 6am. In the city, taxis are ubiquitous and can be hailed in the street at any hour.

City-centre Buses: Antalya has one private bus firm that services all the major urban and many suburban districts. They accept only cash on entry. Many minibuses (dolmuş) also dart around the city and environs.

 Intercity Buses: The central bus terminal (otogar) is to the north of Antalya but bus companies operate free shuttle services to here from their central offices. The city bus service that says 'terminal' goes to the otogar from any city bus Stop. Reliable intercity companies are: Kâmil Koç; tel: 0242-444 0562; www.kamilkoc.com.tr; or Antalya Seyahat; tel: 0242-331 4374; www.antalyaseyahat.com.tr. Reservations are essential and tickets can be booked online.

Tram/LRS: A touristic tram runs about every half hour for 8km (5 miles) through the city centre, ending at the Archaeological Museum. You pay on entry. Antalya has completed the first stage of an 11km (7-mile) overground light rail system, which will eventually cover the city.

★ VILLAGE WEDDINGS

It is not unusual for tourists to be asked to a traditional three-day wedding ceremony. While Turkish city weddings tend to follow Western trends with the wedding held over one day, traditional village weddings will begin on a Friday and stretch until late on Sunday.

Wedding Preparations

In previous years, many marriages were arranged and the bride and groom would barely have laid eyes on each other previously. This happens less now; a girl who wants to continue her education or disapproves of a suitor will register her wishes.

The bride and groom have their respective hen and stag nights on the Friday of the wedding. The stag night is usually boozy and has a jolly last-days-of-freedom ambience. For women, this is the Henna night and girls colour their hands and arms with the ritual paste.

If you attend enough weddings, hands and nails will be constantly orange-tinged. There will be music and some-times dancing, while married women will proffer advice to the bride.

The Wedding Day

Except in the most pious families, alcohol will be served at the wedding ceremony on Saturday. The bride spends the morning having her hair coiffed, make-up and manicure completed and an intimate waxing. As with Western weddings, the bride wears white and has bridesmaids, while the groom has a best

Sending the bride off in style

man. At the ceremony, the bride and groom sit at the head of the table while guests sit in rows or mill around to watch the couple repeat their vows. Each says 'kabul ediyorum', or 'I do,' and signs the official marriage register. This is a civil ceremony but a religious ceremony may (or not) have already been performed. These are not recognised legally except in isolated clannish enclaves.

Turkish Wedding Traditions

A quaint tradition after the signing ceremony is for the couple to trounce each other in a footsy game. The winner is deemed to be the head of the family! Gifts are traditionally given in the form of cash pinned to the bride's dress or gold jewellery. A master of ceremonies broadcasts the gift register, such as: 'Ali Bayrak, 200 Lira.' Guests may try to out-donate each other if the bride or groom are from a prominent, influential family. As a visitor, you will be expected to up the ante. However, contemporary brides often prefer dishwashers and plasma-screen TVs. Then there will be dancing and revelling, usually to the sounds of synthesised organ music.

Saturday is the wedding night when the marriage is consummated. Families these days are more discreet about hanging around for 'evidence' of virginal honour than in days gone by.

Sunday celebrates the bride's leaving her family home and being taken to her husband's residence, usually via a jovial, honking motorcade. There will be more eating and socialising. Modern couples increasingly choose not to share a parent's house.

Expect to dance at a village wedding

Village Weddings

A newly married couple with traditional gifts of money pinned to them

Wandering the old streets in Antalya's Kaleiçi district

and horses charging through; you can still see the wheel ruts.

At the end of Atatürk Caddesi, **Karaalioğlu Park** is a peaceful and shady park overlooking the sea. It is ideal for enjoying a refreshing breather or people-watching. Near the park, the truncated minaret, or **Kesik Minare**, is all that remains of a 13th-century mosque struck by lightning in 1851.

The **Antalya Archaeological Museum** G (Arkeoloji Müzesi; tel: 0242-238 5688; Tue–Sun 9am–6.30pm; charge) on Kenan Evren Bulvarı is one of Turkey's premier museums. Originally created as a depot to prevent Italian occupiers from looting regional treasures, it was later revamped with a global approach. There are 13 superb exhibits, natural history, a statuary hall, a sarcophagus hall with a poignant statue of Stephanos and a purpose-designed children's wing, to name a few of the museum's attractions. The silver collection is particularly dazzling.

A new wing opened in 2008 in the shape of a Lycian tomb, displaying valuable finds previously in storage.

Along the whole western access stretches the grainy beach at **Konyaaltı**. Many hotels have sprung up just behind the seafront, joined by dense residential developments. The boardwalk is interspersed with cafés, bistros and bars and is a focal point for bathers, day trippers and, in the cool dawn, joggers. City planners struck gold along this stylish promenade.

At the eastern end of the boardwalk, Antalya has its own **Minicity** (Arapsu Mahallesi, Konyaaltı;

the bay to the mountains, especially at sunset. It's also the symbol of Antalya and its oldest Seljuk monument, dating from the reign of Sultan Alâeddin Keykubat I (1219–38). Exquisite turquoise-and-blue tiles are set into the 8-metre (26ft)-high minaret, while the pool in front is of marble.

A few blocks away on Atatürk Caddesi, it is hard to miss **Hadrian's Gate**, a symetrically-triple-arched monumental gateway honouring the well-travelled emperor's visit in AD130. Try to imagine the chariots

tel: 0242-229 4545; daily, May–Oct 9am–11pm, Nov–Apr 9am–7pm; charge ), with Lilliputian schemes from all over the world. It is beautifully arranged with a Mediterranean theme. If you can't see all of Turkey's antiquities in flawless condition, they are a *fait accompli* here.

Every October, Antalya stages the **Antalya Golden Orange Film Festival**. Once frivolous entertainment, it is now prestigious and glitzy and a grand time to be in the city. The public can attend any of the films.

The suburb of **Lara** is 6km (3 miles) east of the city with many grandiose hotels, great restaurants and views over the cliffs. There are excellent sandy beaches here. Another attraction is the **Lower Düden Falls** that tumble 20m (65ft) over the cliffs. These are more dramatic if seen by boat from sea level.

Statue treasures at the Antalya
Archaeological Museum

At the opposite end of town, on the western fringes 12km (7 miles) away, **Büyük Çaltıcak** and **Küçük Çaltıcak** are perfect for a relaxing beach day. Try to stake your patch on the beach before the many Turkish families descend.

North of Antalya

A picturesque waterfall, **Düden Şelâlesi,** is found north of Antalya, and has carved out a twisted gorge from the karst rocks. There is a picnic area and several simple fresh trout restaurants. The same topography has formed two notable cave systems in the area, the **Karain Caves** (Karain Mağarası; daily 8.30am–5pm; charge) and the **Kocain Caves** (Kocain Mağarası), both in the vicinity of Burdur.

The most acclaimed inland site is **Termessos** (daily 8am–7pm; charge). There is a lot of walking, scrambling and few signposts or conveniences, but don't let this put you off. Prepare for at least a whole, even if arduous, afternoon to really appreciate the site. This was a Roman Pisidian city that vexed Alexander the Great in 333BC and is known as the Eagle's Nest thanks to its loftiness. The views over the Gulf of Antalya from the theatre are the reason you come here and could detain visitors indefinitely. Be sure to take a camera and a picnic to gather strength for seeing the agora, gymnasium, an odeon, impressive hydraulic system and baths, and hundreds of hillside tombs.

Perge and Aspendos

Known to the Hittites as far back as 1300BC, **Perge** (22km/14 miles east of

Antalya; daily, summer 9am–7.30pm, until 5.30pm in winter; entrance and parking charge) boasts a magnificent 14,000-seat theatre, stadium, Roman baths and a colonnaded street, all from the Pax Romana period. Standing in the agora, it is easy to visualise the power and glory of ancient Rome.

East of Antalya 40km (25 miles) is the jewel of the region, **Aspendos** ❻ (daily, May–Sept 8am–7pm, Oct–Apr 8.30am–5pm; charge), widely regarded as the finest surviving Roman theatre in the world. Built during the reign of Emperor Marcus Aurelius (161–180AD) by architect Zeno, a local whizz kid, it accommodated 15,000 theatre-goers. The elaborate construction is nearly intact. Behind it lie the ruins of the acropolis, agora, nymphaeum, and a wonderful surviving example of a Roman aqueduct with a pressure conduit. The **Aspendos Opera and Ballet Festival** is staged mid-June through July every year but in an adjacent modern arena.

Approaching Aspendos, the Euromedon Bridge over the Köprüçay River is interesting as a 4th-century Roman structure (restored by Seljuks in the 13th century) with a bizarre crick in the construction span.

The coastal resort of **Belek**  just south of Serik off the main highway is a purpose-built tourist region, fashioned around excellent golf courses and convenient to Antalya's Bayındır International Airport. Although busy and touristy, the area has matured graciously and the setting is magic with pine and palm trees, and golf courses bordered by beachfronts.

A short distance beyond Aspendos, a tarmac road cuts off the main coastal highway leading to the beautiful, cool **Köprülü Kanyon**, a much favoured area for white-water rafting, hiking and picturesque sightseeing.

Side

Nowhere else in Turkey combines touristic flair with such a spectacular antique open-air museum like **Side** ❼. Like many of the country's coastal towns endangered by rampant tourism, Side has matured and the once-dire predictions have not materialised; it is still captivating, with good restaurants and seaside appeal, as well as a strong sense of its history.

The access road is littered with Byzantine ruins. Past the entrance gate and

In the Roman baths complex at Perge

Some of the remains of Byzantine structures at Side

Vespasian Monument, the immense Roman theatre (capable of seating 25,000 people) looms into view. Beside it are the **agora**, the remains of a 24-person public lavatory, a Byzantine basilica, episcopal palace, and remnants of the city wall, beyond which one can access the beach. Across the road from the theatre, the former **Roman Baths** are now a good museum (Tue–Sun 9am–noon, 1.30–6.30pm; charge 🏛).

The graceful Temples of Apollo and Athena on the headland are the most romantic place to be when the sun sets.

Leaving Side and heading east towards Alanya, **Manavgat** has a famous waterfall, or *şelâle*. For an exceptional country interlude, take the Konya Highway 695 north and turn off after 70km (43 miles) to **Akseki** (to the right) or **İbradı** (to the left) two beautiful time-capsule villages steeped in tradition and time *(see box, below)*.

Mediterranean Region

The İbradı and Akseki Rural Cousins

Although once on an ancient trading route, the rural outposts of **İbradi** and **Akseki** are not on many agendas today. They are, however, delightful, high-altitude villages that offer a glimpse of life that has been barely brushed by time. Five km (3 miles) east of Manavgat, turn north on the 695 road to Konya. About 25km (16 miles) further along, Akseki is signposted east and İbradi to the west. An all-terrain vehicle lets you follow the dirt track from Akseki to above the tree line to see the harsh life of traditional migrating families. Shepherds wear traditional cloaks, *kepenek*s. The

families make the delicious Akseki ewe's milk cheese, impossible to find elsewhere. Many bulbous plants thrive, the delicate snow drop *(kardelen)* in particular.

Both villages have cobblestone streets and period timber houses with stones and horizontal beams on interior and exterior walls. These were made without mortar to cushion earth tremors. Most houses here date from the 18th century, unlike most remaining Ottoman mansions, which tend to be from the 19th century. Most of these houses are now under a protection order and are being faithfully restored.

Alanya

As you approach **Alanya** ❽, west of the city (20km/12 miles) is a glorious sweep of sand at İncekum (fine sand) Beach ⛟. There is a lot of concrete-on-sea here, but the water is perfect and the sand is brilliant.

Alanya itself lies 121km (75 miles) from Antalya's airport. A new airport at Gazipaşa, 40km (25 miles) east, is expected to benefit this part of the Turkish riviera hugely; opened in 2010 to domestic flights, it is anticipated that international air traffic will be accommodated from summer 2011.

As well as being known for its entrenched European population and lively nightlife, Alanya's city walls, which snake for over 7km (4 miles), and the haughty **Citadel** represent the finest, most extensive examples of Seljuk architecture in Turkey. The

---

Banana Republic

The region around Alanya, in particular, Gazipaşa, is Turkey's premier banana-growing region. Bananas first came to Turkey from Colombia and they flourished in the sea air. The banana terraces staircasing down to the seashore are a remarkable sight. Production is geared to just one crop per year, in February. Banana production worldwide cultivates varieties for ease of transport and shelf life, but the priority in Turkey is a sweet, delicate flavour, making local bananas highly valued. Ask for 'yerli muz' if you want locally grown bananas. The price is similar to imported ones due to severe water shortages caused by the declining water table in much of the fertile Aegean coastal plain.

---

climb to the citadel is a steep 5km (3 miles), so go by taxi. Overseeing the city-centre harbour is the Red Tower, **Kızıl Küle**, built by Sultan Alâeddin Keykubat I in 1226. It protected the strategic docklands, or *tersane*, and the impressive drydocks are still brimming with the buccaneering spirit.

The worthwhile **Alanya Museum** (Alanya Müzesi; Hilmi Balcı Caddesi, Damlataş; tel: 0242-513 1228; Tue–Sun 9am–noon, 1.30–6.30pm; charge) has some decent archaeological and ethnographic displays.

West of the fortress at sea level, next to the **tourist office** (Damlataş Caddesi; tel: 0242-513 1240), is the Weeping Cave, or **Damlataş Mağarası** (daily 10am–7pm; charge), an exquisite grotto with curtains of stalactites and stalagmites that are 15,000–20,000 years old.

Cilicia

Cilicia covers Turkey's most rugged and wrinkled coastline, windswept, battle-scarred and full of Hellenistic, Byzantine and Seljuk remains dotted along the circumflexed coastal highway in what is modern-day Çukurova.

Gazipaşa

Moving across the flat farmland east of Alanya it is easy to bypass **Gazipaşa**. A stop here is rewarding, especially to see the marvellous panorama over the terraced banana plantations. The coastal plain sloping off the Taurus Mountains is fertile and most produce is grown organically. Hardy folk can climb up to the 7th-century **Selinus Castle**, ancient Trajanpolis (open access). If too arduous, a magnificent **aqueduct** bisects

Anamur Castle has been well used as a strategic fortification and, more recently, a film set

Mediterranean Region

the road leading to the seaside, 2km (1 mile) out of town from the mermaid statue. A new marina is located here and there is a blissful beach and boardwalk .

Returning to the main D-400 highway, turn east and 6km (4 miles) ahead on the left is **Hasdere**, an intact Ottoman village with 300-year-old houses. Those who favour wilder shores of independence without the hordes can embark on a marvellous exploratory tour of the region. A car is essential for exploring most places here and walking shoes will also come in handy. **Gazipaşa town hall** (Cumhuriyet Meydanı; tel: 0242-572 1013) has an excellent booklet in English detailing the local sites.

Anemurium and Anamur

Beyond Gazipaşa, tourist numbers dwindle further and the scenery gets wilder around every bend in the road. **Anamur**, 130km (80 miles) east of Alanya and several kilometres inland, is best known for its seaside suburb of **İskele**, 5km (3 miles) south, with a white-sand beach and a small **museum** (İskele Caddesi; tel: 0324-814 1677; Tue–Sun 8am–5pm; charge).

About 5km (3 miles) west are the solemn ruins of ancient **Anemurium** (daily 8am–8pm; charge), a windy cape at the southernmost tip of Asia Minor. The setting and the ruins are intensely atmospheric and butt onto a swimming beach and picnic area.

Two km (1 mile) east of Anamur on the N-400 is **Anamur Castle** (Mamure Kalesi; daily 9am–5.30pm; charge), built over a Byzantine fortress. Crusaders found it strategic; Ottomans used it up until the 20th century and it still stars as a romantic film set.

Silifke and Göksu Delta

The 153km (95 miles) from Anamur to **Silifke**  is the most challenging roller-coaster road to be found in the country. Concentration is required when outstanding scenery threatens to distract. From the little town of **Taşucu**, car ferries regularly make the two-hour journey to and from the Turkish Republic of Northern Cyprus. Using Silifke as a base, one can take in the vast Byzantine **Silifke Castle** (Silifke Kalesi; daily 8.30am–5pm; charge) that lies 4km (2 miles) from the centre. There is a stunning view of the 1st-century AD bridge over the lethargic Göksu River.

The local **tourist office** (Gazi Mahallesi, Veli Gürten Bozbey Caddesi 6; tel: 0324-714 1151) is helpful, and on the main road there is a pleasant **Archaeological Museum** (Arkeoloji Müzesi; Tue–Sun 8am–noon, 1.30–5pm; charge) with a remarkable hoard of Seleucian coins.

South of Silifke is the **Göksu Delta**, a sanctuary for a superb range of water birds amongst the marshes and reeds. The beaches are home to gulls and turtles. Migrating predatory birds feed here en route to Africa.

Twenty-eight km (17 miles) north of Silifke lies **Uzuncaburç** (daily 9am–6pm; charge) and **Olba Diocaesarea** (charge), lonely and ancient outposts of Roman ruins. Uzuncaburç has 30 peristyle Corinthian columns once part of the Temple of Zeus dating from 300BC. There is also a temple to the goddess Tyche.

Continuing on the coastal road about 30km (19 miles) east of Silifke,

The dramatic panorama of the Göksu Delta.

Religious souvenirs mark the St Paul connection at Tarsus

1579. The **Tarsus Museum** (Kubat Paşa Medrese, Tabakhane Mahallesi, 155 Sokak 1; Tue–Sun 9am–5pm) is passable. The city once had an American missionary school (Cengiz Topal Caddesi), dating from 1888, but is today absent-minded about its former Christian inhabitants.

Adana, which is home to 2.8 million people, is a methodical mercantile centre that prospered from the fertile Çukurova plains, especially cotton and other agricultural staples. The American NATO base at nearby İncirlik still hosts missions to Iraq. There is a Roman stone bridge spanning the Seyhan River; a 16th-century mosque contrasts with the 21st-century **Sabancı Mosque**, but the city concerns itself with industry, not tourism. Save your time for the far more intriguing Antakya.

The Hatay

A narrow finger of land pointing south to the Arab lands, the Hatay rings with oriental sights, sounds and smells. It has retained its multicultural ambience more than any other Turkish region.

Karatepe and İskenderun

Between Adana and Antakya, the site most worthy of a diversion is **Karatepe ⓫** (May–Sept 8.30am–5.30pm, Oct–Apr 9am–3.30pm, guided tours only; charge). It is 70km (44 miles) east of Adana, north of Osmaniye, and lies in **Karatepe-Arslantaş National Park**. It was the most important Neo-

limestone karst formations have created cave systems and sinkholes at the **Cennet ve Cehennem** or Corycuan Caves, known as 'the Caves of Heaven and Hell' (daily, sunrise–sunset; charge). Five km (3 miles) east of **Narlıkuyu** are two castles, Korykos and its offshore twin, **Maiden's Castle** (Kız Kalesi), where the sleeping beauty legend persists.

Tarsus and Adana

Tarsus ⓾ is often overlooked but is one of the oldest continuously inhabited cities in the world and was also the birthplace of St Paul. There is an 11th-century church and a well named after the saint, an interesting 'Forty Spoons' covered bazaar and a handsome **Friday Mosque** (Ulu Camii; open access except during prayer times) dating from

The Külliye

At Yakacık, Payas' 1574 Sokullu Mehmet Paşa complex is one of the most prominent examples of an Ottoman community centre, or *külliye*. These had an important social welfare function and were run as charitable foundations. Although its outward appearance is that of a mosque, it incorporated public baths, a bazaar, soup kitchens *(imaret)*, a hostelry, and a theological college *(medrese)*, and usually would have a hospital and public fountains *(çeşme)*. A *külliye* was a vital social catalyst that encouraged a sharing of life and facilities. It stimulated urbanisation in Ottoman times, becoming the focal point of many cities.

One of the outstanding mosaics at the Antakya Archaeological Museum

Hittite centre after the 12th-century BC collapse of the Hittite Empire. Orthostat reliefs are at once divine, whimsical, pastoral and warlike, expressing an incredible degree of cultural scope. The hilltop site is perfect for a picnic overlooking the lake.

İskenderun lies at the easternmost end of the Mediterranean and has a faded finality about it. Twenty-two km (14 miles) north is **Yakacık**, historic **Payas**, and the Sokullu Mehmet Paşa mosque and *caravanserai* complex (daily 9am–noon, 1–5.30pm; charge), worth spending some time at. Sokullu Mehmet was a cultured and revered consultant to imperial Ottoman sultans and his name endows numerous bridges, mosques and *caravanserai* in Ottoman lands. His last ancestral blood relative, Ljubo Kiridzic, died in March 2010.

Antakya

Antakya 12 is a city that will charm and entertain. The material remains of Antakya's (on the site of ancient Antioch) remarkable past have left the city with a potent cosmopolitain atmosphere embedded in and around the narrow alleys, clustered dwellings and the boisterous **bazaar** (Mon–Sat 9am–9/10pm). The delicacy to sample while here is a deliriously rich pastry baked with cheese, called *künefe*. In the centre of the bazaar on Kurtuluş Caddesi is the **Habib-i Neccar Mosque** (Habib-i Neccar Camii), a former Byzantine church with a minaret added in the 17th century.

Antakya is divided neatly in two by the Orontes River; to the left are the wide boulevards and Art Deco style of the French colonial era, 1918–38. To the right is the narrow, noisy Arabic old town.

The **Archaeological Museum** (Arkeoloji Müzesi; Gündüz Caddesi 1; Tue–Sun 8.30am–noon, 1.30–5pm; charge), on the roundabout beside the main bridge, houses a superlative collection of mosaics that once graced upmarket Roman mansions and villas in Harbiye. This is one of the finest mosaic displays in the world and guaranteed to delight.

Near the 3rd-century **Rana Bridge** that spans the River Orontes is the **Friday Mosque** (Ulucamii).

The tiny cave church of **St Peter** (Tue–Sun 8am–noon, 1.30–5.30pm; charge), 2km (1 mile) off Kurtuluş Caddesi, northeast of the city centre, is generally regarded as the first Christian church. It was here that the saints gave their new religion a name, Christianity.

Twenty-five km (16 miles) south-west of Antakya is **Samandağ** and the attraction here is the **St Simeon's Monastery** (Aya Simeon Manastırı; open access), associated with pious ascetics who perched indefinitely on pillars. There is also an interesting subterranean conduit, **Titus' Tunnel** (open access, summer only; charge), a feat of Roman engineering.

Closer to Antakya (8km/5 miles south) is Daphne, now called **Harbiye**. It has a romantic history and was reputedly the wedding place of Antony and Cleopatra. Be sure to take home some of the wonderful pure laurel (*defne*) soap made today and for which the region is famous.

A relatively new airport 22km (14 miles) to the northeast of Antakya, **Hatay Airport** (HTY), has expanded tourist potential in the region.

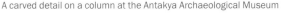

A carved detail on a column at the Antakya Archaeological Museum

ACCOMMODATION

There are hotels, apart-hotels and pensions in every budget category in the Mediterranean region. These are more concentrated and offer a comprehensive range in the western, Lycia and Pamphylia areas but as occidental Turkey slips into oriental, choice diminishes. But so do the all-inclusive package hotels with pegged meals. In Antalya, look in the Old Town, Kaleiçi, for sophisticated boutique hotels close to the harbour. Alanya has its own concrete coastal strip but remains an economical and comfortable venue. By the time you reach the Hatay, it is easy to feel yourself an adventurer and pathfinder; hotel options will reflect this.

Lycia

Aqua Princess Hotel
Hükümet Cad. 71, Kaş
Tel: 0242-836 2026
www.aquaprincess.com/new/antalya_kas_hotel.php
Pretty hotel with simply furnished attractive rooms, their own pool and beach. Stunning views. Open April–Oct only. 🏨 **$$**

Club Patara Prince
P.K. 10, Kaş Yolu, Kalkan, 2km (1 mile) from Kalkan centre
Tel: 0242-844 3920
www.clubpatara.com
Stunning hillside location opposite Kalkan Bay with a hotel and timeshare houses enjoying state-of-the art luxury. Superb swimming on Blue Flag beach. **$$$$**

Diva Residence Hotel
Çukurbağ Peninsula, İbrahim Cingay Sokak,

The stunning views from Hotel Berke Ranch

Kaş
Tel: 0242-836 4255
www.divakas.com
Idyllic locale overlooking the Greek Island of Castellorizo combines smart, professional service with attention to detail. Panoramic sea vistas. **$$$$**

Hotel Berke Ranch
Akcasaz Mevkii, P.K. 186, Çamyuva, Kemer
Tel: 0242-818 0333
www.hotel-berkeranch.com
Serious riders will delight in the facilities, Arabian steeds and the range of trail-riding activities. **$$$**

Hotel Hideaway
Anfitiyatro Sokak 7 (near upper mosque), Kaş
Tel: 0242-836 1887
www.hotelhideaway.com
A city-centre boutique hotel run by a local family. Splendid views from the terrace, small swimming pool and home cooking in the evenings. Highly recommended. **$$**

Kadir's Tree Houses
Olympos, Kemer
Tel: 0242-892 1250
www.kadirstreehouses.com
If you don't fancy sleeping in the trees, there are bungalows, cabins and dorms to choose from, all at budget prices. This is an experience, not just a place to bunk down. Many delicious meals are included in the price. **$$**

Letoonia Hotel and Club
Paçarız Burnu Mevkii, 4km (2 miles) from city centre, Fethiye
Tel: 0252-614 4966
www.letoonia.com/fethiye/eng/konum.htm
A children's paradise at this large, active resort on the pine-fringed outskirts of Fethiye with villas and holiday club units, bars, restaurants and pools. Sports and activities galore. Ⅲ **$$$**

Pirat Otel
Kalkan Marina, Kalkan
Tel: 0242-844 3178
www.hotelpirat.net/english.php
Resort hotel overlooking the harbour with a sun-soaked pool deck and panoramic balconies. Convenient to all sights and activities. Open all year. Ⅲ **$$$$**

Presa Di Finica
Sahil Yolu (4km/2 miles from town centre), Finike
Tel: 0242-855 5500
www.presadifinica.com.tr
Beach-front hotel with 375 beautiful rooms, 52 private suites and sports facilities amid citrus groves. Caters mostly to Corendon Hotel group charters. Ⅲ **$$$$**

Swiss Hotel Göcek Marina and Resort
Cumhuriyet Mahallesi, Göcek, Fethiye
Tel: 0252-645 2760
www.swissotel.com
Superb location for understated style and class. One of Turkey's most glittering marinas is overlooked by the hotel. Great amenities. **$$$$$**

Villa Daffodil
Fevzi Çakmak Caddesi 115, Fethiye
Tel: 0252-614 9595
www.villadaffodil.com
Attractive Ottoman-style *pansiyon* with pool and restaurant. Far enough from the town centre to enjoy peace and quiet. Advance booking is recommended. **$$**

Yalı Pansion
Hastane Caddesi 11, Kaş

The subtly glamorous Swiss Hotel Göcek

Tel: 0242-836 1132
Five basic rooms and shared cooking facilities convenient to centre. Sea views compensate for what it lacks in charm. **$**

Pamphylia
Club Hotel Bedesten
İçkale, Alanya
Tel: 0242-512 123
Restored 13th-century Seljuk *caravanserai* on the castle rock. Great views but mixed reviews; however, this is the only boutique hotel in Alanya. **$$$**

Hotel Grand Kaptan
İskele Caddesi 70, Alanya
Tel: 0242-513 4900
www.kaptanhotels.com
Outwardly dated, the hotel has been going for years and pleasing guests endlessly. A perfect middle-of-the-road choice without pretensions. Harbourside location. **$$**

Onur Pension
Selimiye Mahallesi, Sümbül Sokak 3/A, Side
Tel: 0242-753 2328
www.onur-pansiyon.com
Hospitable, nine-room pension lovingly run by retired police chief. Set amidst lemon groves and offering refreshing simplicity in a congested part of town. **$**

Özmen Pansiyon
Kılıçarslan Mahallesi, Zeytin Çıkmazı 5, Kaleiçi, Antalya
Tel: 0242-241 6505
www.ozmenpension.com

Hugely successful family-run pension with a great roof terrace in the heart of the Old Town. Open all year. Advance booking appreciated. They will fetch you from the airport. **$$**

Park Side Hotel
Cennet Mevkii, Side
Tel: 0242-753 5660
www.hotelparkside.com.tr/en
Rooms, suites and self-catering apartments. Lots of glass, brick and gable roofs, but comfortable, self-contained and handy to everything in Side. Turkish bath and many family activities. 🏫 **$$$**

Şehir Hotel
Elmalı Mahallesi, 2 Sokak 9, Antalya
Tel: 0242-246 1184
www.sehirhotel.com
The most handy budget hotel in Antalya. Everything is clean and neat and new in this small-scale hotel, and but you can walk to all the main sights. Well recommended. **$**

Sheraton Voyager Antalya Hotel and Spa
100 Yıl Bulvarı, Konyaaltı, Antalya
Tel: 0242-249 4949
www.starwoodhotels.com
The views are incredible at this local landmark and there are first-class restaurants on-site. Convenient for the beach and Migros Shopping Centre. 🏫 **$$$$**

Tuvana Hotel
Tuzcular Mahallesi, Karanlık Sokak 18, Antalya
Tel: 0242-244 4054
www.tuvanahotel.com
Secluded and quiet hotel, beautifully restored, once the ancestral dwelling of the owner. Hugely elegant and richly furnished and the scent of jasmine wafts seductively. **$$$$**

Xanadu Resort Hotel
Belek Tourism Centre, Acısu Mevkii P.K. 49, Belek
Tel: 0242-710 0000
www.xanaduresort.com.tr/eng
One of the most romantic venues along the coast. Their many awards for quality and excellence make them a no-compromise choice. **$$$$**

Cilicia
Grand Hotel Hermes
İskele Mevkii, Anamur
Tel: 0324-814 3950
www.grandhotelhermes.com.tr
A large (and bulky) holiday club right on the seaside. Mostly for local Turks, but this kind of place is a cultural experience and the sun and sand are perfect. 🏫 **$$**

Hotel Seyhan
Turhan Cemal Beriker Bulvarı 20/A, Adana
Tel: 0322-455 3030
www.otelseyhan.com.tr/en/index.html
Shiny, mirror-plated tower block in the town centre with urban views, restaurants, bars and fitness facilities. Good venue for business visitors. **$$$**

Selinus Hotel
Gazipaşa Plaj, Yat Limanı, Gazipaşa
Tel: 0242-572 1147
www.selinushotel.com.tr
Not luxurious, but homely charm and convenience to the beach count for more. A budget hotel in an area lacking any other sort of accommodation. **$$**

Hatay
Antik Beyazıt Hotel
Hükümet Caddesi 4, Antakya
Tel: 0326-216 2900
www.antikbeyazitoteli.com
French colonial-era courthouse, now a boutique hotel. It is overdone inside with weighty furniture and out-of-place mosaics but is comfortable and convenient to everything in Antakya. Well recommended. **$$$$**

Savon Hotel
Kurtulus Caddesi 192, Antakya
Tel: 0326-214 6355
www.savonhotel.com.tr
A converted soap factory turned richly-furnished and draped hotel. It is centrally located and rooms are nicely equipped to make your stay comfortable. Great restaurant. **$$$**

RESTAURANTS

The choices in restaurants and other eateries along the Mediterranean are weighted towards the country's western region culinary-wise. Fish is the obvious choice everywhere, but is expensive and often farmed, despite just-off-the-hook vows. Turks are extremely proud of their culinary traditions, but even if you don't see something specific you fancy on the menu, good restaurants all over the region will frequently be willing to prepare whatever you want.

Lycia

Amfora Balık Evi
Kordon Caddesi, Yat Liman Üzeri, Finike
Tel: 0242-855 3888
Very smart linen and silver fish restaurant overlooking the Marina. Friendly service and fresh fish, salads and a large selection of freshly made meze are always on offer. **$$**

Eriş Lokanta
Gürsoy Sokak 13, Kaş
Tel: 0242-836 1057
In an historic Greek house, this is Kaş' most enduring eatery run by the same family since 1956. Seafood, grills and salads are sometimes overshadowed by the fantastic setting. Good value and congenial owner. **$$**

Meğri Lokantası
Eski Cami Gecidi 8–9, within the Bazaar, Fethiye
Tel: 0252-614 4046
This is the liveliest restaurant in Fethiye and the food is fresh, original and unfailingly good quality. Outstanding Turkish fare at affordable prices. **$$**

Oba Ev Yemekleri
Çukurbağlı Caddesi, Kaş
Tel: 0242-836 1687
A mom-and-pop restaurant with a pleasant garden. Limited menu but everything is fresh and nourishing. **$**

Patlıcan Restaurant
Yat Limanı, Kalkan
Tel: 0242-844 3332
www.kalkanaubergine.com
The only restaurant on the coast that has fine dining down to such a meticulous art. The best of Turkish *nouveau* cooking from a brilliant chef. They are open for breakfast, brunch and dinner, with a fireplace in winter. **$$$**

Spinnaker Café and Restaurant
Otel Kemal altı (behind the PTT), Kordon, Fethiye
Tel: 0252-612 0432
This excellent seafood restaurant near the marina with fresh choices has been pleasing customers for years. Open all year. **$$$**

Sultan Garden Restaurant
Yat Liman (harbourfront), Kaş
Tel: 0242-836 3762
www.sultangarden.net

'Shepherd's salad' often accompanies mains

Outstanding alfresco dining and the most romantic setting on the marina. Cooking has an eastern Turkish bias, and the 'Sultan's Sweet' (pancake, cream and apple) is worth multiple return journeys. **$$$**

Pamphylia

Ağaçlı
On coastal highway 35km (22 miles) east of Anamur at turning to Gülnar
Tel: 0324-768 3017
The best stop along this lonely stretch of road. It excels in every way, with welcoming service, freshly cooked dishes and the cleanest facilities east of Antalya. Open 24 hours.  **$**

Amor Restaurant and Bar
Tophane Çay Bahçe altı, Kaleiçi, Yat Limanı, *Antalya*
Tel: 0242-244 3900
Ideal spot to sip cocktails and spoil yourself with a romantic dinner overlooking the picturesque harbour. Elaborate seafood dishes and music until late. **$$$$**

Antalya Balık Evi
Eski Lara Yolu 349, Sokak 1, Lara, Antalya
Tel: 0242-323 1823
www.antalyabalikevi.com.tr
Hard to outpace this slick and stylish seafood restaurant. They serve only fish but it is exquisitely cooked and presented. They also have a reasonable wine list and elegant service. **$$$$**

Cilicia
Yeni Onbaşlar Restaurant, Atatürk Bulvarı, Adana
Tel: 0322-363 2547
This is a long-standing reliable restaurant offering nourishing basic dishes and speedy service. **$$**

Harbour Restaurant and Café Bar
Rıhtım Caddesi, İskele Meydanı (beside the Red Tower), Alanya
Tel: 0242-512 1019
Arguably the best restaurant in Alanya on the harbour serving outstanding seafood and a huge selection of regional dishes.

Booking advised. It is always noisy and busy. Lunch and dinner. **$$$**

Nergiz
Liman Caddesi, Side
Tel: 0242-753 1467
This two-storey restaurant overlooking the harbour attracts mostly tourists, but it has a large terrace and first-rate seafood, stews and colourful salads. Lunch and dinner all year. **$$$**

Orfoz Restaurant
Liman Caddesi 58/B, Side
Tel: 0242-753 1362
Amazingly comprehensive menu in this perfectly located seafront restaurant. They do everything with gusto; the owner is on site and the atmosphere and presentation hit the mark beautifully. Lunch and dinner. **$$$**

Sultan Sofrası
Şahoğlu Sokak, Çolak Apt. 2/C, Güllerpınarı Mevkii, Alanya
Tel: 0242-512 5627
Popular downtown restaurant serving juicy kebaps, sautéed stews, pilavs and much more for slim budgets. **$$**

Yedi (7) Mehmet
Atatürk Kültür Parkı 333, Arapsu, Antalya
Tel: 0242-238 5200
www.7mehmet.com/eng.htm
One of Antalya's most renowned

A spicy take on hummous and olive oil

Antakya's speciality, künefe

restaurants with soup-kitchen beginnings. Everything is slick and sleek and the food flawlessly prepared. Typical Turkish dishes include Antalya's own speciality, a fiery chickpea *meze*, hibeş. **$$$$**

Hatay
Anadolu
Hurriyet Caddesi 30/A, Antakya

Tel: 0326-215 3335
www.anadolurestaurant-haysim.com
Decor of rustic palms and pseudo nature seems tacky, but the eastern Anatolian cuisine here is sensational, albeit a steep and spicy learning curve for foreigners less familiar with this side of Turkey's food; embrace the eastern experience and give it a try. **$$**

Antakya Evi Restoran
Silâhlı Kuvvetler Caddesi 3, Antakya
Tel: 0326-214 1350
An historic Antakya mansion with several private dining rooms. Protocol and etiquette are traditional and heartfelt and foods are spicy and piquant and nicely served. Open for lunch and dinner all year round. **$$**

Samlioğlu Künefe Salonu
Next to Ulu Camii, Antakya
Serving only *künefe*, the local delicacy served freshly baked and piping hot. **$**

NIGHTLIFE

Many visitors come to the Mediterranean as much for the nightlife as for the sun and sea. Nightlife mostly consists of good jump-up fun, bars that convert to discos, great DJ'd music and sometimes live singers and entertainers. Clubs, bars and discos are concentrated in cities like Antalya and Alanya, but smaller towns that cater to tourists, Kaş or Side for example, will also lay on thunderous nightlife, although most areas have a no-noise policy after 3am. If you are staying at one of the mega hotels, nightlife and entertainment will be rolled into one and inclusive in the price. Nightlife is considerably more subdued east of Alanya.

Agora Café Bar
Turgut Reis Caddesi 7, Side
Tel: 0242-753 1040
An enduring and successful café by day that shifts up a gear into the disco and live music scene until late.

Auditorium Open Air Disco
Dimçay Mevkii, Alanya
Noisy, lively open-air disco. Summer only.

Club Bahane
Gençlik Mahallesi, Fevzi Çakmak Cad. No.

30, Antalya
Tel: 0242-244 4475
Popular with young and old, the decibels are pumped out and many guest artists perform live.

Janus Restaurant and Café-Bar
Rıhtım Girişi (harbourfront), Alanya
Tel: 0242-513 2694
An institution in Alanya and still belting out the music and blues until late. They also have a good restaurant.

ENTERTAINMENT

Much entertainment is found in-house at the large, all-inclusive hotels along the coast. Many will have belly-dancing and *1001 Nights* evenings. Antalya and Alanya have plenty of cinemas but these generally show Turkish films or foreign ones that have been dubbed without English subtitles. East of Alanya, spontaneous entertainment is not readily found. However, if you are asked to a village wedding, this is a splendid experience that combines culture and socialising *(see p.156)*.

Antalya Golden Orange Film Festival
Sakıp Sabancı Bulvarı, Atatürk Kltür Parkı
İçi, Antalya
Tel: 0242-238 5444

www.altinportakal.org.tr
This annual festival is open to the public and is increasingly prestigious, garnering more silver-screen celebrities every year.

SPORTS, ACTIVITIES AND TOURS

The Mediterranean coast abounds in water, sky and altitude sports and activities for all the family. Every locale has a speciality inviting you to engage and participate. The Lycian Way hiking route has also alerted outdoors types to the region's more diverse touristic activities *(see p.31)*. All organised tours, whether on a weekly, customised or daily excursion basis, will be arranged by local adventure specialists. Most package a whole range of activities like walking, hiking, canyoning, diving and paragliding. Tailor-made tours can also be arranged to suit individual preferences.

Active Divers
İskele Caddesi, Tophane Sokak 2/2, Alanya
Tel: 0242-513 8811
Diving adventures and day-trip excursions.

Aquapark Water Planet
Okurclar Mevkii, 30km (19 miles) from
Alanya centre,
Tel: 0242-527 5165
www.waterplanet.com.tr/eng/eng.html
Wet and wild thrills and spills for all the family. Shuttle service from centre of Alanya.

Arya Yachting and Tours
Fevzi Çakmak Caddesi, Mahmut Çil 3
Apartment D3, Antalya
Tel: 0242-243 4300
www.aryatours.com/en/contact-us.php
Established professional yacht charter company with many repeat customers. Charters and tailor-made tours.

Blue Peace Dive
Serapsu Hotel Diving School, Konaklı, Alanya
Tel: 0252-565 1621
www.bluepeacedive.com/home.htm
CMAS and PADI dive centre with professional staff and fun daily tours.

Bougainville Adventure Diving
İbrahim Serin Caddesi 10, Kaş
Tel: 0242-836 3737
www.bougainville-turkey.com
A pioneering legend in energetic adventures above the clouds or below the waves.

Climber's Garden
Geyikbayırı, 25km (13 miles) north
of Antalya
Tel: 0242-441 3421
www.climbersgarden.com
Rock-climbing adventures make use of the limestone rocks, dramatic crags and various rock faces and pitches of the coastal heights.

FAJOS A.Ş
Cumhuriyet Meydanı 1/G, Kemer,
Antalya
Tel: 0242-814 3047
www.tahtali.com/english
Panoramic téléphérique/aerial cable-car
excursions to the top of Mt Tahta. 🏔

Get Wet Turizm
Eski Lara Yolu, Ayseli Göksoy Apt. 198/1,
Şirinyalı, Antalya
Tel: 0242-324 0855
www.getwet.com.tr
A long-established and experienced tour
agent with a whole range of trekking,
camping, birdwatching and caving programmes; awards recognise their superb
rafting tours. 🏔

Hotel Berke Ranch
Akcasaz Mevkii, P.K. 186, Kuzdere Köyü,
Çamyuva, Kemer
Tel: 0242-818 0333
www.hotel-berkeranch.com
Guests muck in and enjoy the equestrian
and ranch atmosphere and explore coastal
trails on horseback.

The FAJOS A.Ş. cable car

Kaş Eflatun Art Camp
Çukurbağ Village, 12km/7 miles from Kaş
Tel: 0242-839 5429
www.kasartcamp.com/en_index.htm
Nobody combines cultural art courses, scenery, organically grown food, yoga and trekking
better than this glorious residential retreat.

Middle Earth Travel
Haşim İşcan Mahallesi, 1297 Sokak 14,
Antalya
Tel: 0242-243 1148
www.middleearthtravel.com
Treks on the Lycian Way and St Paul Trail.

Listings

FESTIVALS AND EVENTS

An interesting mix of cultural, sporting and religious festivals abounds in the
Mediterranean region, reflecting its diversity of character.

March
International Öger Antalya Marathon
20 March or nearest Sunday; Antalya
www.runtalya.de/uk/index.php
Competitors run 10km (6 miles) in and
around Antalya.

June
Finike Orange Festival
10–17 June; Finike
Street dancing, handicrafts and fun for all.

International Volleyball Beach Tour
June and July; Alanya
Tel: 0242-519 4361

www.alanyacup.com/?lang=24
Organised by the Town Hall, various
heats and league heats lead up to the
championship.

Aspendos Opera and Ballet Festival
June–mid-July
One of the outstanding regional cultural
events, staged in Aspendos Roman theatre.

December
Demre-Kale
3–7 December (approx)
St Nicholas Symposium and coastal
pilgrimage to Patara.

Ankara and Central Anatolia

A vast open plateau, encircled by mountains, the Anatolian heartland has seen some of Turkey's most fascinating history. Attractions include Çatalhöyük: the oldest Neolithic city; Gordium, home of King Midas of the golden touch; Boğazkale, capital of the Hittite Empire; and Ankara, the country's flourishing capital city.

Ankara

Population: 4 million

Local dialling code: 0312

Tourist Office: Gazi Mustafa Kemal Bulvarı 121, Tandoğan; tel: 0312-231 5572. Esenboğa Airport Tourism Information Office; tel: 0312-398 0348

Time Zone: GMT +2

Police: 155 (call centre), Ankara Emniyet Müdürlüğü, İskitler, Ankara; tel: 0312-303 5465; www.ankara.pol.tr. Tourism Police: İskitler, Ankara; tel: 0312-384 0606

Hospital: Bayındır Hospital, Söğükötü; tel: 0312-287 9000, 0444 7774; www.bayindirhastanesi.com

Post Office: Necatıbey Caddesi 106, Bakanlıklar; tel: 0312-229 8922

Central Anatolia's uplands and plateau region is austere compared to the mountainous or forested Turkish regions or the more relaxed coastal plains. The land is characterised by flat, fertile steppes and gentle rolling hills, broken by occasional mountains such as the snowcapped Mount Erciyes, an extinct volcano rising 3,917m (12,926ft) above sea level.

Mankind's earliest settlements are found in central Anatolia and it was here, about 10,000 years ago, that people moved from being hunter-gatherers to adopting primitive farming techniques and domesticating animals. Dating from 7500BC, Çatalhöyük, located south of Konya, has been scientifically excavated using advanced technology. A little way north, Boğazkale was the capital of the Hittite Empire, which flourished from about 1800BC.

The broad plains make ideal agricultural land, and central Anatolia served as a granary to both the Roman and Byzantine empires. Its capture by the Turks in the 11th century deprived the Byzantine Empire of its agricultural wealth and must have contributed to its decline. Although the area is fertile, modern state farming practices have turned Turkey into a net importer, not an exporter, of staple crops like wheat.

The region reveals innovative Hittite settlements, which are presented to marvel at in the Museum of Anatolian Civilisations. The home of the Whirling Dervishes in Konya is one of Turkey's biggest tourist draws.

Travellers also pay homage to Turkey's founding father, Atatürk, buried in the country's capital, Ankara.

Ankara

İstanbul may flirt and flaunt but **Ankara ❶**, the nation's capital, jealously guards its founding principles of Republican reserve and authority. In 1923, Atatürk chose Ankara to be the newly born nation's capital, mainly to emphasise a secular rather than a religious seat of government.

Atatürk's Mausoleum in Ankara

But this is no drab metropolis. Ankara has a lively social scene, great restaurants and award-winning shopping malls, with a great deal of history dating back to the Romans to top it all off. The nation's capital is the place to eat out in style, go to a club, visit art galleries, museums or explore antiques shops.

Anıtkabir

Before seeing anything else, most visitors to Ankara will be shown Mustafa Kemal Atatürk's mausoleum, or **Anıtkabir ⓐ** (daily 9am–12.30pm, 1.30–5.30pm; evening sound-and-light show in summer), in the Maltepe district of the city. Adjoining the monumental structure is the **Anıtkabir Museum** (charge), which safeguards the ruler's memorabilia and personal items.

Classical Sites

The busy intersection at Ulus Meydanı is a good place to begin your sightseeing. It is dominated by the statue of Kemal Atatürk on horseback surveying his capital. Most of the Roman remains of the city are found here on either side of Çankırı Caddesi.

The **Temple of Augustus ⓑ** (Augustus Tapınağı) was built by the Phrygians in 25BC, and the inscriptions on the walls of the Temple are the official records of the Acts of Augustus. It remains a unique source of knowledge about Augustus and his time. Close by is **Julian's Column** (Jülyanüs Sütunu; open access), erected in about AD360, probably commemorating the Roman Emperor's visit.

The foundations of Ankara's Roman Baths

Further along Çankırı Caddesi, on the left, the **Roman Baths** (Hamamları; daily 8.30am–12.30pm, 1.30–5pm; charge) consist mainly of brick foundations, but there are some pillars, tombstones and other remnants of the Roman city strewn about.

Past the Turkish Central Bank building on Atatürk Bulvarı, on your right at the intersection with Talatpaşa Bulvarı and the State Opera House, **Gençlik Parkı** (dawn–dusk;) is a relaxing green space with a lake and amusement park for children. Tea comes to your table in a regal samovar and you serve yourself. All of Ankara convenes here.

Ankara and Central Anatolia

Ankara City Transport

 Airport: Esenboğa Airport (ESB) is 20km (12 miles) northeast of the city centre (tel: 0312-590 4000; www.esenbogaairport.com/esben). An airport shuttle between the airport and city centre is operated by Havaş (tel: 0312-310 3555). Services run both ways every 25 mins between 3am–9.30pm. A bus service departs every 60 mins between the airport and AŞTİ (the main Ankara bus station; tel: 0312-311 0620; www.asti.com.tr) from 2.30am–9pm. The journey takes about 45 mins and costs 10TL.

 Metro/LRS: Ankara has two intersecting rapid transit systems: the Light Metro, known as Ankaray (tel: 0312-224 1170; www.ankaray.com.tr), and the Ankara Metro. Both lines operate from 6am until midnight.

 Buses: Ankara transport is run by EGO (Emniyet Mahallesi, Hippodrom Caddesi 5, A Blok, Yenimahalle; tel: 0312-507 1000; www.ego.gov.tr). Metro, Ankaray and bus tickets are electronically integrated and can be used on all urban transport. You buy the card at kiosks, main bus/Metro hubs or from vendors near bus stops.

 Trains: The central station is called Ankara Garı and is a major junction between the east and west of Turkey.

 Taxis: Taxis are abundant and can be hailed in the street at any hour. They wait outside airport terminals and have a price-sharing arrangement (Ankara Esenboğa Taxi Drivers And Motor Vehicle Carriers Cooperative; tel: 0312-398 0897; www.esenbogataxi.com); it costs about 60–70TL to the city centre, or a flat-fee US$50 for the 20-minute journey.

 Car Hire Companies: Europcar; Domestic Arrivals Terminal; tel: 0312-398 0503 and Tunus Caddesi 79/2, Kavaklıdere, Ankara; tel: 0312-426 4606; www.europcar.com.tr. Alamo National Car Rental; Ankara Esenboğa Airport; tel: 0312-398 2166.

The glorious interior of Kocatepe mosque

Kocatepe Mosque

Just off the Kızılay intersection, an impressive site in the city is the **Kocatepe Mosque** C (open access except at prayer times). It endured decades of indecision over designs before being completed in 1987. It can hold 100,000 worshippers. For its neo-classical Ottoman architectural style, it is considered by many to be a pinnacle of Islamic architecture. The fashionable department store, **Beğendik**, is located underneath the mosque complex.

Around the Citadel (Ankara Kalesi)

From Ulus, a taxi up to the **citadel** will save you a long and arduous climb. The lofty castle's strategic importance is self-evident. The walls of **Ankara Kalesi** D (Hısarparkı Caddesi; charge) are spectacular: to the west, a line of triangular towers, rather like the prow of a ship, juts out from the wall. Step through the main gate, to a different world unaltered in 100 years. There is a striking view from the base of the (locked) Ottoman Tower.

Directly opposite the entrance to the castle is the **Çengelhan Rahmi M. Koç Museum** (Sutepe Mahallesi, Depo Sokak 1, Altındağ; tel: 0312-309 6800; www.rmk-museum.org.tr. Tue, Wed, Thur 10am–5pm, Sat–Sun 10am–7pm; charge). A restored 16th-century *caravanserai* was where the Koç family's founding father worked as an apprentice. Amongst the family memorabilia are many nostalgic items, machinery and airplanes. This is one of Turkey's most resourceful and interesting privately funded museums.

Down a slope to the west is the **Museum of Anatolian Civilisations** E (Anadolu Medeniyetleri Müzesi, Karaman Sokak, Necatibey Mahallesi, Ulus; tel: 0312-324 3160; Tue–Sun 8.45am–5.15pm; charge). A museum of huge importance, its displays include Palaeolithic and Neolithic finds from Çatalhöyük, the Assyrian traders of Kültepe and pre-Hittite Alacahöyük. Then progress to the ingeniously artistic Phrygians and, finally, the Roman era. The displays are breathtaking, arranged beautifully in chronological order, and will redefine your interpretation of the word 'civilisation' entirely. Easily the finest museum of its kind.

Copper Alley, Kavaklıdere and Çankaya

The side streets in this part of town are atmospheric and full of artisanal shops. Turn into Salman Sokak, to the right of the **Aslanhane Mosque**, and you are in **Copper Alley**, the city's best-known flea market. More trinkets than treasures are up for grabs but the district is animated and noisy and there is much on offer besides copper. Nearby Konya Sokak has similar second-hand wares.

The main shopping areas are along Tunalı Hilmi Caddesi in Kavaklıdere. **Karum**, an exclusive shopping mall, is found here, near the Hilton Hotel. Just opposite Karum is **Kuğulu Park**, a well-known city meeting point, always teeming with people feeding the swans that were a gift from the Chinese government and after whom the park is named.

Many foreign missions are located along Cinnah Caddesi. At the top of this long avenue at the junction with Çankaya Caddesi is **Atakule**, the highest point in Ankara. The restaurant at the top has a panoramic view, but serious shoppers will prefer the choices in the many snazzy malls offering designer merchandise and European brands constantly opening

Eclectic wares for sale in Copper Alley

up in the rapidly expanding suburbs of Ankara. Many of these, like **Armada** (Eskişehir Yolu 6, A Blok, Kat 1 Söğütözü; tel: 0312-219 1319) and **CEPA**, can be reached along the Eskişehir arterial highway.

West of the City

Following the main road, İstanbul Caddesi, out of the city brings you to Alparsrlan Türkeş Caddesi and the entrance to **Atatürk Forest Farm and Zoo** (Atatürk'ün Orman Çiftliği; www.aoc.gov.tr; tel: 0312-211 0170; daily 8am–5pm;). There are vineyards, a nature park, zoo and picnic areas. The Merkez Restaurant sells honey, wine, real ale and fruit juices made on the premises. An interesting replica of the house where Atatürk was born in 1881 in Thessalonica is part of the displays.

North of Ankara

Kızılcahamam, blessed with gentle hills and dense forests, is a favourite picnic and resort spot, also known for its steamy therapeutic mineral springs. It is 85km (52 miles) due north of Ankara in **Soğuksu National Park** (Soğuksu Milli Parkı; tel: 0312-736 1115; dawn–dusk). This makes a calming day out and offers a breather from the clamour of the city.

Northwest Anatolia

The Ankara plateau gives way to the mountains around Bolu to the north, but the lowlands to the west are stark, flat and unpopulated. But this is the heartland of ancient Phrygia and some interesting sights can be seen as a day trip from Ankara.

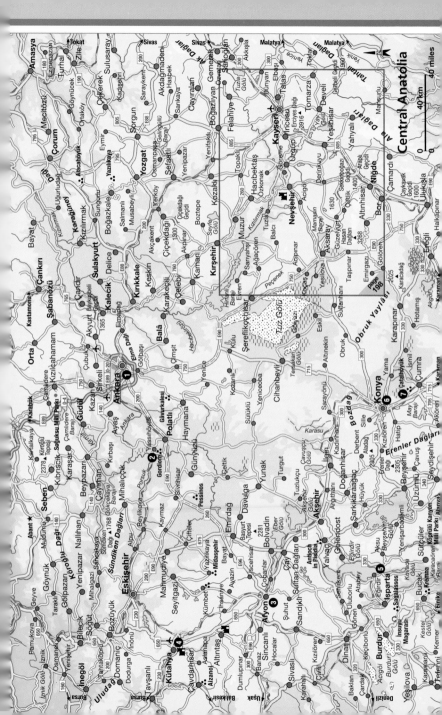

Central Anatolia

0   40 km
0   40 miles

Beypazarı's Ottoman architecture is pretty even on dull days

Three roads head roughly north-west out of Ankara up to the Sea of Marmara and on to İstanbul. The first goes via Eskişehir while the second is a remote ramble through the mountains to Beypazarı. A third follows the main highway north to the Black Sea region.

West from Ankara

The E-90 highway out of Ankara through Polatlı and due west to Eskişehir is the same road that Alexander the Great, the Crusaders and most of the great armies of the Byzantine and Ottoman empires travelled; it is still a major artery.

One hundred km (62 miles) west of Ankara, the remarkable town of **Beypazarı** has roots back to the Hittite era. Now known for the production of carrots and its exquisite Ottoman buildings, this pretty town has cobbled streets, and a day spent here will enrich your historical knowledge and enchant with its architectural heritage.

About an hour southwest out of Ankara, the town of **Polatlı** was the most easterly point reached by the Greek antagonists in Anatolia in 1921. The ruins of **Gordion ❷** and the Tomb of King Midas (daily 8.30am–5.30pm, closed Mon in winter; charge) about 10km (6 miles) northwest, at

Ankara and Central Anatolia

Animals of Ankara

Ankara has three distinct species named after it. The Ankara cat is an ancient breed with white, silky fur and absence of undercoat. It is distinguished by its blue, green or amber eyes; often each eye is a different colour. A meticulous breeding programme protects the prized pedigree.

The Ankara goat is famous for its fleece, used to weave lustrous mohair. Only Turkey, South Africa and the United States produce mohair and, until 1849,

Ankara had a global grip on production. The first Ankara goats to be exported to the US in 1849 were a gift from Sultan Abdül Hamit I in exchange for American advice on cotton production.

The Ankara rabbit is a fluffy cloud of soft, downy wool with a comical appearance. There are four recognised breeds and they are often kept as pets. Only wool from this breed of rabbit can be called Angora wool.

⭐ FLORA

Turkey is well known for its diverse and unusual flora and is a paradise for nature-lovers. Every region has something to offer including some quite unusual ecosystems. More than 9,000 species of plants exist in Turkey, of which 3,000 are native to Anatolia. Investigate them in the country's 40 national parks and forests.

Regional Variation

Heavy rainfall throughout the year, combined with warm summers and mild winters along the eastern Black Sea coast, covers the mountain slopes with beech, oak and maple trees. Between them stretch velvet emerald blankets of tea plantations. Gigantic, ageing sycamore, chestnut and pine forests cover much of northwestern Turkey, turning every autumn into a kaleidoscope of colour. Vivid yellow sunflowers brighten Thrace and Marmara in summer, while cluster pine forests cascade down the mountains to the seashores of the southwest, and fragrant pink and white oleanders grow along the Aegean and Mediterranean. On the steppes of central and eastern Turkey, a wide variety of spiky cacti bloom during the long, dry summers and eventually bear edible fruit, known as Barbarian figs.

Turkey has extensive and valuable wetlands, marshes and reeds that attract birds. Here marsh orchids are found as well as buttercups and delicate water lilies.

Along the Mediterranean coast, the most beautiful Arum lilies grow magnificently in gardens. Note too the elongated carob pod which children suck for its chocolaty flavour.

Uludağ National Park offers a chance to see some of Turkey's wealth of nature

The snowflake is native to Turkey

İstanbul residents seeking respite from the rattle of the city drive to the **Belgrade Forest** (Belgrad Ormanı), 40km (25 miles) north. Within İstanbul there are some superb botanical parks and ponds in the suburbs. Those in Bursa head for **Uludağ National Park**. There are also superb botanical gardens outside both cities, with tulips blooming among the many indigenous flowers.

Natural Crops

Many bulbous plants and flowers, including snowdrops, *Galanthus nivalis* (*kardelen* in Turkish), and the enchanting spring snowflake, *Leucojum vernum*, grow indigenously. Cyclamen are commercially grown and exported. Farmers in Isparta province cultivate roses for their oil (attar of roses), exported to France as an essential ingredient in the perfume industry.

Red Anatolian corn poppies (*gelincik*) grow wild throughout Turkey, but are commercially produced in the Afyon region to be refined into opiates for the pharmaceutical industry.

Oriental tobacco, known for its short stalks, small leaves and aromatic flavour, is grown by thousands of farmers on sun-drenched slopes in western Turkey, Marmara, the Black Sea coast around Samsun and throughout southeastern Turkey. The country is a major producer of oriental tobacco, which requires little irrigation and is sun-dried.

Hazelnuts are cultivated all along the Black Sea coast. Turkey is the world's biggest producer and exporter of hazelnuts, often to be used in the chocolate and baking industries abroad.

Flora

Poppies can be seen growing wild everywhere in the country

Yassıhöyük, are the sights to see. This was the capital of ancient Phrygia in the 8th century BC, and the adjoining museum is more than worthwhile (Tue–Sun 8am–5pm; charge). However, most finds excavated from here are on display elsewhere, such as in Ankara's Museum of Anatolian Civilisations.

A road southeast from Polatlı leads to **Haymana**, famed for its therapeutic hot springs reputedly enjoyed by Romans (daily 7am–midnight; charge).

West of Polatlı, there are two towns of interest. **Sivrihisar** is the birthplace of Nasreddin Hoca, a 13th-century satirical Sufi and witty narrator. The town has an interesting 13th-century **Great Mosque** (Ulu Camii). Fourteen km (9 miles) south are the very scant remains of the remote Phrygian cult site of **Pessinos** (open access).

Nasreddin Hoca

Turkey's most famous folk hero, Nasreddin Hoca, figures in endless jokes throughout the Middle East. His stories, many of which end in a moral twist or clever epigram, are popular among all Turkic peoples. Set in homes, marketplaces, bazaars, streets, courts and mosques, they describe everyday life. His jokes and tales abound with the common sense of the Anatolian people and are subtle without intending to disparage anyone. The real Nasreddin Hoca (1208–85) lived in northwest Anatolia and studied in the religious schools at Sivrihisar and Akşehir, a city 200km (130 miles) southwest of Ankara, at a time when the region was under siege by Mongol invaders. He died in Akşehir and is buried there.

Eskişehir is in the industrial heartland of Anatolia, home of Turkish State Railways (TCDD) and the Turkish Air Force. The white magnesium silicate used in the making of pipes, known as meerschaum, or sea foam, is mined in and around Eskişehir. The excellent **Meerschaum Museum** (Lületaşı Müzesi, İki Eylül Caddesi; daily 10am–5pm; charge) doesn't disappoint.

Southwest Anatolia

Refreshing freshwater lakes, poppies, pottery, migrating birds, whirling dervishes and an historical cast of thousands: there is something for every interest in this region.

Afyon

Afyon ❸, southwest of Ankara, is named after the opium poppy that grows in the region and is refined for the pharmaceutical industry. More palatable is a thick and creamy clotted cream (kaymak), produced in the town and known all over Turkey. If you wander the backstreets, there are quaint residences and characteristic architecture.

Although many civilisations have touched Afyon, the Seljuks left the most potent legacy in the form of the delicately embellished 13th-century **Great Mosque** (Ulu Camii; open access except at prayer times). The **Archaeological Museum** (Kurtuluş Caddesi; Tue–Sun 8am–noon, 1–5.30pm; charge) is surprisingly good, with mainly Roman artefacts.

The overpowering black rock face above Afyon is 225m-(738ft) high and dominates the town. Its strategic

Some of the pottery for which Kütahya is renowned

local workshops. There is an impeccable **Tile Museum** (Gediz Caddesi; Tue–Sun 8am–noon; 1.30–5.30pm; charge) with outstanding 14th-century porcelain items. Like most towns, Kütahya has its Friday Mosque on Gediz Street (*Sokak*) and, adjacent, a small **Archaeology Museum** (Tue–Sun 8.30am–noon, 1.30–5.30pm; charge), but it pales after the tile museum.

The **Kossuth House Museum** (Tue–Sun 8am–noon, 1–6pm; charge) provided refuge for Lajos Kossuth, a Hungarian freedom fighter committed (unsuccessfully) to unyoking his country from Habsburg dominance in 1848. The architecture is classically Ottoman but nothing personal of the Kossuths remains.

importance is not in doubt and the climb up some 700 steps to the **Afyon Citadel** (open access) is for strong legs and robust boots.

North of Afyon the site to allow time for is **Şehitgazi Valley**. The main attraction is the 5th-century rock tomb of King Midas at **Midasşehir** (open access; dawn–dusk).

Kütahya

Kütahya ❹ is the ceramic centre of Turkey. Factories on the outskirts produce commercial dinner plates and tea mugs, but the delicate, prestigious porcelain designs that defined Ottoman artistry are being revived in specialised

Isparta, Eğirdir and the Lake District

Isparta is justifiably famous for rose oil (attar of roses). It takes many kilograms of petals to distil just one gram of the precious liquid used in perfumes. Bulgarian refugees from the Balkans provided the rosewater technology when they came to Isparta in the late 19th century. The town was founded by Greeks from Sparta and remained a Greek town until the mass expatriation of the 1920s. Tourism in the town has been much enhanced from the biblical walking trail of St Paul (www.stpaul trail.com, *see p.31*).

An hour to the east of Isparta are the beautiful lakes known as Turkey's **Lake District**. There are seven significantly large lakes attracting a variety of birds that are migrating or nesting.

The main town is **Eğirdir ❺**, at the southern tip of the lake named after it. The settlement was founded by Hittites and thrived on a vital trade route between Ephesus and Babylon in the 5th century BC. Two tiny islands are joined to the town by a causeway, and one of them, Yeşilada, has attractive pensions and a Greek church that is being restored. The Thursday market is riot of colour selling local produce and handicrafts.

Driving up the eastern side of the lake brings you to **Yalvaç** and its nearby classical site, **Antioch ad Pisidiam** (9am–5pm; charge). Founded around 300BC, it is much visited by Christian pilgrims, as it was where St Paul is said to have made his first sermon to the Gentiles. A basilica dedicated to him still remains, as well as a Roman theatre, baths and an imposing aqueduct. The small **Yalvaç Museum** (Tue–Sun 9am–noon, 1.30–5.30pm; charge) displays relics from the site.

Twenty-five km (15 miles) south from Isparta, travelling through the village of **Ağlasun**, are the spectacular ruins of **Sagalassos** (daylight hours; charge). Few sights in Turkey are so brilliantly excavated, catalogued and restored, by Belgian archaeologists. This is a fascinating place and much can be seen about it at www.sagalassos.be.

Harder to reach, up a steep strategic hill overlooking the Aksu River, little remains of **Kremna**, a Pisidian stronghold (open access; charge) where culture and siege mentality were merged in typical Roman fashion. Kremna is about 10km (6 miles) south of Isparta off the 650 highway.

East of Isparta, the largest freshwater lake in the Lake District is **Beyşehir**, replete with carp and perch. The attraction here is the beautifully proportioned **Eşrefoğlu Mosque** (open access except at prayer times), which has an unusual wooden interior. The tile work is particularly handsome and this style of mosque exemplifies the 14th-century Beylik period.

Konya

Defying its pious, conservative reputation, **Konya** ❻ is a city filled with fun and you will find that alcoholic beverages are alive and well and served here, although not near the famed Mevlâna Museum, Konya's prime attraction. Konya (Roman Iconium) was the capital of the Seljuk Empire between 1071 and 1308, and remains the centre of Sufi teaching and a pilgrimage centre for devout Sunni Muslims. Konya is also recognised for its fine handmade carpets which can be found all over Turkey.

This is the ancestral home of the 'real' Whirling Dervish troupe. They appear here once a year in December to perform but otherwise tour the world. They have recently moved to a fine-looking modern hall to perform their annual whirling *sema* dance that symbolises a mystical union with god. The **Mevlâna Cultural Centre** (Mevlâna Kültür Merkezi) is located 1km (½ mile) east of the **Mevlâna Museum** (Mevlâna Müzesi; Selimiye Caddesi; Mon 10am–5pm, Tue–Sun 9am–5pm; charge) on Selimiye Caddesi. In the Museum itself, the ablutions fountain, or *şadırvan*, is a work of art. The main part of the lodge (*tekke*) contains the sacred tomb of Mevlâna, gloriously embellished.

The famous whirling dervishes perform in their ancestral home of Konya

There is a ceremonial hall which now houses symbolic Mevlânabilia.

Other attractions include the **Alâed-din Mosque** (Alâeddin Camii; daily 9.30am–5pm; entry by donation), named after one of the most creative Seljuk designers, Alaeddin Keykubad I. The mosque stands atop a leafy park in the centre of Konya. The **Karatay Museum** (Hastane Caddesi, Alâed-din; daily 9am–noon, 1–5pm; charge), once an Islamic school (*medrese*) for girls and dating from 1251, displays creative and artistic tiles and ceramics. The often-bypassed **Archaeological Museum** (Arkeoloji Müzesi; Sahip Ata Caddesi; Tue–Sun 9am–noon, 1–5pm; charge) has some fine sarcoph-agi, eye-catching carpets and finds from nearby Çatalhöyük.

Çatalhöyük ❼ (daily 8am–5pm; charge) is 60km (36 miles) south of Konya near the village of Çumra. New technologies and modern science have discredited previous theories about Çatalhöyük's matriarchal society and existence of mother goddesses. The earliest-known textile fragments were discovered here. The community traded in luxury goods and made money from valuable glass-like obsidian. In existence from 7,500BC until 5,300BC, Çatalhöyük is regarded as the best-preserved Neolithic site ever unearthed. There is a museum on site (daily 8am–5pm; charge) with reproduction artefacts. The bona fide pieces are cosseted in the Museum of Anatolian Civilisations in Ankara.

East of Ankara

The journey east of Ankara has less of interest for the average pathfinder than going in other directions from the capital. But several sights are worthy of attention and will appeal to those who like their travel with a twist.

Boğazkale and Yazılıkaya

From Ankara it is a three-hour drive to the vanished Hittite settlement at **Boğazkale** (daily 8am–5pm; charge), located in **Hattuşaş National Park**.

Alacahöyük was a major Hittite site

Ankara and Central Anatolia

The stone sculpted friezes carved into the rock faces at nearby **Yazılıkaya** (entrance included in Boğazkale admission) have tremendous impact as outstanding artistic achievements.

Alacahöyük to Yozgat

Alacahöyük (Sungurlu; Tue–Sun 8am–noon, 1.30–5.30pm; charge) is 30km (19 miles) southeast of Çorum and was another principal Hittite site. Although Alacahöyük is less picturesque than its surrounding Hittite compatriots, the cult mentality is much in evidence. The Sphinx Gate is the most notable sight here and the small **Alacahöyük Museum** (Tue–Sun 8am–noon, 1–5pm; free) has a few pots and burial items on display.

Northeast of Alacahöyük, the city of **Çorum** is 244km (152 miles) east of Ankara. It dates back to before Roman times but mostly escaped the march of history and time. Today it is famous for its dried chickpeas. **Çorum Museum** (Şehir Merkez; Tue–Sun 8.30am–noon, 1–5.30pm; charge) has finds or replicas from Boğazkale.

South of Boğazkale, **Yozgat** was founded by the Çapanoğlu family, powerful regents in the 17th century.

The town is dramatically located and built on two levels. The most striking things to see are the Lion's Gate (Aslanlıkapı) and the King's Gate (Kralkapı). The **Great Temple** (Büyük Mabet) dates from 1400BC and honours a temperamental storm god. In the 13th century the city would have had double fortified walls about 8km- (5 miles-) long. The ruins, as well as the bronze and clay tablets unearthed, provide a real-life impression of Hittite civilisation.

Crazy About Chickpeas

Chickpeas are a staple of Turkish munchdom, and indeed, the country is the world's third-largest producer of them. They have been a food item for as long as mankind has been eating, and remains have been found in ancient Jericho and at Neolithic sites in Turkey. Turks nibble nuts constantly and chickpeas are a favourite. The processed chickpea is called *nohut* and is used in cooking to add texture to stews, sprinkled cold over salads and for making the delicious starter, *hummous*. Dried chickpeas are for snacking; Turks call these *leblebi*. Chickpeas are also sometimes known as garbanzo beans and can be eaten as a sweet. This legume is high in fibre and low in fat, with a host of wholesome, nutritional advantages.

ACCOMMODATION

As the nation's capital, Ankara has many hotels geared to business travellers and visiting diplomats. You can expect all the amenities found in any cosmopolitan capital and a lively nightlife to follow the day's dealings. Ankara also makes the most practical and convenient base for touring the Central Anatolian region.

Accommodation Price Categories

Price categories are per night in high season (May–Oct), for a double room, including taxes.

$ = below 30TL
$$ = 30–50TL
$$$ = 50–100TL
$$$$ = 100–200TL
$$$$$ = Over 200TL

Ankara

Angora House
Kalekapısı Sokak 16, Ankara
Tel: 0312-309 8380
A lovingly restored period house within the walls of Old Ankara near the citadel. Rooms are timber-framed with beamed ceilings, and furnished with lovely antiques and a grand eye for detail. Six rooms. **$$$$**

Ankara Hilton SA Hotel
Tarhan Caddesi 12, Kavaklıdere, Ankara
Tel: 0312-455 0000
www.hilton.co.uk/ankara
Belonging to the Sabancı Group, this is Ankara's signature hotel with 324 rooms and 24 suites. There are well-equipped executive lounges, meeting and conference facilities and the popular Greenhouse Terrace Restaurant. Everything international visitors would want is provided.
$$$$$

Barcelo Ankara Altinel Hotel
Gazi Mustafa Kemal Bulvarı 151, Tandoğan, Ankara
Tel: 0312-231 7760
A really outstanding hotel from the Barcelo Group. The emphasis is on comfort, light, airy rooms and a feeling of not being in a big city. Great gourmet restaurant and the hotel is near all the city attractions and public transport. There are 172 rooms and several classes of suites. This is a great place to stay. Don't expect bargains. **$$$$$**

Gordion Hotel
Tunalı Hilmi Caddesi, Büklüm Sokak 59, Kavaklıdere, Ankara

Tel: 0312-427 8080
www.gordionhotel.com
An intimate boutique hotel with 42 rooms and 3 suites, it is richly furnished inside and rooms are very woody and clubby with touches of marble. But it is highly original, designed by an engineer/diplomat father-and-son team, and the personal Ottoman touch is beautifully incorporated. Moreover, it is supremely comfortable. The rooftop restaurant serves gourmet food with panoramas over the city. **$$$$**

Houston Hotel
Güniz Sokak 26, Kavaklıdere, Ankara
Tel: 0312-466 1680
www.hotelhouston.com.tr/site/index.php?language=en
Comfortable, efficient and friendly hotel in an excellent central location. Fifty rooms with private bathroom, telephone, satellite TV and air conditioning. They also have a restaurant, bar, cafeteria, garden and garage. Suitable for business or pleasure.
🏨 **$$$**

King Güvenlik Hotel
Güvenlik Caddesi 13, Aşağıayrancı, Ankara
Tel: 0312-418 9099
www.kinghotel.com.tr/default.aspx
Just behind the Turkish National Assembly building and off busy Atatürk Bulvarı, the hotel is in an ideal position for sightseeing or business. Rooms are tastefully furnished and everything to make your stay above average is provided. The garden restaurant is divine in summer and staff are determined that you enjoy Turkish hospitality to the utmost. **$$$**

191

Listings

A comfortable room at the Swiss Hotel

Rixos Grand Hotel Ankara
Atatürk Bulvarı 183, Kavaklıdere, Ankara
Tel: 0312-410 5100
www.rixos.com/index.aspx
Located across from the Grand National
Assembly, the Rixos Grand Hotel has some
quirky design features but businesspeople
and tourists rate it highly for its sunny atmosphere and excellent facilities. The owners
are Russian and sometimes the guests are
too. Glitzy evening floor show and a divine
Royal Spa. **$$$$**

Sheraton Hotel and Convention Centre
Noktalı Sokak, Kavaklıdere, Ankara
Tel: 0312-457 6000
www.sheratonankara.com
A luxurious international hotel catering to
business travellers and tourists. The Towers,
run effectively as a separate hotel, offers
even more exclusivity. 414 rooms and
suites. **$$$$$**

Swiss Hotel
Yıldızevler Mahallesi, Jose Marti Caddesi 2,
Çankaya, Ankara
Tel: 0312-409 3000
www.ankaraswissotel.com
Not in the city centre but adjacent to the
upmarket neighbourhoods near the Presidential Palace, this is the best place to
stay in its class in Ankara. Their beautiful
Amrita Spa and Wellness Centre is the
spot to rejuvenate and regenerate. Everything one expects and more from a leading
global hotel. **$$$$**

Northwest Anatolia
Cırcırlar Konağı
İnözü Vadisi Yolu 200 mt, Beypazarı
Tel: 0312-763 3001
www.circirlar.com
Slightly outside of town on the original Silk
Road. Perhaps too rustic for some, this
is authentic country living with a glorious
garden. Great restaurant and home-cooked
traditional dishes. **$$**

Mevların Konağı
Cumhuriyet Mahallesi, Aladdin Sokak,
Beypazarı
Tel: 0312-762 3698
www.mevalarinkonagi.com
This is a beautifully equipped and fur-
nished mansion house converted into a
boutique pension, the best of quite a few in
Beypazarı. In the centre of town, there is an
attractive café downstairs. 🅜 **$$**

Southwest Anatolia
Otel Selçuk
Alâeddin Caddesi, Babalık Sokak 4, Konya
Tel: 0332-353 2525
www.otelselcuk.com.tr/EN/index.htm
This is a comfortable, modern hotel with 82
rooms and suites, centrally located near to
all the sights. Not pretentious but staff are
friendly and eager that you enjoy the hotel
and Konya. Well recommended. **$$**

Presentation and top-quality food are
important in Ankara's restaurants

RESTAURANTS

Restaurants in Ankara are slick and stylish. As much attention is paid to decor and ambience as to preparation and presentation of excellent menus. Being a capital city has refined local tastes and visitors will enjoy superb food in many price categories. Outside Ankara, choice is limited. Konya has some excellent family restaurants but other areas will focus on tried and true local fare. Some may not serve alcohol.

Ankara

Boyacızâde Konağı Kale Restaurant
Berrak Sokak 9, Ankara Kalesi, Ankara
Tel: 0312-310 2525
Turkish cuisine with excellent *mantı*, a delicate ravioli dish served with a spicy tomato sauce topped with yoghurt. Outdoors there is a fountain and splendid city views. **$**

Cafemiz
Arjantin Caddesi 19, Kavaklıdere, Ankara
Tel: 0312-467 7921
Charmingly converted old house with a conservatory café serving French-style crêpes, salads and desserts. **$$**

Kale Washington Restaurant
Doyran Sokak 5/7, Kaleiçi, Ankara
Tel: 0312-311 4344
www.washingtonrestaurant.com.tr
Sophisticated restaurant with excellent Turkish specialities, fixed price and à la carte menus and panoramic views. The dessert menu is excellent, featuring many of Turkey's most traditional sweets, like the creamy caramel-based pudding, *kazandibi*. The restaurant is in a restored Ottoman mansion within the castle. Terrace in summer. Open noon–midnight. **$$$**

Kebap 49
Bulten Sokak 5, Kavaklıdere, Ankara
Tel: 0312-467 4949
Traditional 3-storey kebap house that has been going forever and pleasing customers with their service and specialities. Garden in summer. **$**

Merkez Lokantası
Çiftlik Caddesi, 72/A, Atatürk Orman Çiftliği, Ankara
Tel: 0312-211 0220
The main restaurant at the Atatürk Forest Farm and Zoo complex, 4km (2 miles) from central Ankara, this is a favourite of government bureaucrats in a relaxed outdoor atmosphere. It has excellent grilled meat and vegetable dishes and many products on sale are produced on-site. **$$**

Quente Churrascaria
Filistin Caddesi, Kader Sokak 34/A, Gaziosmanpaşa, Ankara
Tel: 0312-428 3626
www.quente-ankara.com
Ankara's first Brazilian restaurant with the emphasis on beef, beef and more beef, and piquant dishes. It is shiny and elegant with great service and they make the best Mojitos outside of São Paulo. Try the zesty Brazilian national cocktail, the Caipirinha. **$$$**

Zenger Paşa Konağı
Ankara Kalesi Üstü, Doyran Sokak 13, Ulus, Ankara
Tel: 0312-311 7070
www.zengerpasa.com
Perched up on Ankara's citadel in a restored 19th-century Turkish mansion, Zenger Paşa serves traditional Turkish fare, grills, salads, pilav and stews, with a photogenic view of the city. They do a gargantuan village breakfast with all the trimmings. **$$**

Southwest Anatolia

Konya Mevlevi Sofrası

Nazımbey Caddesi, Konya
Tel: 0332-353 3341
This restaurant set in a series of restored houses is very reasonably priced, with a classic Turkish menu and seating at low level. Popular with the local crowd. No alcohol. 🍴 $

Sammaz Usta

Marangozlar Sanayi, Başkışla Caddesi 35, Konya
Tel: 0332-236 2918
Simple but well-cooked kebaps, *pide* baked in the oven, pizzas and salads. Great for a quick lunch or a nourishing snack. 🍴 $

NIGHTLIFE AND ENTERTAINMENT

The Anatolian hinterland is very conservative. Families are home-loving and rarely engage in mixed-gender revelries. Ankara is the place to let your hair down and enjoy dancing 'til dawn. Although politically starchy, Ankara's many universities have young, trendy and restless students that fill up the discos and jazz bars and scout the hippest places to hang out. Ankara has cultural events and a State Opera and Ballet Company. Details of performances and tickets can be seen at www.dobgm.gov.tr. You need to register securely to buy tickets online.

Cabare

Atakule, Çankaya, Ankara
Tel: 0312-440 2374
Elegant club with glorious views, on the second floor of Atakule tower. Live pop music at weekends. Closed on Sundays.

Marilyn Monroe Bar Café and Restaurant

Üsküp Caddesi (Çevre Sokak) 16/2, Çankaya, Ankara
Tel: 0312-466 6630
www.marilynmonroebar.com
A pizza parlour that became so popular with foreigners and young urban party-goers, they gave it a more iconic name on this trendy bar-lined street. Beer and darts go with live music and rock. Open until 4 or 5am on weekends. A great bar-away-from-home for many of Ankara's foreign residents.

North Shield

Guvenlik Caddesi 111, Aşağıayrancı, Ankara
Tel: 0312-466 1266
www.thenorthshield.com
English pub Turkish-style, with British beer, whisky, pub grub and international food. Pleasant and popular. Open daily noon–1am.

Pampero Café

Arjantin Caddesi 24, Gaziosmanpaşa
Tel: 0312-467 8844
A café and restaurant with live Turkish music at the weekends.

Seğmen Bar

Gazi Mustafa Kemal Bulvarı 151, Tandoğan, Ankara
Tel: 0312-231 7760
Features country and western music. This is a good place to meet and socialise with local Turks.

Ankara has a lively student population

TOURS

There are many tour companies based in Ankara, as often Turks prefer not to travel independently but with a tour group. The tour agents below are mostly Turkish but can arrange group tours, day trips or tailor-made tours for foreign visitors to surrounding Anatolian districts. If you travel in groups with Turks, it will be much more economical than tours arranged only for foreign sightseers.

Exploring Ankara's treasures

Alabanda Tourism
Cinnah Caddesi 67, Çankaya, Ankara
Tel: 0312-440 5600
www.alabanda.com.tr
Excursions and outings within Ankara and surrounding regions.

Ay-Fi Tourism
Ali Suavi Sokak 23/54, Maltepe, Ankara
Tel: 0312-232 4820
www.ay-fi.com

Day trips and excursions in the local area and the urban metropolis of Ankara.

Tempotour
Binnaz Sokak 1/4, Kavaklıdere, Ankara
Tel: 0312-428 2096
www.tempotour.com.tr
Weekend excursions, cultural and hiking tours in and around Ankara and other regions of Turkey.

FESTIVALS AND EVENTS

Every town or village has a festival that is significant to its history or that reinvigorates local traditions or personalities. Events are usually cultural, well publicised locally and attract neighbours and visitors alike.

April
Kütahya
April 5
Hungarians revitalise bonds with Turkey at the Kossuth House of the Hungarian Patriot.

June
Beypazarı
Celebrate all aspects of this pristine Ottoman town at the Traditional Historical Houses, Handicrafts and Carrot and Stew Festivals and explore its traditional skills and crafts.

July
Nasreddin Hoca International Festival
Turkey's best-known and loved wit and

philosopher is revered each year in his ancestral village.

September
Eskişehir
Third week in September
Meerschaum Festival highlights the region's mineral wealth and the 'sea foam' that is used to carve elaborately decorated pipes.

December
Konya
10–17 Dec
Whirling Dervishes perform the *sema*, the symbolic whirling dance routine, in their ancestral home.

Cappadocia

Cappadocia is Turkey's most renowned tourist region because of its surreal geological formations and incredibly deep, man-made subterranean sanctuaries. Visitors marvel at the Christian churches that were carved into the soft rock, dating from the 4th century on, and the vivid frescoes within revealing unique evidence of Byzantine art in the post-iconoclastic period.

Kayseri

Population: 1,200,000

Local dialling code: 0352

Tourist Information Office: Cumhuriyet Meydanı, Sivas Caddesi; tel: 0352-222 3903

Time Zone: GMT +2

Police: Kayseri Emniyet Müdürlüğü, Yenimahalle, Erkilet Bulvarı Üzeri; tel: 0352-338 1402; call centre: 155; www.kayseri.pol.tr

Hospitals: Sevgi Hastanesi, Melikgazi Mahallesi, Sevgi Sokak 3; tel: 0352-224 0101; www.kayserisevgihastanesi.com

Post Office: Gavreoğlu Mahallesi, Seyyit Burhanettin Bulvarı; tel: 0352-231 6495

Airports: Erkilet Airport (ASR); tel: 0352-337 5494. There is also Kapadokya Airport (NAV) at Nevşehir; many tourists use this

Buses: Bus Station (Otogar): Osman Kavuncu Bulvarı; tel: 0352-327 4500

Trains: Kayseri Station, Atatürk Bulvarı; tel: 0352-231 1313

Car Hire: Hertz Rent-a-Car; İstasyon Caddesi, Emek Bulvarı 48/C; tel: 0352-222 6829; www.hertz.com.tr

Sitting on a vital tectonic junction, the Cappadocia region was subject to enormous volcanic eruptions from Mt Erciyes and Mt Hasan millions of years ago. The lava blanketed the area and later solidified into a soft rock that eroded easily and is known as tuff. Underneath, younger and harder volcanic rock 'cones' pushed their way to the surface, forming weird mushroom caps balancing precariously on pedestal rocks. Complete erosion results in the conical shape, which today looks like the world's most unworldly phenomenon. The strange formations are called fairy chimneys, or *peri bacaları*. The volcanoes themselves are now extinct but have left lovely moraine lakes and a popular ski centre on the slopes of Mt Erciyes, the backdrop to Kayseri.

From the 4th century AD, Christian hermit communities dug into the soft rock to dig cells. To counter Arab invaders, they built secluded churches and dwellings, sealing themselves below ground in claustrophobic troglodyte cities that could house up to 20,000 people. After the Iconoclast period ended in AD842, allowing freedom of worship with icons, many more rock churches were formed in Cappadocia. There are charming, yet desolate, remains of Christian monasticism found in the Ihlara Valley and at Zelve. At the Göreme Open Air Museum, the churches tinted with poignant frescoes pay inimitable tribute to human creative genius.

Cappadocia lies on prime agricultural land, and vegetables, vines and fruits flourish in the rich soil. Sunflowers nod their heads everywhere. Persians knew the area as Katpatuka, the 'Land of Beautiful Horses'. Today, the spirited and fearless mares used

Hot-air balloons setting off over the peaks of Cappadocia

on the Great Anatolian Ride *(see p.34)* are bred and raised in Avanos. However, the most thrilling way to see the region is from the vantage point of a hot-air balloon.

The Ihlara Valley

The main arterial roads from Ankara and Konya merge at Aksaray, in Roman times known as Archaelais. It is easy to spend the whole day exploring the many churches in the Ihlara Valley. Along with the two *caravanserais* and eerie underground cities, this area sets the scene perfectly for a Cappadocian sojourn.

Around Aksaray

Aksaray ❶ will interest you only for its natural setting underneath Mt Hasan and for its Seljuk buildings, especially the 13th-century **Red Minaret** (*Kızıl Minare*). The mosque itself is built on the region's soft stone and the minaret now inclines obliquely. The 14th-century **Great Mosque** (*Ulu Camii*) has a delicately carved pulpit *(minbar)* (open access except during prayer times).

The terrain in Cappadocia National Park is unlike anywhere else in the world

Caravanserais

Aksaray and Kayseri straddled an ancient trading route; as encouragement for the vital trade in silks, dye stuffs and spices, Seljuk and Ottoman sultans built securely fortified *caravanserais*. These were roadside inns intended to provide shelter and safety for traders, goods and animals from brigands and robbers. Sultanhanı is a good example of an almost intact *caravanserai*. Travellers were welcomed regardless of nationality, religion or class. Soup, bread and a candle were provided, while each horse got a bag of oats. Guests could stay for three days without charge and the innkeeper would know his guest list by the size of the dust cloud kicked up from a distant camel train. *Caravanserais* on major routes were approximately 20km (12 miles) apart, the distance a laden camel could travel in a day.

Thirty km (18 miles) west of Aksaray is an extensive endorheic lake, Salt Lake, or **Tuz Gölü**, filling a tectonic depression and fed by two streams with no outlet. In summer it dries up to form a thick salt crust, and the nearby mines refine about three-quarters of Turkey's salt consumption. The lake is now a protected area and has a colony of breeding flamingos.

Aksaray's position on the Silk Road provided vital trade revenue. To attract the long-haul commercial caravans, *caravanserais* were built, and the 1229 Seljuk **Sultanhanı** is the most magnificent and well preserved of any of these. Forty km (25 miles) west of Aksaray, its intricately carved portal, interior arcades and side vaults are typical of form meets function in the 13th century. There are courtyards, stables and an interesting mini mosque on barrel-

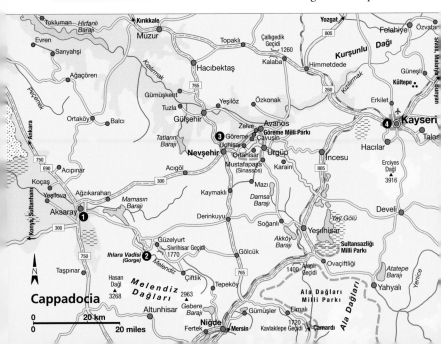

vaulted arches. Gertrude Bell visited the *han* in 1907. **Ağzıkarahan** is another *caravanserai* found 8km (5 miles) east of Aksaray but, comparatively, it is in a rather dismal state of disrepair.

In the Valley

Known in Greek times as the Peristrema Valley, a sheer-sided gorge called **Ihlara Vadisi**  runs alongside the Melendiz River southeast of Aksaray and is excellent for a day's trek to reconnoitre the 60 or so 11th-century churches on the canyon floor (open access; charge). About 10 or 12 of the churches are in sound enough condition to enter, but an overwhelmingly devout atmosphere pervades the 15km (9-mile) -long valley. A few of the tiny churches have pale traces of frescoes. Many have whimsical names like Church of the Black Deer, the Crooked Stone, the Serpents or the Hyacinth Church. Take a hat if you cannot arrive early; there is little shade, although the one-room churches are cool inside.

The underground city of **Kaymaklı**, 20km (12 miles) south of Nevşehir, has underground rooms and storage depots to explore (daily 8.30am–6pm; charge). A further 10km (6 miles) south is the most impressive of the underground cities, aptly named 'deep well' (**Derinkuyu**). A complex network of sleeping quarters, stables, wine presses, kitchens and intriguing air shafts, Derinkuyu has eight subterranean floors descending to a depth of 60m (197ft). It is difficult to imagine this

underground life, as inhabitants left little behind in the way of clues.

At **Güzelyurt**, a beautiful monastery remains from 1856. After the Greek exodus, it was used variously as a primary school, a police station and then a film theatre. Thankfully, today restored as the lovely, highly recommended **Karballa hotel**, the building enjoys national treasure status.

Around Nevşehir

Nevşehir is a focal town in Cappadocia, located 290km (180 miles) southeast of the nation's capital, Ankara. Carpet weaving and viticulture were the traditional economic mainstays of the town, but tourism from the surrounding towns and sights has generated new revenue sources. Leaving

199

Cappadocia

Nevşehir and entering the Disney-esque Göreme is like emerging onto another planet.

Nevşehir

Nevşehir boasts a ruined citadel, the **Kurşunlu Mosque** and seminary complex and the small **Nevşehir Museum** (Tue–Sun 8am–noon, 1–5pm; charge). The town is usually bypassed by those scurrying to reach the mystical and bizarre eroded landform creations, cave churches and dwellings around Göreme, Ürgüp, Uçhisar and Zelve.

Göreme

Göreme ❸, 15km (9 miles) east of Nevşehir, is where many visitors stay in converted caves, close to the star sight of the region, the **Göreme Open-Air Museum** (Göreme Açık Hava Müzesi; daily, summer 8am–5.30pm, winter 8am–5pm; charge plus additional fee for the Buckle and Dark Churches; 🏙). The monastic rupestrine community hollowed out their churches and dwellings above a verdant valley and there are more than 30 churches here dating from the 9th to the early 13th centuries. The delightful paintings and frescoes on the church walls and ceilings depicting biblical scenes are awe-inspiring. Many have been restored and these are infinitely more vibrant than the pale, fairy-dusted frescoes one would expect. The **Dark Church** (*Karanlık Kilisesi*) was used to house pigeons until 1950. Its name derives from the lack of light that entered; this may have actually helped to preserve the primitive pigments used in the frescoes.

The churches are superb in their simplicity and take their names, such as Apple, Maiden, Serpent or Buckle, from an object or image contained in their cramped one-room interiors. Until relatively recently the frescoes and cave chapels fared poorly. Graven images are not approved of by Islam and many were defaced, while early visitors to Göreme could flake bits of them off the walls as 'souvenirs.' Since 1985, however, the Göreme National Park has been protected as a Unesco World Heritage Site.

The intricate detailing in the ceiling of Göreme's Dark Church

See remains from the region's troglodyte past at Zelve

Ürgüp and Around

Ürgüp, 12km (9 miles) from Nevşehir, is tucked into a canyon beneath cliffs riddled with cave dwellings. It is a lively tourist hub with accommodation and good transport. It is known for its handmade carpets and its wines, the white wines being smoother than the red ones. It had a large Greek population up until their mass exodus in 1923.

Zelve is 10km (6 miles) northeast of Nevşehir and tranquil compared to Göreme, but with derelict towns, cave dwellings and churches (only a few with frescoes) in the vicinity. This deserted complex (daily 8am–7pm, until 5pm in winter; charge) is the ideal place for trekking, but come equipped to climb and to navigate narrow rabbit warrens. The most prominent churches are the **Grape (*uzumlu*) Church**, the **Fish (*balık*) Church** and the **Çavuşin Church**.

Avanos on the northern bank of the Kızılırmak River, north of Zelve,

is famed for its pottery skills dating back to the Hittite era. Many shops sell local items and some will let you try your hand at pot-throwing. These shops also often offer priceless export-quality porcelain with classic Ottoman designs.

Ballooning

The most thrilling, extraterrestrial sound to wake you on a Cappadocia morning is not birds but the 'whoosh' of a hot-air balloon being fired by its propane burner, and then to see the soft shadow of an oversized technicolour balloon drifting silently with the updraughts and overhead currents. Despite the tranquillity and laid-back image, hot-air ballooning in Turkey, as elsewhere, is governed by exacting aeronautical standards and rules.

Cappadocia's lunar landscape looks spectacular enough on the ground but the wow factor increases with altitude and the feeling of freedom generated by being in the clouds. Most hot-air balloon pilots can manoeuvre their craft to allow you to pluck an apricot from a tree. Once you are aloft, you will want to be Phileas Fogg for 80 days, but, in reality, you will eventually hit the ground with a controlled bump and sip champagne on de-ballooning.

⭐ CAVE LIFE

Cappadocia's 4th-century cave dwellers were either in hiding or fleeing persecution, but nature was on their side when they found that the soft volcanic residue in the region could be carved out to provide refuge for monks and holy people. They moulded nature's handiwork into their underground rock churches and rupestral shelters, allowing them to practise their Christian faith clandestinely. While the Göreme churches are now secured under the umbrella of Unesco, many of the dwellings are still being dwelt in, both as hotels and as private homes.

The New Cave-Dwellers

Even before the region gained touristic prominence, local people used the hollowed-out caves of Cappadocia as houses. One major advantage was that they were free; there was no rent to pay and nobody knew who the real owners were. Squatters' rights prevailed and title deeds were, in general, lacking in Turkey. On a physicaly practical level, caves had innate advantages;

they were warm in winter and cool in summer, with the sandstone regulating an ambient temperature year-round.

When foreigners and expats began to put down roots in Turkey in the 1980s, the idea of subterranean living seemed quaint and quirky. There was a growing market for these historic rabbit warrens and it did not take long before a new generation of neo-troglodytes were adorning their grottoes with

The basic interior of a house in Cappadocia

the designer trappings of the modern age. Stables that once sheltered donkeys and camels had mangers in-built that were perfect for diffusing soft lighting. Ancient tandoor ovens were discovered and regenerated for contemporary use.

Delicate frescoes in Göreme's churches are well maintained today

Converting the Caves

The process of making Cappadocia's ancient caves suitable for contemporary living was not straightforward. The cooking fires of civilisations past tended to layer the cave walls with soot and ash, preventing the natural stone from breathing. Often, caves were on different levels, with dank air vents or stairs concealed in the chimneys, so immense design challenges turned up. With no blueprints to hand, restoration of these old dwellings was a continual experiment with the unknown.

Even once conversions were complete, there could be disadvantages. It is known by those living in these former troglodyte homes that rainwater tends to have a mind of its own, often drizzling into a neighbour's kitchen or bedroom. The less attractive emblems of global development, such as satellite dishes, rear their heads too, somewhat detracting from the fairy-tale ambience!

Despite all this, many cave houses have become living showcases, tended with great care and even sometimes like museums, filled with exquisite antique carpets and textiles treasured by their owners. The synergy of cultures adds another layer of history to the caves' evolving time line.

The fairy chimney of a cave dwelling; these ancient structures are still in use

Avanos is known for its pottery, sold at many of its shops

Uçhisar, 7km (4 miles) east of Nevşehir, has an immense fist-shaped tower of volcanic tuff, pockmarked with chambers. The **citadel** (daily 8am–sunset; charge), is the highest point in Cappadocia. There is a spectacular view of the unworldly Göreme valley below and this is the perfect place to watc,h the brilliant Cappadocian sunsets.

Ürgüp is within reach of several other villages. **Mustafapaşa**, 6km (4 miles) and **Soğanlı**, 38km (24 miles) south of Ürgüp, are quintessentially Greek, largely untouched since their owners departed in 1922–3. There are churches to visit in Soğanlı with subtle frescoes and an atmosphere of times past permeates the area. It

is a great place to walk or cycle. Trail riding is immensely popular here for horse enthusiasts.

Hacıbektaş Lodge

One of the most impressive antiquities in the region is the **Hacıbektaş Lodge** (Tekke; Tue–Sun 8.30am–12.30pm, 1.30–5.30pm; charge), found about 20 minutes north of Gülşehir towards Kırşehir. Closed in 1924 in line with Turkey's secular development, the Bektaşi Sufi Order moved its headquarters to Albania, but the building is now a splendid museum. Hacı Bektaş was a 13th-century philosopher whose beliefs melded Islamic and Christian principles. He was the guiding light of the Bektaşi Sufi Order and a prominent mentor of Alevism, which still has an estimated 15 million followers in Turkey. His religion offered an 'Islam Light' alternative to the more stringent precepts of pure Islam. The Bektaşi dervishes served as chaplains to the janissaries, the storm-troopers of the Ottoman Empire. The museum here is known as the Founder's House (**Pirevi**), and thoughout the whole complex you will find courtyards, tombs, a refectory and excellent woodcarvings. The tomb is much visited by Muslims from both the Sunni and Alevi sects.

Around Kayseri

Situated on a vast plain overlooked by Mt Erciyes, Kayseri is one of the oldest cities in Anatolia. It served as the capital of the Graeco-Roman province of Cappadocia from 380BC to AD17 and was conquered by Roman Emperor Tiberius. Within the region, the handicraft town of Bünyan, a major bird sanctuary at Sultansazlık, an Assyrian trading post and a Byzantine monastic church round out the tourist options in one of Turkey's most fabled areas.

Kayseri

Kayseri ❹ is Cappadocia's largest city with the region's main airport, Erkilet (ASR), located 12km (7 miles) north of the city. On a strategic ancient trading route, Kayseri practised a sharp eye for commerce and, today, a new breed of small and nimble business tycoons has lent it credence, collectively rebranding themselves the Anatolian Tigers and pouring investment into the city. But this is Turkey's most devout municipality and a staunchly alcohol-free zone. In any case, it is the city's Seljuk past and remains that will interest visitors most. Unless, of course, you fancy the shoe-leather cured sausage known as *pastırma*, a local delicacy.

Amongst the Seljuk monuments are the **Twin-Turreted Seminary** (*Çifte Medresesi*) in **Sinan Park** (Wed–Sun 8am–5pm), the mausoleum of Seljuk Sultan Alâeddin Keykubat's wife, the **Huand Hatun** mosque complex and the adjacent educational institution, or *külliye* (daily 9am–5.30pm), which is one of the most superb examples of Seljuk religious architecture in Anatolia. The supremely symmetrical octagonal tomb (*Döner Kümbet*) on Talas Caddesi dates from 1250 and is the tomb of a Seljuk princess.

The **Archaeological Museum** (Arkeoloji Müzesi; Gültepe Mahallesi, Kışla Caddesi; Tue–Sun 9am–noon, 1–5.30pm; charge) is worth a peek inside, as is a well laid-out ethnographic museum of Ottoman life in a restored 15th-century mansion house, **Güpüpoğlu Konağı** (Tennuri Sokak, Cumhuriyet Mahallesi; Tue–Sun 8.30am–noon, 1.30–5pm; charge). There are three intertwined **bazaars** in Kayseri (Mon–Sat) that maintain a trading mentality and where bartering and haggling endure. There are plenty of (over) eager carpet sellers here.

Outdoor activities are hugely popular in this region; cycling is a great way to see Göreme

Evidence of a trading colony has been excavated at Kültepe

Kültepe

Twenty-two km (14 miles) northeast of Kayseri are the remains of **Kültepe**, a Bronze Age Assyrian merchant financial centre *(kârum kaneş)*. This was a prehistoric freetrade zone, the most compelling evidence of trade being the baked clay tablets and cylinder seals (now in the Museum of Anatolian Civilisations in Ankara, *p.180*) used to stamp legal and trade documents. The texts found here are the oldest written documents found in Anatolia.

Niğde

Niğde is worth much more time than visitors spend there, if indeed they do so at all. There are numerous 13th- and 14th-century Islamic tombs and monuments, including an 11th-century castle, once a prison. There is also a quirky clock tower and lively ethnic bazaar. Like most of the Armenian churches, the best ones near here are isolated or impossibly remote, but the monastery at **Eski Gümüşler** (daily 9am–6.30pm; charge) in the village of **Gümüşler**, 9km (6 miles) north of Niğde, has been restored. The frescoes here disregard time with their artistry. Outside, a wine press and baths have been discovered.

The **Sultansazlığı Bird Sanctuary** (Sultansazlığı Milli Parkı; daily 5am–midnight; charge), 50km (31 miles) northeast of Niğde, represents one of the most important wetlands in Europe, is protected under the RAMSAR Convention and supports over 300 species of birds. The reeds and marshes are a haven for birds and, of course, those who like to observe them.

Bünyan

Bünyan is about 35km (22 miles) northeast of Kayseri; it is known for its handicrafts. It is great for a day trip and a pastoral break from the Seljuk sights and the pumiced landscapes of the rest of Cappadocia. The town produces hand-woven carpets with distinctive large floral patterns and some contemporary designs (www.bunyan.com.tr).

ACCOMMODATION

It would be a shame to come to Cappadocia and not stay in one of the neo-troglodyte dwellings that are so characteristic of the region. Some were once family homes, and are now restored as boutique hotels. Others are grottoes given the designer touch and these are the ideal places to 'encave'.

The Ihlara Valley

Hotel Karballa
Çarşı içi, Güzelyurt
Tel: 0382-451 2103
www.karballahotel.com
The village just east of the Ihlara Valley is beautiful and much more tranquil than the rest of Cappadocia. The focal point of Güzelyurt is a monastery dating from 1856, now converted to an unusually comfortable inn. Most of the rooms occupy the vaulted monks' cells and have been designed as two-storey apartments, with a sitting area on one level and a sleeping loft above. Meals are served in the former refectory, and a swimming pool occupies one end of the tree-shaded gardens. 20 rooms. **$$$$**

Around Nevşehir

Ataman Hotel and Restaurant
Uzundere Caddesi 37, Orta Mahallesi, Göreme

In a Göreme cave hotel

Tel: 0384-271 2310
www.atamanhotel.com
This small cave hotel has 16 rooms, decorated in a very woody style and somewhat over-adorned with kilims, but comfortable enough. There is quite a good restaurant, and it is close to everything that matters in Göreme. **$$$**

Cappadocia Göreme House Hotel
Esbelli Mahallesi 47, Göreme, Nevşehir
Tel: 0384-271 2060
www.goremehouse.com
Once a lovely family home built around a calm and leafy courtyard five minutes from the centre of Göreme, the hotel is open all year round and surveys stunning views from the terrace restaurant. Rooms provide refuge for modern travellers to a high standard of comfort. All 13 rooms have central heating and some have a jacuzzi. **$$$**

Dedeman Kapadokya Hotel and Convention Centre
2km (1 mile) from Nevşehir on the Ürgüp Road, Nevşehir
Tel: 0384-213 9900
www.dedeman.com/Kapadokya.aspx
Cappadocia has its own branch of this well-respected Turkish hotle chain. Don't expect the cosiness of caves, but rooms are comfortably furnished; there are restaurants, bars and a disco. Turkish bath and fitness centre. Booking early rewards you with large discounts. 🏨 **$$$**

Esbelli Evi
Esbelli Sokak 8, P.K. 2, Ürgüp
Tel: 0384-341 3395

www.esbelli.com

Probably the most comfortable and illustrious of all the cave hotels, the old stone house opens onto expansive courtyards. There is a honeymoon suite and guests are treated as friends. A favourite of many high-profile diplomats, the hotel also has an impressive classical music collection and marvellous vista over the magic of Cappadocia. $$$$$

Les Maisons de Cappadoce

Belediye Meydani #6, Uçhisar, Nevşehir,
Tel: 0384-219 2782
www.cappadocia.info/cappadocia-boutique-hotel.html

Meticulously restored by a French architect to harmonise with the region's natural stone, 16 houses and cave studios set the highest standards in the Cappadocia region. These have been lauded by many upmarket publications and personalities. Fully equipped and marvellously furnished, many houses sleep six to nine people, have fireplaces and some are equipped with barbecues. A breakfast hamper is also provided. There is a fully equipped conference room for up to 70 people. 🏛 $$$$$

Museum Hotel

Tekeli Mahallesi 1, Uçhisar
Tel: 0384-219 2220
www.museum-hotel.com

Rated among the finest hotels in the world, Museum Hotel is truly a tribute to nature, the environment and Cappadocian style. No expense has been spared to make this an outstanding boutique hotel furnished with exceptional textiles and Anatolian antiques. There are grand views, a picturesque swimming pool and an award-winning restaurant that cultivates its own organic produce. Royalty and regents have stayed here. Highly recommended. $$$$$

Serinn House

Esbelli Sokak 36, Ürgüp
Tel: 0384-341 6076
www.serinnhouse.com

Brimming with immense natural charm and

Stunning views of the landscape and attention to detail are on offer at the Museum Hotel

contemporary interior style from a Turkish architect, this tiny cave hotel (only five rooms) is Cappadocia at its chicest and is well known as a bijou boutique hotel. A stay here will be memorable. $$$$

Sofa Hotel

Orta Mahallesi, Avanos
Tel: 0384-511 5186

In a restored period Turkish house with 34 rooms, Sofa Hotel has an outdoor restaurant, snack bar, cafeteria and outdoor bar. 🏛 $$

Üçhisar Kaya Hotel

Üçhisar
Tel: 0384-219 2007

Built on the side of a hill, this hotel has a grand view of Üçhisar and the volcanic tuff formations and backs right onto the rocks. It has 62 rooms, a swimming pool, meeting room, restaurant and bar. Open 25 April–15 October. 🏛 $$

RESTAURANTS

Local eateries have proliferated in the Göreme region in response to tourism but adhere to their authentic Turkish roots, and some focus brilliantly on exquisite Anatolian cooking. Many boutique hotels also feature gourmet restaurants in an authentic setting and welcome non-resident guests.

Around Nevşehir

A La Turka
Meydanı (Main Square), Göreme
Tel: 0384-271 2882
www.alaturca.com.tr
Offering over 60 traditional Anatolian dishes in authentic surroundings, this restaurant lives up to, if not exceeds, all expectations and reviews. It is huge fun to eat here and they do breakfast, lunch and dinner with great style and flair. It is hard to find better atmosphere and cooking in the area. ⓜ **$$$**

Elai Restaurant
Tekelli Mahallesi, Uçhisar
Tel: 0384-219 3181
Beyond İstanbul or Ankara, foreign cuisine is rare in Turkey, but Elai is peaceful and wonderfully formal with the emphasis on French cuisine. There are many classic French dishes and a fine view from the bottom of the village's imposing fortress. **$$$**

Harmandalı Restoran
Kavak Yolu Üzeri, Üçhisar
Tel: 0384-219 2364
The signature dish at this budget eatery is *fırın kuzu*, succulent over-roasted lamb. **$**

Old Greek House Restaurant and Hotel
Sinasos Village, Mustafapaşa
Tel: 0384-353 5141
www.oldgreekhouse.com
A short drive from Ürgüp, this delightfully authentic restaurant turns out some of the most typical and tasty village fare anywhere. Try the aubergine dishes, the haricot beans in olive oil and any of the chickpea creations. There is sweet and syrupy baklava for dessert. **$$**

Şömine Restoran
Cumhuriyet Meydanı, Merkez Pasajı Üstü, Ürgüp
Tel: 0384-341 8442
Traditional and well-presented Turkish fare with the accent on freshness and choice. The dish to have here is the *testi* kebap, a spicy lamb with tomatoes, onions and peppers cooked in an earthenware pot. ⓜ **$$**

Around Kayseri

Tuana Restoran
Mehmet Alemdar İş Hanı, Sivas Caddesi, Cumhuriyet Meydanı, Kayseri
Tel: 0352-222 0565
The Tuana speciality is beef steak with mashed potatoes. It is a popular choice with locals too. ⓜ **$$**

A romantic setting for dining in Göreme

Listings

NIGHTLIFE AND ENTERTAINMENT

Most nightlife and entertainment in Cappadocia is on an all-inclusive basis, packaging scores of tourists into a whirl of Turkish and *1001 Nights* action. They are good fun; the food may be mediocre but the atmosphere will be animated.

Karakuş Restoran
$$$
Mustafa Paşa Yolu Üzeri, Pancarlık Mevkii, Ürgüp
Tel: 0384-341 5353
www.karakusrestaurant.com
The Black Bird Restaurant excels in large-scale Turkish evenings complete with a grand selection of starters *(meze)* and main courses, followed by folk troupes, singing and belly dancing, and the occasional whirling dervish. Popular with package tour groups, and for business dinners, weddings and any special-occasion celebrations.

SPORTS AND ACTIVITIES

Most visitors spend time seeing the caves and open-air museum in Göreme, but Cappadocia offers some more participatory sports, and this is one of the best regions to hit the trail on some feisty steeds. Ballooning may be a leisure pursuit but it is also a sport – even if you cannot fly your own balloon.

Akhal Teke Horse Centre
Aydın Altı Mahallesi, Gesteric Sokak 21, Avanos
Tel: 0384-511 5171
www.akhal-tekehorsecentre.com
The Akhal Teke is a special breed of Caucasian/Turkomen horse being bred and raised here. The centre organises exciting trail rides and longer riding tours on the lovely and spirited beasts, the same ones used on the Great Anatolian Ride *(see p.34)*.

Kapadokya Balloons
Nevşehir Yolu 14/A, Göreme
Tel: 0384-271 2442
www.kapadokyaballoons.com
The pioneering hot-air balloon specialists are still gusting over the Cappadocian moonscape. This is the most professional and fully licensed company in the region and they continue to enchant clients with their panoramic aeronautical tours, complete with champagne on landing. April–October only.

TOURS

The travel agents below are the best in the business and have impeccable credentials and professional accreditation. From the simplest to most complicated request, they will oblige.

Argeus Tourism and Travel
İstiklâl Caddesi 7, Ürgüp, Nevşehir
Tel: 0384-341 4688
www.argeus.com.tr
Argeus arranges the most imaginative tours all over Turkey. They specialise in small, personal and close-up mountain biking excursions, culinary journeys and biblical tours, including Mevlana excursions to Konya. They have immaculate references and many happy customers. Also handles shuttle services from Nevşehir and Kayseri airports.

Middle Earth Travel
Gaferli Mahallesi, Cevizler Sokak 20,
Göreme
Tel: 0384-271 2559
www.middleearthtravel.com
Hiking in Cappadocia is on offer as well as
local tours and sightseeing.

Proper Travel
Suat Hayri Ürgüplü Caddesi, Onur İşhanı,
Kat 2 Daire 8, Ürgüp, Nevşehir
Tel: 0384-341 6520
www.propertravel.com
www.travelatelier.com
One of the friendliest and most proficient
of the many tour companies in the area,
Proper Travel can make the difference
between a memorable visit or a mediocre
one. They arrange everything from rental
cars up, and specialise in historical tours
and honeymoon packages in, around and
outside of Cappadocia.

Taking to the skies on a balloon ride

FESTIVALS AND EVENTS

Every town or village has a festival that is significant to its history or that
reinvigorates local traditions. Events are cultural, religious or gastronomic and are
well publicised locally. Visitors are always welcome.

April
Erciyes Winter Festival
1–7 Apr, Kayseri
Erciyes Winter Festival highlights the pistes
and ski runs of Kayseri and the dry-cold
winter climate of this region of Turkey.

May
Yoghurt Festival
18 May, Bünyan
Tha annual Yoghurt Festival focuses on one
of the healthiest staples of Turkish cuisine.

Tepecuması Folklore and Country Festival
27 May, Niğde
This local festival celebrates folk culture
and delights visitors with its variety of ethnic
skills and local colour.

August
Hacıbektaş Veli Commemoration Festival
16–18 Aug, Hacıbektaş
The colourful and ceremonial Hacıbektaş
Veli Commemoration Festival is held in the
town named after the 14th-century Sufi
philosopher and is the largest public event
celebrating Alevism in Turkey. Traditional
theatrical and musical performances are
also staged.

September
Pastırma Festival
15 Sept, Kayseri
Pastırma Festival is a unique local event
that pays homage to the pressed and dried
beef (cured in shoe leather) for which
Kayseri is famous.

Black Sea Region

The Black Sea region is defined by its misty and verdant highlands, streams cascading freefall down dark canyons, folklore, and ethnic customs and traditions that make it distinct from the rest of Turkey. This is Turkey's most reticent region, which often keeps its mystery and secrets to itself, but once discovered, the area draws visitors back time and time again with its stimulating environment.

Trabzon

Population: 800,000		1/A; tel: 0-462 326 4760	
Local dialling code: 0462		**Police Station:** tel: 0-462 230 1985; Call Centre: 155	
Time Zone: GMT +2			
Tourist Office: İskenderpaşa Mahallesi, Ali Naki Effendi Sokak		**Airport** Trabzon Airport (TZX); tel: 0462-328 0940	

Ancient Greek accounts of the Black Sea concern the legendary adventures of the rebel Jason and his Argonauts around 1000BC. This region was the kingdom of Colchis and the home of the legend of the Golden Fleece. Underwater archaeological excavations suggest this could be the site of the great flood of biblical fame, and remains of human settlements more than 7,000 years old are being studied. The Black Sea was once a freshwater lake but today is known for its brackishness and 'blackness'.

Black Sea people, with their unrepressed music and dance traditions, have a culture shaped by geography and the environment. Aquiline profiles, fair colouring and a keen sense of humour are frequent amongst the Laz, as Black Sea people are known. In the northeast mountain villages, people still speak a dialect of Armenian, while those in Çaykara and the town of Of speak Pontic Greek. Many inhabitants are Alevi rather than the more populous Sunni Muslims. Georgian is still spoken in the Borçka frontier area and many Georgians also speak their own form of Turkish.

Coastal Lowlands

With 1,250km (780 miles) of coastline, there are many undiscovered beaches, bays and pristine fishing villages west of Samsun. Travellers imagining the 'shimmering towers of Trebizond' may be disappointed, but turn inland, however, and a maze of winding roads leads to a feast of unspoilt green, damp wilderness, ancient castles and churches, fairy-tale forests and villages full of local spirit and colour.

Near İstanbul

Geographically, the Black Sea holiday resorts begin just outside İstanbul. **Şile** is popular for weekend outings. The coastal resort of **Akçakoca** was much affected by the 1999 earthquake but has interesting domestic architecture. To skirt this stretch of coast, head inland on the E-80 towards Bolu. To the south is a spa complex at Abant and the ski resort at Kartalkaya; to the north is the Seven Lakes National Forest, **Yedigöller Milli Parkı**, worthwhile for the scenic drive alone.

The Black Sea coast is lined with tranquil beaches and villages

Safranbolu

The first unmissable stop is the city of **Safranbolu ❶** *(see also Walking Tour, p.216)*, included in Unesco's World Heritage List, with some 800 of the finest 19th-century Ottoman houses,

Safranbolu is famed for its well-preserved Ottoman architecture

or *konaks*, in Turkey. Many have been beautifully restored as period hotels or pensions. As its name suggests, Safranbolu is also noted for saffron. There are quaint ethnic shops and cultural attractions in the old market quarter, or *Arasta*. There is also a very pretty mosque and ablutions fountain dating from 1780 which is a focal point of the town, the **Kazdağlı Mosque** (Kazdağlı Camii). The **Governor's House Museum** (Kaymakamlar Evi; daily 8.30am–12.30pm, 1.30–5.30pm; charge) is just near the 350-year-old **Cinci Han**, a notable and imposing *caravanserai*. The city's largest mansion, **Havuzlar Konak**, has become a spectacular hotel whose main attraction is a large indoor fountain (the original household's water supply) in the main salon.

There is a craft exhibition in the Muvakkithane section of the **Köprülü Mehmet Paşa Mosque**, and the 17th-century Ottoman bath, **Cinci Hamamı** (bathhouse), has been artfully restored with a splendid marble interior. The **Yemeniciler Arastası** was the original shoemakers' bazaar.

The colourful and attractive beachfront town of Amasra

Amasra

Amasra ❷ is 91km (56 miles) north of Safranbolu, an historic town between two fortified promontories with Hellenistic foundations and surviving Byzantine walls. The town is dominated by a magnificent 14th-century **Genoese fortress**, a reminder that the town was once a commercial and trading powerhouse. There is a charming mosque on the quay, **İskele Mosque**, and a former Byzantine church converted to **Fatih Mosque**. Two offshore islands, **Rabbit** *(Tavşan)* **Island** and **Grand** *(Büyük)* **Island**, are not inhabited but are good for a picnic by boat.

Sinop and Around

Some 150km (90 miles) along the coast towards Sinop, **İnebolu** is on the beach. There are few antiquities and the remaining Ottoman or Greek houses suffer from neglect. İnebolu has some economical beachside hotels ℍ. You really need your own transport to keep coasting along to **Sinop ❸**, situated on a peninsula jutting far out to sea. It has a superb natural harbour and is the base for underwater excavations that include Byzantine shipwrecks. The oldest city on the coast, Sinop was settled by Greeks from Miletus in the 7th century BC

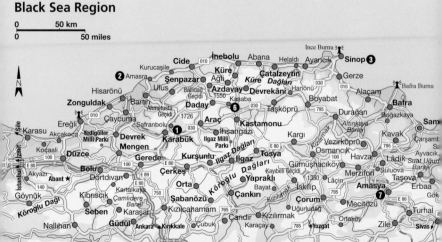

Black Sea Region

0   50 km
0   50 miles

and legend has it that it was founded by the Amazon Queen Sinova. There are around 39 prehistoric sites in the region, one dating from 4500BC. The remains of a 2nd-century BC **Temple of Serapis** stand in the town centre, but the mask of the god himself has been removed to the local museum (currently closed).

Continuing on the coast road, one of the prettiest of the fishing villages is **Gerze**, 40km (24 miles) from Sinop. This is a calm haven for true lovers of the sea, although the beach is rather stony. The best places to stay are those situated along the point, where you can sit on a balcony watching the fishermen harvest mackerel (*palamut*).

Bafra, at the mouth of the Kızılırmak River, has a geothermal spring that made it an ideal location for a 13th-century hamam. There is also a 15th-century mosque and theological school that are worth a stop. **Samsun** is a major centre and has a reasonable **Archaeological and Ethnographic Museum** (Arkeoloji-Etnografya Müzesi; Cumhuriyet Meydanı; Tue–Sun 9am–noon, 1–5.30pm; charge), with a fine collection of 2nd-century BC gold jewellery. There is also the **Atatürk Museum** (Atatürk Müzesi Atatürk Bulvarı; Tue–Sun 9am–noon, 1–5.30pm; charge), with many objects owned by and relating to Turkey's founding father.

Ünye to Tirebolu

Heading east from Samsun, the coastal highway runs along the shore right to the Georgian border and this is a major transport route. Off the beaten track there are still some lovely, wild places. **Ünye** has a good beach and tourist facilities 🏨, and, further along, a temple to the leader of the Argonauts once stood at the tip of Cape Jason (Yasun). **Ordu** is another coastal town displaying much-of-a-muchness charm but here one can turn off to the spectacular beach-encircled crater lake at **Cambaşı**, about 70km (45 miles) south. In **Giresun**, the main attraction is the Aksu

Black Sea Region

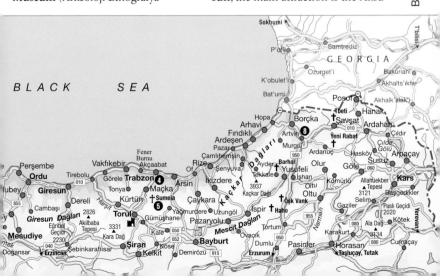

A walking tour of historic Safranbolu takes about an hour and is the best way to immerse yourself in the ambience of a working Ottoman town, with intact 17th-century mosques, *caravanserais* and hamams.

Begin your walk at the **Kazdağlı Mosque** (Kazdağlı Camii) at the town's northern end. From here, head down Arasta Sokak (Market Street) and just on the left is the covered precinct which houses the **Tourism Information** office and little shops selling artisanal handicrafts. Resuming your direction on narrow Arasta Sokak where bay windows and

Tips

- Safranbolu is easily reached by intercity bus from Ankara. The journey takes 3 hours and goes to the upper part of Safranbolu. A connecting *dolmuş*, shuttle bus or taxi service descends 4km (2 miles) down the hill to this, the historic town, where Ottoman residents decamped for the summer. Turkish Railways, TCDD, has a train service to nearby Karabük but this is not recommended.

- Curious walkers can deviate from the walking route to explore the quaint alleyways embedded in bygone times.

- Government House is on the hill under the castle *(Kale)* above the main market *(Arasta)* area. The clock tower has a functioning clock, a fascinating mechanism and a knowledgeable custodian.

balconies lean against each other, ahead on the left is Cebeci Street (Cebici Sokak). A splendid namesake (**Cebeciler Evi**, or the Cebeci's House) dominates the junction. The mansion is a beautiful example of Ottoman secular architecture of the period. You can only view the exterior, but the interior is heavily decorated in pine wood and features separate areas for men, *selamlık*, and women, *haremlik*.

Just opposite on the corner of Kara-üzüm Sokak (Black Grape Street), a public fountain, or *çeşme*, is the loveliest of at least eight natural springs that dignified the town. They were named after a local benefactor and this decorative example was a gentleman named Şükrü. Before piped water, spring water was precious. On the left, just ahead is Old Hamam Street (Eski Hamam Sokak). The remains of the Ottoman bath are on the left. Once an assertive urban icon, it is now defunct.

This street becomes Kunduracılar Sokak and has a pleasant vista looking down to the central business district. Many of the streets and alleyways were named according to their trade and this is Shoemakers' Lane. Safranbolu had a thriving tannery and leather was used for footwear production.

Shoemakers' Lane runs up to **Cinci Han**, a classic 17th-century hostelry that would have been a welcome refuge on a prosperous east-west trading route. Today, it is a classy boutique hotel but without camels and commodities. Enjoy a coffee break in the cool courtyard.

Behind the *caravanserai*, Hıdırlık Yokusu Sokak leads to the **Governer's**

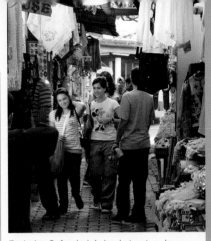

House Museum (Kaymakamlar Evi). Returning to Cinci Han, proceed into the little lane directly outside the main portico. This is Şekerciler Sokak, or Confectioners' Street, where traditional sweet treats, like baklava, are still sold.

The lane opens out onto Upper Hamam Sokak and on the left is the 1656 masterpiece **Köprülü Mehmet Paşa Mosque**, named after an exalted advisor to the sultan. There is an interesting sundial in the courtyard but the mature plane trees bathe it in shade.

Returning along Upper Hamam Street (Üst Hammam Caddesi), the **Cinci Hamam** with its goblet-shaped skylights and domed ceilings is on the right. It dates from 1645 and still flaunts the dignity, style and superb craftsmanship

Exploring Safranbolu's backstreets, where life is lived much as it ever was

of its time. This is the town's main hamam, where anyone can partake in the experience of a Turkish bath.

This street brings you back to Kazdağlı Mosque, with an attractive square-plan design and şadırvan (ablutions fountain) in the forecourt. It dates from 1779 and was superimposed on a much older mosque.

Safranbolu old town is filled with half-timbered Ottoman mansions

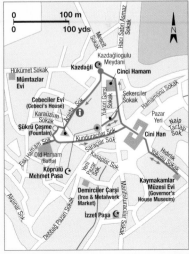

Arts and Culture Festival on Giresun Island (third weekend in May). The area is a rich agricultural one and grows most of Turkey's hazelnuts, a large export item. There is a beach here, many bars and a relaxed attitude to alcohol and dress codes not found in other Black Sea towns. Atatürk chose his presidential guards from Giresun because they were said to have an instilled trait of fierce loyalty.

Back on the coast, **Tirebolu** (formerly Tripolis) occupies a crescent-shaped bay; on a rocky promontory to the east is a Byzantine fortress, possibly built by the Grand Comneni of Trebizond. This has been a substantial trading port since antiquity, especially for the silver mined inland; it became an important Genoese outpost in the Middle Ages. With two other fortresses nearby, it is now considered to be one of the prettiest and most tranquil towns on the central eastern coast; it also relies much on hazelnut production for its economy.

Trabzon

Founded as a Greek colony in the 6th century BC, **Trabzon** (Trebizond) ❹ was to reach its cultural zenith when Alexius Comnenus and his Georgian supporters took control in 1204 after the Crusader invasion of Constantinople. The Comneni dynasty lasted 257 years. Mongol raids forced the diversion of the Silk Road through here, fostering a flourishing trade with the Genoese and Venetians.

Trabzon's central and harbour area reveals nothing of the once-shimmering towers mentioned in

Selling the catch of the day in Trabzon

Rose Macaulay's famous book, *The Towers of Trebizond*. Many crumbling, uninhabited Greek mansions line the quay and little remains of the grandiose city walls, the citadel or the Imperial Palace. The most important site is the 13th-century Byzantine **Church and Museum of Aya Sofia** (Haghia-Müzesi Sofia; İnönü Caddesi; Tue–Sun 8.30am–noon–5.30pm, until 5pm in winter; charge), which was built by Emperor Manuel VII Palaeologus. It is beautifully situated on a seaside bluff and has astonishing interior frescoes. The Chrysocephalos, the cathedral of Trabzon during Comneni rule, is now the **Fatih Mosque** (Fatih Camii). Like the **Church of St Eugenius** (Yeni Cuma Camii since 1461, located on Kasım Sokak), it may have contained important mosaics and imperial portraits of the Comneni. The oldest church in the city, the 9th-century Armenian **Church of St Anne** (Karamanmaraş Caddesi), is permanently locked. The **Trabzon Museum** (Zeytinlik Cadesi; Tue–Sun 9am–noon, 1–5.30pm; charge) has a small collection of local archaeological finds housed in a magnificent 19th-century mansion, once a convent but later the home of a wealthy Greek banker.

Two km (1 mile) outside Trabzon is Atatürk's handsomely ornate villa **Atatürk'un Köşkü** (daily 8.30am–4.30pm; charge), built in 1903. Trabzon had an extraordinarily cosmopolitan and skilled Christian population up until the early 1900s and its current ultra-nationalistic mentality does not sit well with its past. Trabzon is not the most highly

Trabzon's town centre

recommended place to stay and locals are little interested in tourism or, in fact, in foreigners, unless they are Russian and female.

Monastery Ruins

Trabzon is a convenient point from which to set out for a day trip to the Black Sea region's most spectacular site, **Sumela Monastery ❺** (daily; Nov–Apr 9am–3pm, May–Oct 8am–6pm; charge), located in the secluded depths of Altındere National Park. Also known as the Monastery of the Black Virgin, Sumela is 55km (34 miles) southeast of Trabzon. It is a towering, seven-storey structure that perches dramatically on a ledge between heaven and earth, halfway up a sheer rock face above roaring waters. Legends tells that it was built by two monks from Athens acting on a visitation of the Virgin Mary. The last resident monks were transported, along with other Greek Ottomans, back to Greece in the population exchange of 1923. The present buildings date from the 12th century and

The Sumela monastery is covered in layers of frescoes

Bayburt

Fifty km (31 miles) further east, **Bayburt**, a provincial capital, boasts the remains of a Byzantine castle, significant mosques, tombs and hamams. A new culture museum has opened here, the **Baksı Museum** (Baksı Kültür Sanat Vakfı ve Müzesi, Çayırlar Mevkii, Bayraktar Köyü, Bayburt; www.baksi. org; daily 9am–5pm; charge). It aims to restore local crafts and customs to their former prominence and revive traditions. The local food speciality in Bayburt is rosehips; be sure to sample the rosehip marmalade.

The Inland Route – High Road

The supreme reason for being in the Black Sea region is the lure of unspoilt nature. For those with time and their own transport, there is magic in the pine forests and the Alpine lakes found in the Kaçkar range of mountains and the Hemşin area. This is a land 1,300m (4,265ft) high with rolling mists, steep valleys, rivers and waterfalls. Ayder is the high-altitude centre of tourism here. The region is justifiably known as the 'Lungs of Turkey'.

Kastamonu and Ilgaz National Park

Taking the inland route eastwards from Safranbolu, your first stop should be **Kastamonu**, a 10th-century town, once the feudal stronghold of the Comneni family, aristocratic officers who captured the Byzantine crown in 1081. There are also a number of Seljuk and Ottoman monuments. Seventeen km (10 miles)

contain many layers of frescoes; most of those still visible date from the 1700s. Although shamefully vandalised, Sumela is being restored and remains one of the Black Sea's most spectacular attractions. Getting there is an arduous trek up a 1km- (½-mile-) long forest path.

Beyond Trabzon are found many more monastic ruins in the Maçka district, such as **Peristera**, near Şimşili, and **Vazelon**, 14km (8 miles) above Maçka, but access is steep and challenging. Continuing on, you travel through the Harşit valley and over the **Zigana Pass**, along the old caravan route towards Erzurum (see p.237) and Asia to Torul, where there is a castle once controlled by a 15th-century mountain lord. **Gümüşhane** was an important silver trading town whose remains are set among fruit groves and wild rose fields.

northwest, the village of **Kasaba** ❻ is home to one of the finest mosques in Turkey, the carved wooden **Mahmut Bey Camii**, a superb Seljuk structure built in 1366 and retaining almost all its original features. Head south from Kastamonu for 63km (39 miles) and you reach the **Ilgaz National Park** (Ilgaz Milli Parkı), which has a popular ski resort (year-round; entry charge for vehicles). The seemingly mundane village of **Devrek**, 60km (37 miles) west of the National Park, makes famous and ornately carved wooden canes, including one for the Sultan of Brunei.

Amasya

You can continue southeast through the pretty Ottoman villages of Tosya and Osmancık to **Amasya** ❼, one of

Local children in Amasya

Getting Around

In the Black Sea region, the most spectacular places are invariably the hardest to reach. Public transport is limited and erratic once you leave the east-west coastal road axis. The forests and plateaux are intersected by deep valleys and transport may be daily or weekly. Locals use a type of electrified 'skycart' called a *vargel* to traverse the valleys. To get the most out of the area, it pays to hire your own car, preferably a four-wheel drive or all-terrain vehicle, or go with a reputable tour group. Be sure to pack sensible clothes and good hiking boots.

the most attractive towns in Turkey and very much under-appreciated. It is 130km (80 miles) inland and was the first capital of the Pontic Kingdom until its rulers moved to Sinop in 120BC. Overlooking the Yeşilırmak River, heritage Ottoman houses have bow windows overhanging the water, which is why they are known as waterfront (*yalıboyu*) houses. At night, floodlights beam up the cliffs near the citadel to highlight the well-preserved Pontic tombs. This was the ancestral home of the classical geographer, Strabo. Later, held as Seljuk territory, it was sacked by Genghis Khan's Mongols in the mid-13th century.

There are two impressive Seljuk mosques: the **Mosque of the Twisted Minaret** (Burmalı Minare Camii) and the **Blue Seminary** (Gök Medrese), a theological institution with outstanding 13th-century Seljuk architecture. There is also a

The waterfront *(yalıboyu)* houses in Amasya *(see p.221)*

16th-century covered bazaar *(bedesten)* between Ziya Paşı Bulvarı and Atatürk Caddesi and a 7th-century Byzantine church converted to a mosque in 1116. Across from the **Sultan Beyazıt Mosque** (Sultan Beyazıt Camii), on Atatürk Caddesi, the **Amasya Archaeology and Ethnography Museum** (Arkeoloji/ Etnografya Müzesi; Tue–Sun 9am– noon, 1.30–5.30pm; charge) contains an extensive collection of artefacts from the nine different civilisations that have ruled the city. It has been renovated and is a very fine museum.

It is a steep climb up to the **Citadel**, but there is a teahouse at the top to entice you and the view makes it supremely worthwhile. The **Hazeranlar Mansion** (Hazeranlar Konağı; Hattuniye Mahallesi; Tue–Sun 9am–5pm, until 7pm in summer; charge) is a restored Ottoman mansion of 1865, carefully furnished in period style.

Into the Mountains

Twenty km (12 miles) north of Amasya, **Lâdık** and its neighbouring town to the east, **Havza**, both have steamy hot thermal springs. These are primitive but still in use today for therapeutic treatments.

To continue along the ridge road towards Niksar, an all-terrain vehicle is recommended. For those with time, the spectacularly scenic 93km (58-mile) expedition across the Eğribel Pass to **Şebinkarahisar** may be the highlight of your trip. Şebinkarahisar sits on a lofty bluff overlooking the beautiful Kelkit valley. It was identified as Pompey's ancient city of Koloneia, established after the Mithridatic Wars in 63BC.

The Hemşin Valley

The Hemşin inhabitants are not Laz but were descendants of Christian Armenians who converted to Islam. They still speak a dialect of

Armenian. Hemşinlis are known for their skill as confectioners and pastry chefs. One of the warming and hearty foods of the region is a special type of cheese and cornmeal fondue known as *mıhlama*, a staple of many households and eaten immediately after preparation.

Çamlıhemşin is an attractive little town built on the roaring **Fırtına Çayı** (Storm River) over which, further up towards **Şenyuva**, are several splendid stone bridges, some dating from the 17th century. On the rugged road leading onwards from Şenyuva, the impressive **Zilkale** (Bell Castle) has fairy-tale spires and a mysterious history. Some claim it dates from the 6th century, but it could be one of hundreds of Armenian and Georgian churches hidden in deep valleys, many forgotten and undiscovered.

Yusufeli to Artvin

Yusufeli stands at the centre of a region where a 200-year renaissance of Georgian medieval culture flourished. Two km (1 mile) southwest of Yusufeli are the **Four Churches** (*Dört Kilise*), amazing basilica ruins

in a village off the road to İspir. Those with vehicles (it is a long and tortuous route) can also reach **Barhal** along the Çoruh River valley. There is a well-preserved 10th-century church here. However, one is strongly advised to access the hiking trails of the **Kaçkar Mountains** (www.kackar.com), Çamlıhemşin and the lovely retreat and thermal pools at **Ayder** from the coast road. Hardy professionals may want to attempt reaching **Barhal** or **Yusufeli** on foot or horseback from Ayder, but a guide is advised unless you are familiar with the terrain and valleys, as damp fogs can roll in without warning. There is a heavily flawed plan to dam the **Çoruh River** at Yusufeli and displace residents. Currently, this is the most exciting and challenging place to join a group for white-water rafting.

Forty km (25 miles) from Yusufeli on the 950 road, **Artvin ❽** is still quintessentially Caucasian and the surrounding region offers some of the most impressive 9th- to 11th-century religious architecture to be found anywhere. For local people, folk music, traditional dancing, bagpipe (*tulum*)

Trekking from Ayder

With at least half a dozen mountain ranges in the Black Sea region, ecotourism and trekking are attracting outdoor sports enthusiasts in unprecedented numbers, particularly to the Hemşin area, where guides are readily available. The lush Kaçkar Mountains are marvellous for climbing and hiking. The ideal base camp is Ayder, 17km (10 miles) southeast of Çamlıhemşin, and this can be reached by bus from Trabzon. Local accommodation is in basic wooden chalets, but many people choose to camp anyway. Handily, Ayder has a steamy hot thermal spa (57°C/135°F) to soothe aching muscles after a long trek. Note that trekking the mountains and valleys around Ayder is for summer months only. The area is inaccessible in winter.

music and culture feature hugely in their ethnic repertoire.

The town of **Artvin** itself is not exactly charming, but it's a friendly place and the surrounding land is beautiful, covered with forests, and walnut, apple, cherry and mulberry orchards. The town has a castle, many Ottoman-era houses, fountains and mosques. What people come here for is the annual Caucasian (Kakfasör) Festival with its traditional bull-butting competitions. Also attracting visitors is the *hıdrellez* ceremony held on the high plateaux (*yaylas*) in May (*see box, right*).

Mountain Villages

Borçka and **Şavşat** are Alpine villages that will remind you of the Swiss Alps. Environmental programmes are in place to protect them and encourage controlled tourism that respects the often tenuous way of life.

There are excellent tourist facilities here for white-water rafting, trekking, mountain climbing and hunting (brown bears), and one must not forget wildflower tourism or photography. This is the place to immerse yourself in nature. The wild Caucasian bee is being nurtured and bred here and the honey has head-spinning properties.

> ### Hıdrellez – Spontaneous Migration
>
> One of the most delightful traditions in and around the Black Sea is the annual migration rite held every year in May, *hıdrellez*. It symbolises the move to the high summer plateaux for shepherds, their families and flocks. As career shepherds have dwindled from thousands to just a few hundred, the ceremony nowadays is largely symbolic. However, the fun traditions continue – picnics, singing, folkloric customs and traditional dancing. Extended families gather, mingle and consume staggering amounts of delicious local dishes.

The stunning and ancient town of Şebinkarahisar (*see p.222*)

ACCOMMODATION

Those preferring elegant accommodation and frills should look elsewhere. The Black Sea is about nature, the environment and keeping it that way. The most ecological accommodation is in wooden chalets or bungalows built in typical regional style. Most of these are remote and difficult to access by car. They are modestly furnished and offer a beacon of friendship after a day's trekking. Trabzon has larger hotels minus the mountain vistas or rolling mists.

Coastal Lowlands

Amastris
Büyük Liman Caddesi, Amasra
Tel: 0378-315 2465
Rather quaint, 1930s spa-style accommodation overlooking the sea. Basic en-suite rooms with balconies but pleasant and laid-back. Closed in winter. **$$**

Belde Otel
Kirazlımanı Mahallesi, Ordu
Tel: 0452-214 3987
Located on a small point of land off the highway, this is Ordu's grandest holiday complex and has its own swimming pool. **$$**

Belvü Palas Otel
Küçük Liman Caddesi 20, Amasra
Tel: 0378-315 1237
Although the accommodation is very basic, the tiny rooms all have balconies and what it lacks in charm it more than makes up for with the superb views. Closed in winter. **$**

Cinci Han Hotel
Eski Çarşı Çeşme Sokak, Safranbolu
Tel: 0370-712 0680
www.cincihan.com.com
The most original and luxurious place to stay in Safranbolu. It was a *caravanserai* for traders in the 17th century and now welcomes modern travellers in similar style and graciousness but with more conveniences. There is an excellent restaurant and bar. **$$$$**

Havuzlu Asmazlar Konağı
Hacı Halil Mahallesi, Çelik Gülersoy Caddesi 18, Safranbolu
Tel: 0372-725 2883
One of the most elegant mansion hotels in the town, the Havuzlu Konak is named after its indoor pool *(havuz)*. A fountain also provided water for the original 18th-century owners and is the centrepiece of a little café. It is easy to imagine yourself an Ottoman notable being waited on in high style. It has 18 rooms and five suites. **$$$$**

Karakum Motel
Gelincik Mevkii, Sinop
Tel: 0368-261 8777
Motels are not so much an accommodation choice in Turkey but these 60 basic

Elegant Ottoman style awaits

Delectable local cheeses may make an appearance at breakfast

waterfront bungalows front onto their own beach and there is a restaurant with few frills or flounces. **$**

Tahsin Bey Konağı and Paşa Konağı
Çarşı Mahallesi, Safranbolu
Tel: 0372-712 6062
Two connected historic mansions, one 19th century and one from the 18th century, operated under one personable management. Eleven rooms and an atmospheric and pleasant garden café. **$$$**

Villa Rose
Ada Mahallesi, Kartal Caddesi 9, Sinop
Tel: 0368-261 1923
Villa Rose is a comfortable home as much as a hotel, full of the travel memoirs and personality of the owner. Delicious home-prepared meals, a master suite with sauna, and the villa is close to the beach. Six rooms. **$$$**

Yağmur Pansiyon
Zindan Mahallesi, Kemere Sokak 6, Amasra
Tel: 0378-315 1603
Cheerful, family-run house with several 3-bedroom apartments and a view. Kitchens are fully equipped and this is a lovely little place to stay. Central heating. Open all year round. **$$**

Zorlu Grand Hotel
Maraş Caddesi 9, Trabzon
Tel: 0462-326 8400
www.zorlugrand.com
The city's first five-star hotel is still going strong and has 160 rooms. The add-ons include mini-suites, a royal suite, patisserie, vitamin bar and an English pub. This is the best place to stay in Trabzon for foreigners. **$$$$**

The Inland Route – High Road
Cancik Hotel
Çat, Çamlıhemşin
Tel: 0464-654 4120
There are only seven rooms in this ultra-basic little Alpine pension at the end of a narrow valley. This makes it a focal point for meeting and chatting and even seeing that someone else exists in this remote hideaway. Unbeatable for the fresh mountain air, rather a lot of mist but grand views when the sun shines. **$$**

Emin Efendi Pansiyon
Hatuniye Mahallesi, Hazeranlar Sokak 66, Amasya
Tel: 0358-212 0852
Fine 200-year-old Ottoman house jutting out over the Yeşilırmak River, in the town's historical section, below the Pontic tombs. There are five rooms and some are en suite. A highlight is the lovely courtyard, and don't forget to check out the common room and its piano. There is also a small café. **$$**

Fora Pension
Çamlıhemsin
Tel: 0464-651 7570
To really appreciate this region, stay in this simple but cosy pension, which will imprint itself on your mind long after your visit. It is run by Türkü Turizm Travel Agency who manage many other small pensions and can arrange everything to do in and around Çamlıhemşin. Highly recommended. **$$**

Hotel Karahan
İnönü Caddesi 16, Artvin
Tel: 0466-212 1800

The most comfortable hotel in a town unconcerned about accommodation. This hotel is a haven after a long journey from the coast, and the owners will organise everything for you in the region. **$$**

İlk Pansiyon
Gümüşlü Mahallesi, Hitit Sokak 1 (opposite the tourist office), Amasya
Tel: 0358-218 1689
www.ilkpension.com
This old Armenian mansion is one of the most beautifully restored houses in Amasya, refurbished by its owner-architect, an urban-renewal guru. The six rooms are different sizes and beautifully and individually decorated to exceed their previous status. The courtyard is cool and also a period feature of the house. **$–$$$**

Karagöl Pension
Karagöl Mevkii (on the lake), Meşeli, Şavşat
Tel: 0466-531 2137
Located 23km (14 miles) from Şavşat village, this lovely pension has great facilities in one of Turkey's most remote eastern corners. Don't expect five-star service, but there are lush forests and hunting and fishing opportunities, six rooms and some camping facilities. Brown bears roam the woods. **$$$**

Karahan Pension
Barhal Köyü, Yusufeli
Tel: 0466-826 2071
An attractive pension located in a remote and atmospheric spot, famous for its 10th-century Georgian church. Trekking is the best way to get here; otherwise by horse-back or a four-wheel-drive vehicle. Authentic and nicely furnished chalets. Summer only. **$$**

Kuşpuni Otel
Ayder
Tel: 0464-657 2052
Located near the thermal hot springs at Ayder, this is a verdant Alpine retreat with the owner on site. It is eco-friendly to the hilt and built in the typical mountain style of many Black Sea chalets. Wonderfully recommended for simplicity and friendliness. **$$$**

RESTAURANTS

One should expect simple, local cooking rather than sophisticated fare or fancy restaurants. Black Sea specialities include a corn meal and cheese fondue (*mıhlama*) and you will see that local anchovies (*hamsi*) feature prominently on many menus, if not every one. Trekkers and backpackers will feast on picnics and tuck into hearty meals at their pension or chalet, while large hotels will have their own restaurants and cafés with more varied cuisine.

Restaurant Price Categories

Price categories are based on a three-course meal for one (including *meze*, grilled meat, bread, salad and fruit) and non-alcoholic drinks.

$ = under 20TL
$$ = 20–40TL
$$$ = 40–60TL
$$$$ = 60–100TL

Coastal Lowlands
Canlıbalık
Küçük Liman Caddesi 8, Amasra
Tel: 0378-315 2606
Coastal restaurant serving fresh, unusual fish dishes. Lively atmosphere and sea views. **$**

Kadıoğlu Şehzade Sofrası
Çeşme Mahallesi, Arasta Sokak 8, Safranbolu
Tel: 0372-712 5091
Specialities include lamb (*kuzu*) kebap with a difference – the lamb is roasted in

a clay pit. Other local dishes are also well cooked and presented. **$$**

The Inland Route – High Road
Horon Hotel
Rooftop Restaurant and Bar
Siramagazalar Caddesi 125
Trabzon
Tel: 0462-326 6455
www.hotelhoron.com
This modest hotel boasts a splendid rooftop bar and restaurant. They serve excellent regional dishes and some ambitious international cuisine. Excellent views of the city. **$$$**

İnan Kardeşler Trout Farm and Motel
60km (37 miles) inland from the town of Of, Uzungöl
Tel: 0462-656 6021
A favoured fishing retreat that has been pleasing hikers and trekkers for ages. The restaurant and tea garden are scenic and the food basic but fresh and tasty. Highly recommended and popular. **$$**

Karadeniz Dalyan Restaurant
Harbour Entrance (opposite the PTT)
Akçakoca
Tel: 0380-611 9656
A basic main-street restaurant specialising in fish of every variety including the regional Black Sea sardine speciality, anchovies *(hamsi)*. What it lacks in finesse is more than made up for in the impressive selection of freshly caught fish each day. Alcohol is not served. 🏨 **$$**

SPORTS, ACTIVITIES AND TOURS

Sporting and activities are as effervescent as the Çoruh River itself. You cannot do white-water rafting or trekking on our own and it is essential that an experienced and professional tour agency packages your requirements with your skills and ensures that you have an exhilarating time and respect the environment. The tour companies below are all well known and respected in this region.

Bukla Travel Agency
İnebolu Sokak 55/6, Kabataş, Beyoğlu, İstanbul
Tel: 0212-245 0635
www.bukla.com/pdfler/eng.pdf
This is a leading-edge travel firm highly specialised in eco-rekking, extreme nature and photo safaris in the Black Sea and Eastern Turkey. They will tailor any trek (or climb) to requirements.

Dağ Raft Rafting and Tourism
Ayder (on the Çamlıhemşin Road), Rize
Tel: 0464-752 4070
www.dagraft.com
They arrange and organise a fine array of the most exciting and amazing white-water rafting expeditions on the Çoruh River and in the Fırtına Valley.

Matiana Travel
Asmalı Mescit Mahallesi, Meşrutiyet Caddesi 7/2, Beyoğlu, İstanbul
Tel: 0212-245 9559
www.matiana.com

White-water rafting is a popular activity here

Fishing off the Black Sea Coast

Private tours to the Sumela Monastery, Çamlıhemşin and other Black Sea heritage sites. Matiana arrange tours on a group or privately tailored basis. They have been doing this for a long time and are accredited by all the main global travel associations.

Middle Earth Travel
Göreme
Tel: 0384-271 2559
www.middleearthtravel.com
This reputable company is one of the leading tour organisers in the country, and in the Black Sea region they can offer rural hiking holidays or packages along the Kaçkar way-marked trail route, www.kackarlar.org.

Türkü Turizm Travel Agency
İnönü Caddesi 47, Çamlıhemşin.
Tel: 0464-651 7230
www.turkutour.com
This is a reliable and comprehensive tourism agency in the Çamlıhemşin's high plateau region. They have maps available, can arrange four- or five-day mountain tours and trail riding, and also have pensions where you can stay and a nature camp. In an area where untamed nature rules, outdoor types and nature-lovers can concentrate on the spectacular scenery by letting this sort of agency do some groundwork for you.

FESTIVALS AND EVENTS

Turkey loves its festivals and celebrations and nowhere does this as fervently as the Black Sea region. Everyone is encouraged to participate in the jovial events, and visitors, especially, are not expected just to be onlookers.

May
Hıdrellez
6 May, Artvin
The *hıdrellez* annual migration to high-altitude summer pastures is centred around Artvin but also held in many towns and villages, as it has been for hundreds, if not thousands, of years.

June
Caucasian (Kafkasör) Festival
27-30 June, Artvin
Held every summer at the Kafkasor High Plateau.

July
Devrek Walking Stick and Cultural Festival
8–9 July, Devrek
It may seem strange to have a festival devoted to walking sticks and canes, but these represent one of the dominant skills of Ottoman artisans, woodcarving. The town celebrates its heritage skills every year.

August
Watermelon Festival
25–30 Aug, Bafra
Join in the festivities at this local two-day watermelon festival.

Eastern Anatolia

Vast and unknown to most travellers, the grandeur and stirring history of Turkey's eastern reaches excite and inspire visitors and devotees of historical legend. Two of the world's noblest rivers, the Tigris and the Euphrates, rise in Eastern Anatolia, and this region has been variously known as the 'Cradle of Civilisation', the 'Fertile Crescent' and the location of the legendary Mesopotamian plain.

Gaziantep

Population: 1,300,000

Local Dialling Code: 0342

Tourist Office: Yüzyıl Atatürk Kültür Parkı: tel: 0342-230 5969

Time Zone: GMT +2

Police Station: tel: 0342-230 1830; Call Centre: 155

Airport: Gaziantep (GZT) airport; tel: 0342-582 1111

Car Hire: Avis; tel: 0342-336 1194. Iremtur Oto Kiralama; tel: 0342-339 036

The vast expanse that is eastern Turkey is better divided into two regions. The Near East is dominated by the Euphrates and Tigris rivers, which are excessively dominated by a series of giant dams, tunnels and irrigation canals engineered to turn barren flatlands into prime agricultural land. Already more reliant on natural gas, Turkey's future energy needs will in fact probably be met by nuclear, rather than hydroelectric, power in future.

One of the highlights of the East is Nemrut Dağı, said by some to be a greater feat of engineering than the Pyramids. Even today, the peak is a dominating landmark and the question of how King Antiochus of the Commagene managed to build this impressive and monumental cult site continues to mystify.

The region has several important cities. Gaziantep, a regional hub known for producing pistachio nuts and textiles, also boasts a dazzling mosaic museum. Ancient Şanlıurfa is the city of prophets and is claimed as the birthplace of Abraham.

The Far East begins with the southern lowlands, rising through the rugged southeastern corner and intercepted by plateau pastures where nomadic tribesmen graze their animals. There are dizzying and snow-covered mountain passes as well as the upper Anatolian plateau. Mount Ararat, on the Armenian border, dominates the northeast corner of the country.

The urban centres of the east are fascinatingly diverse. Erzurum is the biggest city in the northeast, and, in the far south, near the Syrian border, lie the cities of Diyarbakır and Mardin. In the east, Van hugs the southeast corner of emerald-green Lake Van, and Kars is an interesting city in its own right, while also being a jump-off point for the fascinating ruins of Anı.

The Near East

This vast tract of central Turkey offers fabulous scenery, from sprawling plains to towering mountains. Then there are the museums that showcase how the region has been home to a plethora of remarkable civilisations, each of which has left its distinctive footprint.

Kahramanmaraş to Divriği

Formerly known as Maraş, **Kahramanmaraş ❶** acquired the honorific 'Kahraman' (heroic) due to bravery in the Turkish War of Independence. Historically an important outpost guarding the second major pass over the Taurus Mountains, it has an exceptional 15th-century **Great Mosque** (Ulu Camii), the **Taş Medrese**, and a citadel which houses the municipal **museum** (Tue–Sun 9am–5pm; charge) and its collection of Hittite reliefs.

A fresco detail at the Church of St Gregory at Anı (see p.237)

Eastern Anatolia

An interesting local town is **Sivas ❷**, which deserves a stop for its thriving crafts bazaar and magnificent clutch of Seljuk architecture. The 12th-century **Great Mosque** (Ulu Camii) and the four theological and medical colleges of **Gök**, **Çifte Minareli**, **Şifahiye** and **Bürüciye Medrese** all have elaborately decorative foundations and were built by Seljuk and Mongol governors. The city has a large Alevi population.

Some 75km (46 miles) south of Sivas, **Kangal** is the home of a fiercely loyal breed of shepherd dog with a curled tail. Fifteen km (10 miles) east

The site of Anı (see p.237) stands on a deserted plateau near the Armenian border

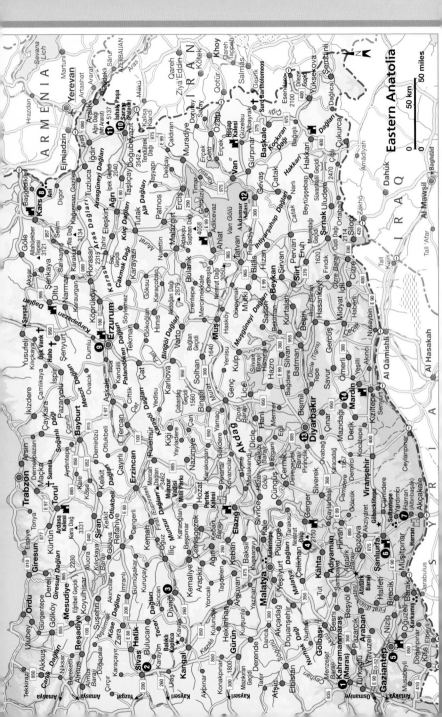

Eastern Anatolia

are the **Balıklı Kaplıca** (Fish Springs Psoriasis Healing Centre), renowned for a unique species of skin-eating fish. Psoriasis sufferers come here from around the world (www.balikli.org).

The sleepy iron-mining town of **Divriği** ❸ to the east houses a masterpiece example of Seljuk architecture in Anatolia. The mosque and grand hospital complex became a Unesco World Heritage Site in 1985 and the mosque itself was founded in 1228. The highlight is the remarkably sophisticated vault construction, one of the most brilliant features of Islamic architecture.

Kemaliye and the Upper Euphrates

South of Divriği and a former Armenian town named Eğin, **Kemaliye** is an abrupt architectural change from the surrounding traditional Muslim settlements. Former residents had a high standard of living and a keen eye for fine decor; it is still a delightful town with trim, cobbled streets. There is a small museum in an Armenian **church** (Tue–Sun 9am–noon, 1–5pm; charge). Note that the road out of Kemaliye to İliç is tortuous and the mountain pass difficult to cross, although it is only 32km (20 miles) on the map.

Elazığ, on the south shore of Lake Keban, is a clean and orderly town, useful for transit. A ferry station some 16km (10 miles) north of Elazığ provides transport across the lake, past **Harput Castle**. Elazığ has a 12th-century mosque. The town was called Harput when Armenians lived there.

Malatya and, to a lesser extent, **Adıyaman**, have illustrious histories but today there is little to detain the

The ritual ablutions fountain outside Malatya's old mosque

traveller. Apart from being Turkey's premier apricot producer, Malatya's claim to fame was as the home town of Atatürk's chief lieutenant, İsmet İnönü. The local archaeological museum houses a small Hittite collection. The old part of Malatya is called **Eski Malatya**; Byzantine and Seljuk remains have been found here. There is also a 17th-century *caravanserai*.

South of Elazığ, the Upper Euphrates region is dominated, physically and emotionally, by Mount Nimrod, or **Nemrut Dağı** ❹. The outline of the Commagene King Antiochus's tumulus can be seen from nearly 150km (100 miles) in every direction. This is a star sight of the eastern region; time is required to access the steep ascent and absorb the enormity of the huge basalt

Eastern Anatolia

figures. Late evenings allow a superlative viewing of the most spectacular sunsets in Turkey.

The Commagene kingdom was a buffer state on the Upper Euphrates, pinched between the fleet cavalry of ancient Parthia and the inexorable legions of Rome. It flourished briefly during the Roman civil wars but was crushed and absorbed into the Roman Empire, disappearing from history as Christianity took hold.

Commagene carved its place in history from the living rock. Visitors make the trek, or perhaps pilgrimage, to view the colossal tumulus and statues of the major gods arranged on terraces built by Antiochus to glorify himself in perpetuity. They have a similar mystical and haunting glory to the Pyramids. There was once a horoscope here attracting many people. It has now been moved to a museum for safety.

The nearest places to stay are in Kâhta, at the base of the mountain, or in Adıyaman, a large town with more choice of accommodation.

A Gaziantep shoemaker at work

Gaziantep and Around

The next stop, **Gaziantep ❺**, is one of the oldest continuously inhabited settlements in the world. Today, it is the eastern region's economic powerhouse, a bustling modern city brimming with history and civic pride; it has also been the recipient of much European Union 'revival' finance.

Its shining star is the **Archaeological Museum** (Arkeoloji Müzesi; İstasyon Caddesi; Tue–Sun 8am–noon, 1–5.30pm; charge). The Zeugma mosaics excavated from the nearby dig at Nizip are unbelievable, and many visitors come specifically to see these. They are breathtaking in their whimsical artistry and their beautifully labelled displays. This is a world-class museum that you won't want to bypass. The most enigmatic mosaic is the *Gypsy Girl*, a symbol of Gaziantep. A stunning collection of clay seals, or *bulla*, is impressive. During excavations, one of the archaeological team members unearthed the wistful *Statue of Mars* from an amphora. It now stands as the centrepiece of the museum.

Squarely in the middle of town are the citadel and several fine 15th-century mosques, *caravanserais* and Turkish baths. The **Covered Bazaar** is one of the best in Turkey. Try to locate the shoemaker (*yemenici*) here who made Harry Potter's shoes for the film series. It is easy to do, as everybody knows him; you will probably end up coming away with a pair too.

One of the finest 19th-century mansions now houses the excellent **Hasan Süzer Ethnography Museum** (Hasan Süzer Etnografi Müzesi; Hanifioğlu Sokak, Eyupoğlu, Şahinbey; Tue–Sun 8.30am–12.30pm, 1.30–4.30pm; charge). It is a beautifully restored house with ashlar walls and a tiled roof built around a typical courtyard with a mosaic floor.

Outside Gaziantep, some 35km (21 miles) away is an open-air sculpture museum at **Yesemek** featuring late Hittite sculptures. A Neolithic site at **Doliche** is located 11km (7 miles) north of the city. Nearby **Kilis** is one of the most perfectly intact Ottoman towns, with picturesque streets, Ottoman baths and inhabitants who speak their own distinct dialect.

At **Birecik** there is a bird sanctuary (daily 9am–5pm; charge) specifically for the Bald Ibis, or *kelaynak*, one of the world's ugliest birds. It was built to attract Ibises migrating to and from Africa, but instead birds found the Turkish climate agreeable and the food laid on and abandoned migration.

From the Birecik reservoir, the most panoramic trip is along the lake formed by one of the region's many dams, past the submerged mosque and up to **Halfeti** and **Rumkale**, a dramatic and fearsome fortress on the hillside. You need to find a local boatman (and many will offer) to take you up the lake by boat to see the sights.

Şanlıurfa and Around

About 75km (50 miles) south of the lake formed by damming the Euphrates River lies lovely **Şanlıurfa** ❻. Known as the birthplace of Abraham, visitors can explore the mosque complex surrounding **Abraham's Cave** (İbrahim Halilullah Dergâhı; daily 8am–5.30pm; charge) and visit the pools of holy carp.

The city was once known as Edessa, and it remained an important garrison town well into Roman times. The city has over 200 historic houses and mansions in beautiful golden sandstone. There is a lively bazaar (*bedesten*) where haggling continues as it has always done. There are several notable mosques like the Rızvaniye, and the local **Şanlıurfa Museum** (Çamlık Caddesi; Tue–Sun 8.30am–noon, 1.30–5.30pm; charge) displays Assyrian, Babylonian and Hittite artefacts and several animal figures from the nearby Neolithic site of **Göbekli Tepe**, where excavations are currently uncovering significant findings.

Eastern Anatolia

Şanlıurfa	
🌐	**Population:** 800,000
📞	**Local Dialling Code:** 0414
ℹ️	**Tourist Office:** Atatürk Bulvarı; tel: 0414-312 5332
🌐	**Time Zone:** GMT +2
🚗	**Police Station:** tel: 0414-313 0000; Call Centre: 155
🚗	**Car Hire:** Avis; tel: 0414-315 0040. Euro Rent A Car; tel: 0414-313 5620
🚕	**Taxis:** Bus Station Taxi; tel: 0414-215 5346. Şanlıurfa Airport; tel: 0414-247 0278

Camels survey the beehive structures of Harran

South of Şanlıurfa, the landscape once more flattens into the Mesopotamian plain and the crossroads of civilisations. Apart from the historic atmosphere, the village of beehive houses, **Harran ❼**, will interest visitors the most. This walled city has origins that date back to the 4th millennium BC. Standing above the ruins of the ancient citadel, you overlook the scattered bits of rock and the remains of the Temple of Sin, once famous for its star-readers and savants. The distinctive houses are mostly used for storage or animal shelter now, although a couple of complexes have been done up as cafés.

Sıra Geçesi – A Şanlıurfa Soirée

A musical gathering known as a *Sıra Geçesi* is an important occasion in regional social life, particularly around Şanlıurfa. These are generally held at night and were once an opportunity for men to assemble in a non-coffee-house setting, sit on the floor, eat, dance and listen to music and discuss political issues and community problems. A *Sıra Geçesi* is now a fun-filled touristy event, extending to both genders, and including families and small children. The live band may play traditional music or there may be a DJ churning out the latest pop. Everyone can get up and dance or sing.

The Far East

Turkey's Far East is fascinating and mystical. It is a region of frontiers, conflict, cosmopolitan populations and religions that date back to biblical times. This cultural cauldron nurtured every civilisation and Mesopotamia was known as the land between two rivers.

Kars to Sarıkamış

Kars has a peculiar aura of being utterly out of place and out of time. The grid layout speaks of a Russian legacy, as does some of the city's graceful but grey neoclassical architecture;

Russians occupied Kars for 41 years until 1919. The city is dominated by a **citadel** and castle rock giving great views over the bleak plateau. It was also the setting for the award-winning novel *Snow* by Turkish Nobel Laureate Orhan Pamuk.

Forty-five km (28 miles) east of Kars, the skeleton of the medieval metropolis of **Anı ❽**, an 11th-century Armenian city sprawled across the meadows of the plateau, is one of the most impressive sights of the eastern region. At the height of its fortunes, it was a city of 100,000 inhabitants and 1,000 churches. The remains include **Anı Cathedral**, the collapsed **Church of the Holy Redeemer** (Prkitch), the **Church of St Gregory of the Abughamrents** (Tigran Honents), a mosque and the city walls. This is one of the most haunting sights anywhere, with bare remnants of the skilled architecture at which Armenians excelled.

About 65km (40 miles) southwest of Kars, gloomy **Sarıkamış** huddles into giant pines amidst the remains of old Russian barracks, a reminder of a World War I defeat without parallel (two-thirds of an army of 90,000 died from winter exposure and reckless logistical decisions) against Russian adversaries in 1915. There is a pleasant skiing piste at Cibiltepe.

Erzurum

Erzurum ❾ is Turkey's coldest city, described as a city that never recovers from its winters. It merits a stop for its glorious setting in the shadow of the giant **Palandöken** mountain range, giving it one of the most superb and challenging ski runs in Turkey.

The city's historical monuments have survived a barrage of constant warfare and destruction and most have Islamic origins, such as the three-domed tomb (Üç Kümbet), the 1179 **Great Mosque** (Ulu Camii) and the town's Seljuk architectural masterpiece, the **Twin Minaret Seminary** (Çifte Minareli Medrese). The Mongols, in their turn, built the **Yakutiye Seminary** (Yakutiye Medrese) in 1310. The Ottomans contributed the graceful **Lala Paşa Mosque** (Lala Paşa Camii) in 1562.

The city is the base for the thrilling equestrian sport of *cirit*, a Caucasian game that found its way to Turkey. In 2011, Erzurum will host the 25th Games of the Winter Universiade.

Doğubeyazıt and Mount Ararat

Outside **Doğubeyazıt** on a once-vital Turkey-Iran caravan route is the 366-room **İşak Paşa Palace** (Sarayı) **❿**. It is hauntingly grandiose and recalls ancient warlords. The impregnable position of the palatial stronghold suggests the source of their wealth.

The peak of Mount Ararat

★ THE ŞAHMERAN LEGEND

It is not possible to visit Mardin without spying a Şahmeran figure, the half-woman, half-fish icon, etched under glass. In the market, every vendor has one more ornate and more vivid than the next. Despite the conservative nature of Islam, Turkish Muslims are superstitious, and fear of *djinns* and goblins calls for talismans or amulets to ward off mythical harmful beings who might spring into real life. The Şahmeran tale has appeared frequently in the culture of Asia Minor and is an emblem of the local folklore still prevalent in the eastern part of Turkey.

Traditional Legends

The Şahmeran fish-woman, or snake-woman, is interrelated with some European mythology that involves fairies, water sprites, animal brides or Melusine fairy themes. Legends associated with the Şahmeran have specific themes and characters underpinned by oriental spirits. The name Şahmeran is possibly of Persian origin but in Turkey relates physically to the

Castle of Serpents *(Yılan Kalesi)* near Adana. It was the name given by Çukurova people to the ruined castle reputedly inhabited by a snake charmer as late as 1956.

Contemporary oral narratives in Anatolia involve a traditional scenario; the hero, a sly antagonist, conditional love with ultimatums, transgression, and separation if conditions are not met or promises broken. The serpentine

An artist painting a Şahmeran figure on glass

nature of the supernatural Şahmeran is discovered by transgression and there is usually an underlying moral, somewhat like La Fontaine fables. But predestined doom is lacking and the tales never end with retribution or calamity as is the case with so many popular fairy tales. Similar legends in European lore include Lorelei, a Rhine maiden who enticed sailors to their deaths, and the famed Sirens, bird-women water nymphs who chanted an irresistible song. The Şahmeran resembles these mythical characters in that they were invariably female, but the endings of her tales tend to be less forlorn.

The potent image of the Şahmeran

Literary Representations

The Şahmeran weaves history, oral legends and artistry all into one. On a literary level, the Şahmeran legends are often compared to *Arabian Nights*, especially in episodes with an underworld princess, feudal fairies or a spirit bride. Delve into the legends further to discover the synergy that exists between the *Tales of the Seven Sleepers* at Ephesus and *Arabian Nights*.

Glass Souvenirs

The technique used of painting under glass is one of the features of Mardin's Şahmerans. This technique is also known as *sous-verre* and was used in the 19th century and early 20th century in Turkey. The craft was a skilled one, so its survival was tenuous but is today thriving in Mardin. The glass-etched Şahmeran is a blend of folklore and fancy, a potent keepsake of the magic of Mardin.

Şahmeran images on glass and copper, for sale in Mardin's market

Just before Doğubeyazıt, unwary travellers are mesmerised by the spectre of **Mount Ararat** (Ağrı Dağı) ⓫ soaring above the clouds with snow pasting the peaks even in summer. The towering volcanic peak stands at 5,137m (16,853ft), making it one of the sheerest profiles in the world. Legend says Noah's ark grounded here, but Islamic tradition believes the Ark came to rest on the slopes of Mount Cudi in the province of Siirt.

Lake Van

Lake Van (Van Gölü) is Turkey's largest inland body of water, a saline and soda lake, 1,650m (5,450ft) above sea level. It is an endorheic lake with no outlet, topped up with the run-off from mountain streams. There is a train ferry across the lake, but in 2008 talks began with Iran to co-engineer a double-track electrified causeway. **Tatvan** is the easiest place from which to reach some of the smaller towns on the north shore of the lake, such as **Ahlat**, which is well worth a visit.

The primary reason for any visit to Lake Van is to see the 10th-century Armenian **Church of the Holy Cross** (Akdamar Kilisesi) on **Akdamar Island** ⓬. Much money was spent in 2006 to renovate this historical treasure, but Turkish authorities insisted it be a museum, not a church. Akdamar Island is reached by a 5km (3 mile) boat ride from the town of Gevaş, some 40km (24 miles) southwest of Van.

Diyarbakır

South of Van, 48km (30 miles) away, is **Hoşap Castle** (daily 8.30am–7pm; charge), built by a Kurdish despot.

Between Batman and Midyat, **Hasankeyf** was a 12th-century Artutid capital. The remains of the magnificent medieval bridge here once spanned the Tigris (Dicle) River. Reports persist of flooding the village for the Ilusu Dam (part of the state hydraulic project), but lack of investor confidence and alternative energy source development probably means a reprieve.

Locals like to call **Diyarbakır** ⓭, Turkey's most Kurdish-populated city, situated 90km (56 miles) north of Mardin, the Paris of the East. Much of the city is actually quite dreary, but European Union investment under the *acquis* protocol has indeed made the main tourist area look more like Vienna than any city in Turkey.

The most distinctive of the town's 22 older mosques is the **Grand Mosque** (Ulu Camii) halfway down Gazi Caddesi, Diyarbakır's main thoroughfare. It is similar in design to the much grander Umayyad Mosque in Damascus, a city that in many ways resembles

---

Telkari – Mardin's Syriac Jewellery

Telkari is a beautifully wrought kind of filigree jewellery that uses gold and silver wire. It was developed and is practised by the Syriac community, who are still living in the environs of Mardin. Thin strands of gold and silver are laced and braided into ornate, symbolic patterns, to be worn as necklaces, earrings, rings and even belt buckles. The craft is extremely intricate and the delicate designs require great skill. Items are much sought after and prices are by no means cheap. See the fascinating designs at www.tamtamis.com.tr.tc and www.telkarimerkezi.com.

Lake Van's vast body of water contains many small islands

Diyarbakır. The city has many other historic 'chequerboard' mosques in the black and white Syrian style.

Stretching for almost 6km (4 miles) unbroken around the old city, and once possessing 82 defensive towers, the forbidding **basalt walls** were erected during the reign of Constantine but have been restored repeatedly. They are in remarkable shape with inscriptions, geometrical and animal designs, but impart an ominous atmosphere to the city. Atatürk's villa (**Gazi Köşkü**) has been lovingly renovated as a communal centre with splendid gardens, musical entertainment and a café. A passable **Archaeology Museum** (Arkeoloji Müzesi; Elazığ Caddesi; Tue–Sun 9am–noon, 1–5.30pm; charge) contains artefacts from almost every period of history.

Mardin to Midyat

Standing on a bluff above the Mesopotamian flats, **Mardin** ⑭ is the most cosmopolitan town in Turkey with a heavy Arab influence; you will hear Arabic, Kurdish and Turkish spoken in the streets and bazaar. It has been the home of Suriyani (Jacobite) Christians since the 5th century. The **Deyrül Zarafan Monastery** (Deyr-az-Zaferan; daily 8am–noon, 1–5pm), 6km (4 miles) east of the town, was founded in AD495 on the remains of a sun temple. Still an important Syrian Orthodox parish, the monastery includes a 1,500-year-old mosaic floor. Services are held in Aramaic, the language of the Bible. The vista afforded from the town's **citadel** is magical, stretching across the vast pancake of the Syrian plain. Mardin's newest addition is the light and airy **Sakıp Sabancı Mardin City Museum** (Gül Mahallesi, 1 Caddesi, Cumhuriyet Alanı; www.sabancivakfi.org/eng; Tue–Sun 8am–7pm; charge), renovated to Mesopotamia-meets-Modern status.

Some 60km (37 miles) east, **Midyat** is the centre of the remaining but beleaguered Suriyani community. The splendid **Mor Gabriel Orthodox Monastery** is biblical in essence and fascinating in impression.

ACCOMMODATION

As eastern regions increasingly become accessible to tourists, many mansion houses have been turned into superb boutique hotels. These are the places to stay especially comfortably and authentically. But most hotels offer basic comforts and sometimes the local hotel may also be the best place for a meal.

The Near East

Anadolu Evleri
Köroğlu Sokak 6, Şahinbey, Gaziantep
Tel: 0342-220 9525
www.anadoluevleri.com
The owner has turned this magnificent old mansion into the best place to stay locally. Rooms and suites have a cool elegance. **$$$**

Edessa Hotel
Balıklıgöl Mevkii, Hasanpaşa Mevkii Karşısı, Şanlıurfa
Tel: 0414-216 4460
www.hoteledessa.com
A charming hotel renovated in traditional Urfa style, adhering to the sandstone architecture of the city's many stately homes. It has a swimming pool, fitness centre and excellent restaurant. Beautifully restored and the best place to make a base in the region. **$$$$**

Grand Hotel Gaziantep
Ali Fuat Cebesoy Bulvarı 32, Şehitkâmil
Tel: 0342-325 6565
www.gaziantepgrandhotel.com

In Mardin's stunning Erdoba Konakları hotel

One of Gaziantep's premier hotels. Plush and velvety inside, it is comfortable and close to all parts of town. Well recommended. **$$$$**

Gülizar Konukevi (Guesthouse)
İrfaniye Sokak 22, Şanlıurfa
Tel: 0414-215 0505
In the centre of the city, this lovely Syrian-Arabic-style building has a main restaurant with live Turkish entertainment. One comes here more for the relaxed, leisurely dinners (but no alcohol) than accommodation. There are eight rooms, but none has en-suite facilities. **$$$**

Harran Oteli
Sarayönü Caddesi, Atatürk Bulvarı 5, Şanlıurfa
Tel: 0414-313 2860
www.hotelharran.com/en/index.html
Located in the city centre, the Harran Oteli is one of the best-known hotels in Urfa, with the 87 rooms and 20 suites beautifully appointed; the hotel also incorporates a bar, Turkish bath, sauna and fitness centre. **$$$$**

New Merhaba Hotel
Çarşı Caddesi 49, Kâhta, Adıyaman
Tel: 0416-725 7111
A convenient base for the 3am hike up to Nemrut Dağı. **$**

Otel Kervansaray Nemrut
Karakut Köyü, Nemrut Dağı, 8km (5 miles) from the summit, Kâhta
Tel: 0416-737 2190
Low-slung old stone *caravanserai* near a waterfall on the slopes of Nemrut Dağı, with 14 simple but comfortable rooms, restaurant, pool and camping. **$$**

Tuğcan Hotel
Atatürk Bulvarı 34, Şahinbey, Gaziantep
Tel: 0342-220 4323
One of the most comfortable and well-recommended hotels in the east, complete with pool, sauna, disco, fitness centre, bar, restaurant and cocktail room. 🅼 **$$$$**

Urfa Valiliği Konukevi
Vali Fuat Caddesi, Şanlıurfa
Tel: 0414-215 9377
Built around a beautiful courtyard, this old mansion has been much done up by the provincial governor as a state guesthouse, but prices are reasonable. Service is relaxed, sometimes too much so, and hospitable. No alcohol served. **$$**

The Far East
Büyük Mardin Oteli
Next to Meteoroloji, 2 Caddesi, Mardin
Tel: 0482-213 1047
This is a great place to stay just off the busy main street in Mardin but close to all sights, shops and some sounds. **$$$**

Büyük Urartu
Cumhuriyet Caddesi, Van
Tel: 0432-212 0660
The hotel is well known in the area with two restaurants, bars and a disco. A good base for touring the Van and Akdamar sights. **$$**

Dedeman Dıyarbakır Hotel
Elazığ Caddesi, Yeni Belediye Sarayı Yanı, Diyarbakır
Tel: 0412-229 0000
www.dedemen.com.tr
The city's best accommodation, with a restaurant-cum-bar, fitness centre and pool. **$$**

Dedeman Palandöken Ski Centre
Palandöken Dağı PK 115, Erzurum
Tel: 0442-316 2414
www.dedemen.com.tr
Set in a mountainous ski resort with Turkey's longest ski run, the hotel has 196 rooms and every facility. Open all year, but the ski season is usually from mid-November to May. 🅼 **$$$**

Erdoba Konakları
1 Caddesi 135, Mardin
Tel: 0482-213 7787
www.erdoba.com.tr
One of Mardin's beautiful houses converted into an hotel along traditional lines. Furnishings are in keeping with the old building. Views stretch across the Syrian plain. **$$$$**

Otel Büyük Kervansaray
Gazi Caddesi, Diyarbakır
Tel: 0412-228 9606
A 16th-century sandstone *caravanserai* recently refurbished into atmospheric glory. Courtyard garden, restaurant and pool. **$$$$**

RESTAURANTS

The glory of Eastern Turkey is food, food and fabulous food. This is not the Ottoman style of 'palace' cuisine but earthy, nutty flavours. Gaziantep in particular is fanatical about its food. The use of spices is wonderfully refined in the east, and wherever you eat, you can expect it to be hot.

Restaurant Price Categories
Price categories are based on a three-course meal for one (including *meze*, grilled meat, bread, salad and fruit) and non-alcoholic drinks.

$ = under 20TL
$$ = 20–40TL
$$$ = 40–60TL
$$$$ = 60–100TL

The Near East
Doğan Et Lokantası (Meat Restaurant)
Gözde 2 Sitesi Altı 7, Kahramanmaraş
Tel: 0344-225 2929

www.doganetlokantasi.com
Simple restaurant specialising in kebaps and succulent meats and vegetables baked in earthenware pots. **$$**

Harran Otel Restoran
Harran Otel, Sarayönü Caddesi, Atatürk
Bulvarı 5, Şanlıurfa
Tel: 0414-313 2860
www.hotelharran.com/en/index.html
Famed for its Urfa kebaps, but the restaurant is outstandingly good at spicy Eastern dishes. **$$$**

İmam Cağdaş Kebap ve Baklava Restoran
Uzunçarşı 49, Gaziantep
Tel: 0342-220 4545
www.imamcagdas.com
Wide range of meat and vegetable dishes freshly prepared. You choose your food cafeteria style; it gets busy at lunch time. One of the most economical places to eat. Closed Sun and religious holidays. 🍴 **$**

Orkide Pastaneleri ve Café
Gazi Muhtar Paşa Bulvarı 17, Şehitkâmil,
Gaziantep
Tel: 0342-215 1500
www.orkidepastanesi.com
If you had to go to only one place in Gaziantep, it would be Orkide. They make the richest, most delectable *baklava* in Turkey, loaded with the local pistachios, and the café maintains scrupulous health and hygiene standards. The café menu is also innovative enough to tempt you away from the baklava. 🍴 **$$$**

Turaç Ocakbaşı
Cahit Zarifoğlu Bulvarı, Kahramanmaraş
Tel: 0344-214 1483
www.turacocakbasi.com
Local food and tasty meats grilled over an open charcoal fire. **$**

Tandır Restoran
Sarayonu Caddesi, Şanlıurfa
Tel: 0414-215 5378
Impressive choice of Urfa kebaps, *lahmacun* and meatballs *(çiğ köfte)*. **$$**

Üçler Kebap ve Baklava Salonu
Zübeyde Hanım Bulvarı (behind SSK hospital), Şehitkâmil, Gaziantep
Tel: 0342-338 1828

Friendly and bustling family restaurant with simple but succulent home-made cuisine to match. Closed Sun and religious holidays. **$$**

The Far East
Cercis Murat Konağı
1 Caddesi 517, Mardin
Tel: 0482-213 6841
www.cercismurat.com
Fabulous views right across to Syria from the terrace. Once an old Syriac mansion and now, as a restaurant, this is a top eatery. It is always busy from morning until late, meaning waiters are rushed and can be snooty. The place to imagine yourself in the 'Fertile (gourmet) Crescent'. **$$$$**

Gazi Köşkü Köşk Sofrası
(Atatürk Villa)
Tel: 0412-226 3333
The founding father's original villa done up for everybody to enjoy with low-level seating, music and convivial atmosphere. 🍴 **$**

Gel-Gör Çağ Kebap
Salonları Kongre Caddesi, Nazik Çarşı 10,
Erzurum
Tel: 0442-213 3253
Traditional Turkish kebap salon. **$**

Güzelyurt Restoran
Cumhuriyet Caddesi 54, Erzurum
Tel: 0442-235 5001
Famed for its juicy and tasty kebaps and as one of the most enduring restaurants in the city. **$$**

İsot Lahmacun
Gevran Caddesi, Diyarbakır
Tel: 0412-224 7439
Specialises in tasty Turkish pizza with meat and tomato sauce on a delicate crust. *İsot* is a fiery hot Eastern dried pepper said to improve vocal cords! 🍴 **$**

Selim Amca
Ali Emiri Caddesi 22, Diyarbakır
Tel: 0412-224 4447
Spicy kebaps and a good selection of starters *(meze)*. **$**

TOURS

If you come to the eastern reaches of Turkey, chances are you are already on a comprehensive tour and this is another stop along the way. But if you come independently, local agents are a source of knowledge and information. Many travel agents can also organise day trips to Aleppo in Syria.

Arota Turizm
Değirmicem Mahallesi, Gazi Mustafa Kemal Paşa Bulvarı 31/C, Gaziantep
Tel: 0342-230 3010
Organises tours of the holy city of Şanlıurfa and of Nemrut Dağı, as well as to southeast Turkey.

Erek Turizm
Donat İşhanı, Kat 2, Beşyol, Van
Tel: 0432-214 3800
Sightseeing tours of the Van area including the lake, town, Akdamar Island and Hoşap Castle.

Kantara Turizm
Atatürk Bulvarı, Şaban Sokak 2/3, Gaziantep
Tel: 0342-220 6300
www.kantara.com.tr
Special tours of the dam projects of the massive southeastern Anatolia Project.

Şahinbey Turizm
Gaziler Caddesi, Kirişci Sokak 17/1, Gaziantep
Tel: 0342-230 3152
Local tours of Gaziantep, Şanlıurfa and Nemrut Dağı.

Listings

FESTIVALS AND EVENTS

The eastern region has many ethnic festivals that are often to do with food or local produce, such as watermelons or pistachios. They are worth promoting because they bring revenue to the area, but festivals are also a satisfactory way of having fun while experiencing an alternative culture.

March
Nevruz
Southeast Turkey, 18–21 Mar
Celebration of Kurdish New Year and the rites of spring.

May
Bald Ibis Festival
Birecik, 8 May
An annual event celebrating the bald ibis *(kelaynak)* on the day they are said to always return to Birecik.

July
Malatya Apricot Festival
Malatya, 2 July
An event to promote Malatya and apricots, with various festivities, sports, activities, concerts and apricot contests organised.

September
Watermelon Festival
Diyarbakır, 5 Sept
Watermelon Festival to judge the weightiest, heftiest melons.

Gaziantep Pistachio Festival
Gaziantep, 1–5 Sept
What began as a gourmet festival to promote Antep cuisine has become a small-scale arts and culture event.

Taste the juiciest watermelons in Diyarbakır

Accommodation

Turkey offers accommodation in all budget ranges from camping sites to the most luxurious and sensuous hotels. Many period houses are increasingly being renovated as hotels and boutique accommodation, but may not have lifts, which may be a problem for some visitors, so it pays to check if this is important to you.

The Aegean and Mediterranean coasts are replete with many expansive and lavish resorts which can get quite crowded in the high summer season (May to October). Many Europeans who have become second-home owners in Turkey have self-catering villas to rent out by the week or month; this provides an intriguing alternative to all-inclusive packages at the many coastal resorts. Expect most prices to be about 15 or 20 percent lower between October and April, but smaller hotels or pensions may close in October and not reopen until April (see p.12–3).

CHOOSING A HOTEL

Your choice will be affected by the kind of holiday you wish to have, how much money you wish to spend and the amenities you are looking for. Whichever hotel you choose, booking in advance using an online form will be cheaper. Even if you ring up a day or so in advance, this will still be more economical than the walk-in price. If you are on a package tour, especially one with all-inclusive meals and activities, the price is most often ridiculously cheap even for high-end and high-season accommodation. In off-season periods, you may find deals where hotels or travel agencies will even throw in the return cost of a flight from European start points. Whether you book independently or through an operator, note that the vast majority of hotels quote prices per room, including breakfast.

Local Turkish tourist offices will give you a list of available accommodation, rooms or apartments. Unlike many countries, they will not book hotel accommodation for you. To secure a room, you will need to give your credit card number. Read the terms on the hotel's website if you are booking independently, especially regarding cancellation. If you arrive before noon, chances are your room

Even smart hotels may offer inexpensive rates in the off-season

will not yet be ready. If this matters, then book a day earlier.

If you are a peace-lover rather than a party animal and choosing a hotel during the day, think about the proximity of night-time activity; somewhere that is peaceful at 10am may be throbbing with disco music through the night.

Many İstanbul hotels boast fantastic views from roof terraces

HOTEL CATEGORIES

The Ministry of Tourism, as well as local municipalities, used to classify hotels and pensions by a star rating system. This was confusing as tourists did not know which star was which or given by what authority and so the system was open to abuse. The star rating system is far less important today though, as almost every hotel can let you see your room, restaurants, bars and swimming pools and beaches online. Many give you a 360-degree virtual tour, allowing you to be familiar with the hotel of your choice before you arrive. Even what local people rated as Turkey's 'S' (for Special) Hotels, a category that covered renovated period houses, are now called boutique hotels, like everywhere else.

A five-star hotel in Turkey will conform to the luxury level of any of the international chains such as Inter Continental, Hilton, Hyatt and Swissotel. Although their rooms are expensive, they all offer very attractive weekend, special occasion or spa packages.

APART-HOTELS

An apart-hotel offers some of the independence of being in your own flat, but with the services associated with a comfortable hotel. In İstanbul this form of accommodation has been developed as a way of renovating and adapting attractive older apartment buildings without substantially changing their character. Many of the luxury-grade hotels also offer residential suites within the hotel complex. If you choose an apart-hotel in a seaside area or at a more moderate price, check carefully what the price includes. You may be expected to pay extra for hot water, electricity or gas canisters for cooking.

Accommodation

A pension stay can be a good way to interact with Turkish families in a characterful environment

PENSIONS

A Turkish *pansiyon* is somewhere between a simple hotel and a bed-and-breakfast. They can be lovely places to stay, especially if they are run by a family. At the seaside resorts you will find that they are often used by Turkish families on their summer holidays and only offer full-board or half-board terms in high season. The more expensive will have en-suite facilities attached to every room. In some, hot water is heated by solar panels on the roof and may run out, at least until the next sunrise. What they lack in facilities they will more than make up for in charm and camaraderie.

YOUTH HOSTELS

Accommodation is so reasonably priced in Turkey that there are very few youth hostels as such. It is possible, out of term time, to stay in empty student dormitories or halls of residence or in teachers' accommodation

(*öğretmen evi*), but the rooms will be spartan with few facilities.

CAMPING

The best camping areas are close to the seaside resorts, and have all the necessary amenities, including showers, shops, restaurants and activities. They welcome caravans, tents or those who want a simple cabin. Camping is surprisingly well developed and hugely popular. Costs are generally on a par with a modest hotel or pension.

The best place to learn about camp-sites in every region of Turkey is from the website www.nereyenereden.com, undoubtedly Turkey's most informative and accurate forum in many languages. Many campsites are closed in winter. Camping should only be done on designated grounds; wild camping is not illegal but not recommended other than when trekking, as the police may come to investigate or move you on.

Transport

GETTING TO TURKEY

No matter which way you are thinking of getting to Turkey, by air, sea, coach or your own car, don't leave home until you have checked out the country's best and most comprehensive transport site www.neredennereye.com. This means 'from where to where' and will be one of the most valuable and up-to-date travel tools you will encounter.

By Air

The flight time to İstanbul from London is about 4 hours; from New York about 9 hours. The national carrier, Turkish Airlines (www.thy.com), has three flights per week direct between Toronto and İstanbul. Most international airlines have scheduled direct or connecting flights to İstanbul's **Atatürk International Airport** from major European and Asian cities. Some budget carriers, like Easy Jet and Pegasus, have flights between London and İstanbul's second airport on the Asian side, **Sabiha Gökçen**. Onur Air also flies between German destinations and Antalya and İstanbul.

If they don't begin and end their tour in İstanbul, many charter flights bring holiday-makers and group tours direct to İzmir, Bodrum-Milas, Antalya and Dalaman. To reach the eastern cities such as Adana, Trabzon or Antakya involves a connection through İstanbul.

Turkish Airlines has kept the gloves on in protecting their domestic routes, but these are slowly opening up to smaller operators like Pegasus, and also providing some more east-west routes rather than having to fly first to Ankara or İstanbul.

Travel To and From the Airport

Whichever airport you fly in to, the easiest option to get from the airport to town is by taxi, of which there is never a shortage. Many taxi drivers will not know the city but can get you to main hubs or to major hotels. Ask them to telephone your hotel if you think they are drifting around clocking up time; the fare is registered on the meter by km and time. Hotels can arrange transfers, but this can be much more expensive, although they may also do it for free, so it pays to check.

All the major cities use the Havaş shuttle-bus service between the airport and city-centre drop-off points. These have regular schedules, don't cost more than 10TL and are comfortable and safe. In İstanbul, the service

Inside Esenboga Airport in Ankara

operates every 30 minutes between 5.30am and 1am. However, if you are going to İstanbul, the easiest way into town is on the Metro, which departs from right inside the airport international terminal.

When leaving Turkey, allow plenty of time for checking in, especially in the high season. Long queues can build up both for the security checks and for passport formalities.

By Sea

With flying the main travel mode of choice, sea travel has diminished in Turkey. For a nation surrounded by water, it seems odd that this form of transport is not developed and that this is not the best way for visitors to come to Turkey, but old routes such as the Antalya to Brindisi ferry line were uneconomical and passengers were sparse. Those carrying cars were even fewer. Unless you are on a cruise ship that calls in briefly to the deep-water port in Kuşadası or the floating fortresses which increasingly dominate the İstanbul skyline,

Tram in Istanbul

the only international ferry service still operating is from Çeşme to Ancona between May and October. They sail on Saturdays and Thursdays and the journey takes two to three days. You can take your car. The best up-to-date information on ferry travel can be seen at http://ferries-turkey.com.

By Rail

The İstanbul Express travels into İstanbul from Munich, Vienna and Athens, with connecting services in Belgrade and Sofia. There are also weekly departures for İstanbul from Budapest, Bucharest and Moscow. Inter-rail tickets are valid in Turkey, but Eurail passes are not. In the UK, for information on fares contact Rail Europe: tel: 0870-837 1371; www.raileurope.co.uk. In the USA, contact Rail Europe: tel: 1877-257 2887; www.raileurope.com.

Trains from Europe arrive at **Sirkeci Station** in Eminönü, on the European side of İstanbul. If you want to proceed anywhere else in Turkey by train, you need to cross the Bosphorus to **Haydarpaşa Station** on the Asian side of the city. Train schedules and booking online can be found on www.tcdd.gov.tr or www.neredennereye.com.

By Bus or Coach

Bus services operate from major European cities, especially from Germany, Austria and Greece. They arrive at the **Esenler Coach Station**, Bayrampaşa, in western İstanbul; tel: 0212-658 0505. Varan and some other Turkish coach operators travel to Athens daily. There are free bus services that get you into the centre of İstanbul, and an overground light rail system that goes to Aksaray before linking up with the Metro.

By Car

Many visitors arrive by car through Bulgaria or Greece. At the point of entry you will need to show the car's registration documents and your driving licence. It is no longer necessary to have the car stamped in your passport but it is recorded digitally on entry that you entered with a vehicle. Normally, you cannot keep the car in Turkey for any longer than six months.

In addition to a valid local or international driving licence, you will need the car, caravan or motorcycle's proof of ownership, such as a sales invoice. A Green Insurance Card is also necessary from your insurance company. This should also be valid for the Asian side of Turkey. To be on the safe side, bring as many documents as you can in case you need to show them at police road checks or demonstrate that you have not stolen the vehicle.

GETTING AROUND TURKEY

By Air

Turkish Airlines services the bulk of cities and locales throughout the country with a good network of scheduled flights. Their supremacy is being challenged by a number of smaller airlines which has helped to bring prices down somewhat. But planes are heavily booked and you are advised to book in advance if possible. Early-morning and evening flights between Ankara and İstanbul fill up quickly. But there are often cancellations and no-shows and it is usually

Setting off for a journey from Sirkeci train station, İstanbul

possible to get a last-minute booking or wait for the next flight, which, on heavily travelled routes in and out of Ankara or İstanbul, may be a matter of an hour or so. Note that, even if you have checked baggage, you must identify it on the tarmac before you board and before it will be loaded onto the plane, particularly at smaller regional airports.

It is easy to book through any local travel agent but it is far easier and quicker to book online. The booking can often be confirmed on your mobile phone and the ticket picked up and paid for just before you collect your boarding card.

You can fly direct to the following cities from İstanbul: Adana, Ankara, Antalya, Bodrum, Bursa, Dalaman, Denizli, Diyarbakır, Erzurum, Hatay, Gaziantep, İzmir, Kayseri, Konya, Malatya, Samsun, Trabzon and Van. For many of the Anatolian destinations, it is necessary to fly via Ankara.

Ferries

Ferry transport is not the way to make progress in getting around Turkey. Only in İstanbul is the service well developed for commuters and for getting to and from the Princes Islands and several destinations on the Aegean. See details of routes and schedules at www.ido.com.tr.

Trains

Turkey has an extensive rail network with over 9,000km (5,600 miles) of track. Some of the top tourist attractions (Esphesus, to name one) can be reached by rail. Travelling by train is leisurely and pleasant, but far slower than intercity buses. However, if you book a berth on an overnight sleeper train, an excellent meal will be served in quite a formal style.

After a few false starts, Turkey is investing seriously in high-speed commuter rail services between Ankara, İstanbul and Eskişehir. Due to the lateral mountain ranges, there is no rail link to the coastal lowlands. Only Adana, Tarsus and Mersin are served by Turkish Railways from the hinterland. Rail cards or concessions are so far unavailable to non-Turks, but rail travel is extremely cheap in any case. See the Turkish State Railways website for details: www.tcdd.gov.tr. Services and schedules are more easily located in English on www.neredennereye.com/rail.

Intercity Coaches

Turkey is wonderfully served by luxurious bus companies on many routes. It is fairly economical but based on price-fixing formulas, so bargaining

An Aegean coast ferry service

isn't acceptable. Most of the long-haul bus routes leave and travel through the night. Note that buses are fully booked at religious or holiday times. When the annual military conscription intake begins, gridlock occurs and it is safer and more peaceful to travel on another day.

The major bus companies on main routes in Turkey are Pamukkale (tel: 444 3535; www.pamukkaleturizm.com.tr), Varan (tel: 444 8999; www.varan.com.tr), Ulusoy (tel: 444 1888; www.ulusoy.com.tr), Kâmil Koç (tel: 444 0562; www.kamilkoc.com.tr) and Metro (tel: 444 3455; www.metroturizm.com.tr). When booking, put the local area code in front of the country-wide (444) telephone number to book at the nearest local office of each company. All the companies above process online bookings and accept credit-card payments but tickets can only be collected by the purchaser and ID must be shown, making it impractical for visitors or tourists. Turks pay on their mobile phones. Some coaches have closed-circuit entertainment, on-board Wi-fi and even hostesses.

Driving and Fuel

Don't let alarming road tales put you off driving in Turkey. Just take your time and be calm and cautious. Turks drive on the right, but, when making a left turn, often veer hard right beforehand. Worse, vehicles entering from the right often take for granted they have priority, despite the law. It is better to be chivalrous than authoritative. If you are alert and drive as if all other drivers are raw recruits, you will be fine. Flooding, unlit vehicles and animals crossing the road are the hazards to be most aware of.

Seat belts are compulsory, as is carrying a warning triangle. Turkey has a 'zero tolerance' policy in force for drinking and driving. One drink puts you over the limit. Monetary penalties are severe and foreigners have their licences taken away and sent back to their home country's licensing authority. Talking on your mobile phone or texting whilst driving are also punishable offences. You will be vulnerable to punishment as a foreigner. If you break down, somebody will always stop to help, call a tow truck, or a local garage, who may be his friend or relative.

Turkey sells only unleaded petrol and there are very few areas that don't have an abundance of filling stations. Garages fill the tank for you and wash the windscreen into the bargain. Turkey has the most expensive petrol of any European country, approximately 3TL per litre, about £4 per gallon, or US$6.

Any foreigner with a valid licence can hire a car, although the Turkish driving age is 18. Credit-card payments are accepted universally but ask for a discount if you pay cash. If anything goes wrong, a credit-card payment helps with compensation.

Car hire is expensive (US$50–60 per day inclusive of VAT) but it helps if you book a fly-drive package. If you are more flexible, it is always cheaper to hire locally from non-brand names. Ask around or from a local tourist office, or see the Places chapters' city fact files.

Local taxi drivers are an excellent option for a day's outing to see local sites without the hassle of driving yourself. Agree the price beforehand, expect to proffer a tip and to include your driver if you stop for a meal.

Accessibility

Turkey has little in the way of conveniences for physically challenged people, except some adapted hotel rooms, making this a difficult country in which to be a disabled tourist. Every mode of transport and most museums and shopping districts are unaware of disabled needs. The good news is that compliance laws are finally in place under newly enacted 'Barrier Free İstanbul' legislation, to be phased in over the next seven years.

Keep alert on Turkey's roads

Health and Safety

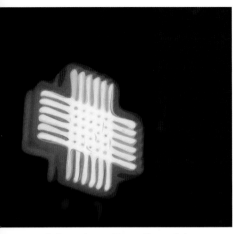

In larger towns, there will usually be a pharmacy open through the night

HEALTH CONCERNS AND MEDICAL CARE

It is not necessary to worry too much about diseases and unhealthy dangers in Turkey. In most cities and built-up areas, the standard of medical care is, at worst, adequate and, at best, very good. Doctors who have expat patients and are remote from big-city facilities today have defibrillators and sophisticated surgeries unimagined only a few years ago. Many towns have tourism doctors who speak several languages, including English. Turkey has many private hospitals and some procedures that outshine Western counterparts. Many nationalities come to Turkey for medical tourism, particularly eye surgery, with a holiday thrown in too. You have to pay up front (credit cards are accepted everywhere) but, if you have a reciprocal health plan (Britain's

National Health Service has reciprocal protocol in place with at least 10 Turkish hospitals), keep receipts and doctors' invoices to present on your return. Insurance is something you should arrange before you leave. For the vast majority of people, the worst that may happen, barring emergencies, is food poisoning, which is unpleasant but can happen anywhere.

For minor ailments, your first stop should be a pharmacy. There is always one open on a rota basis and the duty one is written up prominently in other pharmacies' windows, or displayed on a digital 'town crier' screen. If unsure of a diagnosis, the pharmacist will refer you to a doctor. All the brand-name pharmaceuticals are found in Turkey: generic drugs are vastly cheaper and just as effective. Doctors have prominent signs in any town, and even small enclaves may have a state hospital. Except opiates, all drugs and medications are available over the counter at a reasonable price; many foreigners even stock up on their paying medications.

Sunstroke, snake or scorpion bites or encounters with a sea urchin (*deniz kestane*) are dangers that should be avoided where possible. A sandfly bite is particularly dangerous and needs to be disinfected immediately. Mosquitoes are the most annoying pests and still found in many areas despite eradication programmes. If you have serious allergies, a suction kit to extract venom is essential for insect stings or bites.

It is best not to drink tap water in hotels. Some hotels put up a sign that says 'İçilmez'. This means non-potable. You may see locals drinking from public fountains, but it is better to ask if the water is from a reliable source and tested, if only because your stomach will not be used to the Turkish water. If you are not sure or want to play it safe, bottled water is available everywhere.

The best thing you can do to avoid food poisoning is to see your meal cooked freshly; get up from the table and go and look at the starters and the kitchen. If many locals are at a place, this is a positive sign. Note though that hygiene is very important for Muslims, especially in food preparation. Most places will be scrupulously clean. Use wet wipes for hands; they are available everywhere and given in restaurants (*kolonyalı mendili*). Try to avoid street food: mussels and almonds on wheels are almost guaranteed to disrupt. Anything with mayonnaise that has been ripening all day is best bypassed.

Emergency Hospitals

Ankara:
Bayındır Hospital, Söğütözü;
tel: 0312-287 9000
Çankaya Hospital, Kavaklıdere;
tel: 0312-426 1450
Güven Hospital, Aşağı Ayrancı;
tel: 0312-457 2525

Antalya:
Akdeniz University Teaching Hospital; tel: 0242-227 4343

Bodrum:
Özel Hastanesi, Mars Mabedi Caddesi, Çesmebasi Mevkii 22-43; tel: 0252-313 6566

İstanbul:
American Hospital, Güzelbahçe Sokak, Nişantaşı; tel: 0212-444 3777
Florence Nightingale Hospital, Abide-i Hürriyet Caddesi 290, Şişli; tel: 0212-224 4950
German Hospital, Sıraselviler Caddesi 119, Taksim; tel: 0212-293 2150

İzmir:
Başkent Hospital, Bostanlı Karşıyaka; tel: 0232-330 5230
Sağlık Hospital, 1399 Sokak 25, Alsancak; tel: 0232-463 7700

Health and Safety

Take precautions with the strong Turkish sun to avoid burning and sunstroke

A local 'Polis' car on patrol

CRIME AND SAFETY

Turkey overall has an enviably low crime record. Foreigners and tourists are regarded as guests, so are very well treated. But in big cities, there are the obvious temptations when foreigners appear prosperous or well off. Pickpocketing or bag snatching are increasing in İstanbul. Keep money safe, not in outer pockets. Keep your bag secure and never leave it looped over the back of a chair in public places. Big cities have tourist police and these are polite and try to be helpful. Some may speak other languages but, in general, Turkish police are there to protect the state and, unless you have committed a criminal offence, may seem uninterested. Indeed, Turkish people call the police only in the most desperate emergencies.

Like other countries, Turkey has strict laws in place for possession of, or dealing in, narcotics. Even if you see or know Turks doing this, as a foreigner you could take the rap. The same goes for gay travellers. Homosexuality is scarcely new to Turkey and is legal, while İstanbul has a thriving gay community and quarter. But it is one of the anomalies of Turkish life that it is fine for locals but not so OK for visitors; harassment and even physical abuse are a risk. Be discreet and avoid overt displays of affection.

Ominous warnings are given about terrorist activities, but rarely are foreign tourists involved. The British Foreign Office and US Department of State issue travel advice that highlights incidents or no-go areas (UK: www.fco.gov.uk/travel; US: http://travel.state.gov) and provide consular assistance details.

Much of Turkey is in an earthquake zone. Many hotels now include leaflets and instructions on what to do in the unlikely event of this happening. In particular, don't shelter in wardrobes!

FOREIGN MISSIONS AND HONORARY CONSULATES

Australian Embassy:
MNG Building, Uğur Mumcu
Caddesi 88, 7th Floor, Gaziosmanpaşa;
tel: 0312-459 9521
Honorary Consulate: Asker Ocağı
Caddesi, 15, Elmadağı Şişli, İstanbul;
tel: 0212-243 1333

Canadian Embassy:
l Cinnah Caddesi 58, Çankaya,
Ankara; tel: 0312-409 2700
Honorary Consulate: Istiklâl Caddesi
189/5, Beyoğlu, İstanbul; tel: 0212-251
9838

New Zealand Embassy:
İran Caddesi. 13/4, Kavaklıdere,
Ankara; tel: 0312-467 9054

UK Embassy:
l Şehit Ersan Caddesi 46/A, Çankaya,
Ankara; tel: 0312-455 3344; http://
ukinturkey.fco.gov.uk/en
Honorary Consulate: Mesrutiyet
Caddesi 34, Tepebaşı, Beyoğlu,
İstanbul; tel: 0212-334 6400
British Vice Consulate: Antalya;
tel: 0242-244 5313;
email: britconant@turk.net

Emergency Contact

Wherever you are in Turkey, the 3-digit
numbers will answer local emergency
calls from any telephone, including your
mobile. Not all will speak English.

Ambulance: 112
Fire: 110
Police: (urban areas) 155
Gendarme: (rural areas) 156
Forest Fires: 177
Coastguard: 158
Health Information: 184
Traffic Information: 154
Municipal Services: 133

British Honorary Consulate:
Fethiye; tel: 0252-614 6302; email:
bhcfethiye@superonline.com
Marmaris: tel: 0252-412 6486, ext: 36
and 39; email: brithonmar@superon-
line.com

US Embassy:
l Atatürk Boulevard 110, Kavaklıdere,
Ankara; tel: 0312-455 5555
Honorary Consulate: l Kaplıcalor
Mevkii 2, İstinye, İstanbul;
tel: 0212-335 9000

Beware of the popular street-food mussels if you're worried about your stomach *(see p.257)*

Money and Budgeting

CURRENCY

The currency is the Turkish lira. Notes come in units of 5, 10, 20, 50, 100 and 200 lira denominations. A feature of the notes is that each denomination is a different size to prevent forgery. The lira is divided into 100 kuruş and metal coins are in 1, 5, 10, 25, 50 kuruş and one-lira divisions. Check the most recent exchange rates on www.xe.com.

Unlimited foreign currency can be brought into Turkey and US$5,000 can be taken out in cash. Other amounts need to be brought in via a bank.

If you change money from a foreign currency into Turkish lira in Turkey or at the airport on arrival, you will find a much better exchange rate than outside the country. Banks give poor rates and you can always find a somewhat better rate at a change office, or *döviz*. Additionally, the Turkish Post Office, PTT, has change facilities. The rate is often good but they charge a commission on top, where others do not.

CASH AND CARDS

Both state and private banks are ubiquitous all over Turkey. They all have ATMs for withdrawal of cash 24/7. Most will dispense a maximum of 900TL daily on one card. Expect to pay a premium for withdrawing money abroad or not from your own bank. Most ATMs dispense money in TL but increasingly offer other currency choices like the euro or the US dollar. ATMs are all multilingual.

Traveller's cheques, like faxes, are limping on their last legs. It is as safe to use your debit or credit card at ATMs. At bazaars, most traders will drool over hard cash. If you also don't want a receipt, you will have the upper hand in bargaining on anything that does not have state-controlled prices. Diner's Club is less acceptable in Turkey and is rarely seen or used, but other credit cards are accepted everywhere for almost every service.

Credit-card fraud is on the rise, as everywhere. Take care when plugging into an ATM and take note of people who crowd you or look too closely as you enter your PIN. Keep all credit cards safe and be sure to keep numbers with you on where to call if your card is lost or stolen.

TIPPING

It is customary to tip anyone who does you a small service, such as porters, a doorman or concierge who calls you a taxi or books a theatre ticket. If you want something special or important, expect to tip more. If

Hard cash is king in the bazaars

someone has brought your bags up to the room for you, just a few lira will be welcome. Turks have become used to tips and many now expect them.

At restaurants it is customary to leave a 10 to 15 percent tip. Waiters will always remember you if you give it direct to them in cash. Don't feel obligated to leave any tip for restaurants who add it to the bill, itemised as *servis*. The word for tip in Turkish is *bahşiş*.

Taxi fares are usually rounded up without the concept of giving a tip. If a taxi driver has unloaded your bags or found your hotel without driving all around the city, tip a few lira. However, if a taxi driver is rude and haughty, don't feel obligated to augment the meter charge.

TAX

Turkey's most lucrative tax is Value Added Tax, or VAT. It is called KDV in Turkish and is inclusive in all touristic and retail purchases and services. It is currently charged at 18 percent. Many stores offer Tax-Free shopping under the Global Refund scheme and display a logo in the window of the shop. It saves you money on large purchases like carpets, as you must spend over 200 Turkish lira to benefit. Although nothing is entirely duty-free, you can claim back about 16 percent of the tax on your purchase. You need to fill out the required forms (a retailer will supply and stamp them) and present them to Customs on exit to receive your refund.

BUDGETING FOR YOUR TRIP

Food may seem cheaper, but adding on alcohol can make a meal expensive. Hotels tend to charge standard

European prices (upwards of €100 for a room). However, an all-inclusive package holiday that includes meals and transfers can make Turkey seem very economical, with the price of an hotel in a 5-star resort being as low as US$60 to US$100 (£40 to £65) per night.

Budget package holidays from the UK to Turkey are advertised extensively in all newspapers in the travel section, in magazines and on the internet. It is possible to find bargain flights and it pays to shop around. From the USA, travel agents or tour operators offer all-inclusive group packages to Turkey. Expect to pay anything above US$4,000 (£2,660) for a 10-day tour including flight, hotels and meals, but exclusive of alcohol. Read the small print carefully.

For a budget, backpacker-style holiday you will need to set aside £400/US$600) per person per week. A standard family holiday for four will cost around £1,200 /US$1,800) per week. A high-class, no-expense-spared break could cost anything up to £10,000/US$15,100 per person, more on a luxury yacht.

Responsible Travel

On the waymarked Lycian Way

GREEN TRAVEL

Environmentally friendly concepts have come quite late to Turkey. Recycling and the like are discussed in the news and there are many activists, but if there is money to be made, environmental concepts tend to go out the window. Carbon offsetting is, thus far, mainly the domain of enthusiasts and has not filtered down to Turkish tourism sources as yet. Ecotourism has been fostered more by outsiders, but the success of opening up trails and waymarking them professionally as with the Lycian Way Walk and St Paul's Trail, along with promoting spa and health tourism, has given the Culture and Tourism Ministry a heads up on alternative tourism potential.

ETHICAL TOURISM

Whilst many travel firms arrange tours in a natural environment, there is only one Turkish agent that sets out specifically to promote conservation and sustainable development. This is **TEMA** (Turkish Foundation for Combating Soil Erosion), a non-profit foundation that has opened up remote regions of Turkey, Borçka and Barhal on the Georgian border. They are dynamically engaged in ventures that promote biodiversity in small hamlets, providing a lifeline to dwindling populations whilst preserving the traditions that make these people unique.

Biyotematur is TEMA's own boutique travel agency specialising in exceptional ecological tours to traditional districts (TEMA Tours; Çayır Çimen Sokak, Emlak Kredi Blokları, A-2 Blok, D: 10, Levent, İstanbul; tel: 0212-283 7816; www.biyotematur. com). They also support and revive spring-water sources in remote places. Some of their tours include a Dendrological Tour to observe Alpine and sub-Alpine flora and herbaceous shrubs. There are also geological and birding-themed tours and a fascinating Oak Tree tour over the border in Georgia. They are also committed to preserving the Caucasian honey bee and offer an exclusive bee safari.

VOLUNTEERING

Reputable volunteering holidays in the destination include those through **Handsup Holidays** (http://www.handsupholidays.com), who offer 15-day volunteer trips focused on community development projects. **Cadip** (http://cadip.org/volunteer-in-turkey.htm) arrange various teenage projects that connect foreign and Turkish kids on volunteer work projects.

Family Holidays

TRAVELLING WITH CHILDREN

Close-knit families are the backbone of Turkish life and this is probably why Turks extend the warmest welcome to visitors who come with children. It is unnecessary to even wonder if you can bring children to Turkey. Better to say that, if you don't like children, then Turkey may not be the place for you. Marriage and having children are a milestone in life and everything is geared to families being together. Many people bring small babies on holiday and Turkey has all the baby foods, formula and brand-name accessories found at home, so don't bother lugging them along. They may be a bit more expensive in Turkey, but even small supermarkets have a well-stocked infants section. Note that it is safer to mix formula with bottled water. Bring your own light pushchair for tots.

HOTELS AND RESTAURANTS

Hotels will always put up an extra cot for kids, and up until the age of 12 years there is no charge for children in a room with their parents. Restaurants, too, welcome children. They will make a great fuss of them, draw up extra chairs or high chairs. You will find that many restaurants have unruly children running around ad-lib, so meeting other children is easy.

Most children will enjoy Turkish grills and some *meze*, but many restaurants feature a children's menu, even if it comprises something 'fast' with chips. Turks adore children and indulge them; so if there is nothing on the menu they fancy, a chef will usually make them something else.

CHILDREN'S ACTIVITIES

Activities and sports are laid on for children at holiday clubs in many hotels, but in cities, there are not a lot of activities designed specifically with children in mind. However, children will probably enjoy the mini cities in Antalya and İstanbul, or the many zoos, fun fairs *(lunapark)* or aquaparks, not to mention museums like İstanbul's Ataman Car Museum or the Rahmi Koç Industrial Museum.

For older children, activities such as water-skiing have no age restrictions as long as the child can swim and wears a life preserver, but paragliding, canyoning and other extreme sports are officially restricted to over 18s.

Kayaking on Dalaman beach

History

Turkey is rich in tales of conquest and glory and the country overflows with historical remains from every period. The findings of many extensive excavations have shed light on ancient civilizations, while the country has also been the setting of several more mythological tales: Homer's *Iliad* relates the legend of Odysseus' wooden horse, presented as a gift to the Trojans, but filled with soldiers who crept out under cover of darkness, freeing the kidnapped Helen and her 'face that launched a thousand ships', and sacking Troy in the process.

Greater veracity can be accorded to the discoveries of how life was once lived at Pergamon and Ephesus, farther south along the Aegean coast. Here, great libraries once attracted the ancient world's scholars. Indeed, Byzantines, Seljuks and Ottomans have left their creative or civic footprints around most of Turkey. In more recent times, Gallipoli is known for the tragic World War I campaign in 1915, in which more than 500,000 Allied troops and Turks died. Turkey's history and more political approach to it today is inextricably linked to the revolution soon after, which saw the birth of the modern state under the founding father of Mustafa Kemal Atatürk.

CONQUERORS AND THE CONQUERED

Some of the oldest human remains outside Africa (about 1 million years old) have been found in Anatolia. By 10,000 years ago, Palaeolithic peoples

Clay sculpture of a Mother Goddess

were painting caves at Beldibi near Antalya. By 6,250BC, there were flourishing towns. Çatalhöyük, south of Konya, is officially listed as the second-oldest town in the world, trailing Jericho. It had a population of around 5,000, and is the first place in the world known to have used irrigation and domesticated sheep and pigs.

By the 2nd millennium BC, written history was in the making. In the west, the early Greek Empire was flourishing; Troy was already 1,000 years old. The Hittites, who crossed the Caucasus to establish a stronghold in central Anatolia, were waging war against Egypt and Mesopotamia, leaving behind them sites such as Boğazköy (Hattuşaş), Yazılıkaya, Alacahöyük and Karatepe, not to mention an effervescence of culture and creative works.

From the 13th century BC, the wave of invading armies and navies from Greece saw colonisation intensifying. The Phrygians moved down from Thrace, taking over most of central and western Turkey. Little now remains of their empire other than the ruined city at Gordium, home of King Midas of the golden touch.

The Lydians settled in Sardis near the Aegean coast, their fortunes reaching a pinnacle under the staggeringly rich King Croesus, who invented coins and dice. The wild coast of the southwest Mediterranean was the territory of the Lycians, described by the Hittites as a proudly independent, ungovernable, matriarchal society. The people of Xanthos twice took this desire for independence to extremes, preferring collective suicide to surrender. As Greek city-states sprang up around the coast from Pergamon to Aspendos, theatres, temples, colonnades and bathhouses showed that life was becoming extremely comfortable, helped by growing international trade, both east to Asia and west to Europe.

This affluent society tempted envious outsiders, and in 546BC the Persians, led by Cyrus II, swept west from Persepolis, conquering much of Anatolia. Their stranglehold was only broken in 334BC by the nexr great imperialist, the young Macedonian king, Alexander the Great. Over the next two centuries, the original cultures and languages of ancient Anatolia were gradually engulfed by classical Greek civilisation.

In 133BC, the king of Pergamon left his kingdom to the Romans. From this toehold, the Romans expanded rapidly, creating many city-states and kingdoms throughout Anatolia. This was Asia Minor. With the Romans came the relative calm and prosperity of the *pax romana*. All was not entirely peaceful, however. The 3rd century AD saw violent invasions by the Goths and Persians.

EARLY CHRISTIANS TO THE SELJUKS

Southeastern Turkey has long nursed biblical history. Legend places Abraham as living at Harran in eastern Anatolia and Noah's Ark as having grounded on Mount Ararat. From the 1st century AD, Christianity began to take a tenuous hold across the Roman Empire. It was in Antakya (Antioch) that saints Peter, Paul and Barnabas first founded and named the Christian religion. St Paul, brought up in Tarsus as Saul the tax collector before his revelation on the road to Damascus, followed an itinerary that may well be the envy of a modern traveller,

The soft rock of Cappadocia sheltered early and persecuted Christians

preaching at Alexandria Troas, Assos, Ephesus, Patara, Myra and elsewhere in Asia Minor. St John the Evangelist settled in Ephesus. Some of the most dramatic stories of the early Christians are those of Cappadocia, whose inhabitants found the cave-riddled landscape ideally suited to hermetic monasticism and the construction of simple underground churches. Almost 600 of these remain.

In AD313, Emperor Constantine gave up the unequal struggle and declared Christianity the official religion of the empire, although he himself only converted on his death-bed in 337. By 325, Christianity had split into so many factions that Constantine convened a conference, held at Nicaea (modern İznik), that laid down the basic tenets of the faith, including the Nicene Creed.

Meanwhile, the western part of the empire was under increasing pressure from invaders. In 330, Constantine moved from Rome to his new capital, Constantinople, built on and around Byzantium. The empire split into independently ruled eastern and western halves a few decades after Constantine's death in 337. The western half, still ruled from Rome but starved of cash, limped on until its demise in the 6th century.

The eastern (Byzantine) empire flourished. Constantinople grew ever more splendid with vast palaces and great churches, the finest being Hagia Sofia, built by Emperor Justinian in AD527 and still a star attraction. However, the borders of the empire were tested by the Slavs in the west, the Avars from Central Asia and the Sassanid Persians in the southeast. In 654, religion again began to rupture the land with the first arrival of Islam. This came via ferocious Arab warriors who reached all the way to the gates of Constantinople before they were repulsed. A second attack in 717–18 gained the Arabs most of the empire's eastern provinces. Islam brought a new civilisation, a different religion, language and script.

By AD1000, Asia Minor was overrun by a new threat in the form of the Seljuks, warriors who traced their origins to the Asian steppes. In 1071 at the Battle of Manzikert, they routed the Byzantine army, capturing the emperor who was deposed while in captivity. The 13th century saw the heyday of the Seljuks, who, from the Sultanate of Rum based in Konya, swallowed up vast swathes of the Byzantine Empire. What remains of the *caravanserais* (hostelries), bridges and roads built in their territories to facilitate trade along the Silk Route, attests to their immense but short-lived power. They were toppled by the 13th-century Mongol invasions of Genghis Khan.

The beleaguered Byzantines faced annihilation from all directions. In the northeast, the Armenians took advantage of the empire's weakness to carve out an independent state. In the west, Christian Europe marched east on a Holy Crusade. Frederick Barbarossa persuaded the Seljuks to attack Constantinople in 1175, and, in 1204, the Fourth Crusade ransacked Constantinople and set up a new Norman Empire. The Byzantine emperors, who fled to Nicaea, only recovered their city in 1261.

THE OTTOMANS

There is still historical conjecture about the origins of the Ottoman dynasty, which seemingly sprang from nowhere. Ottomans helped the Seljuks defeat the Mongol invaders and were given land near Eskişehir in central Anatolia in gratitude. Over the next 200 years or so, the armies of one sultan after another raised the Ottoman standard on new territories. In 1402, the Mongols reappeared led by Tamerlane, and very nearly succeeded in stopping the Ottoman advance. But in 1453, Mehmet II, the Conqueror, captured Constantinople, renaming it İstanbul. He built a grand new palace, the Topkapı. It was the end of the Byzantine empire.

By 1520, Sultan Selim I had brought Palestine, Egypt and Syria under Ottoman control. Between 1520 and 1566, the Ottoman Empire flourished under the enlightened reign of Süleyman the Magnificent, who advanced frontiers and added territory from northern Africa and Iraq and the Balkans. The Holy cities of Medina and Mecca were under Ottoman rule and Constantinople became the keeper of the Islamic faith. Süleyman was regarded as a just administrator and a cultured ruler. With the help of his Imperial architect, Mimar Sinan, he built some of the empire's greatest mosques, Turkish baths and civic buildings. Unfortunately, his favourite wife, Roxelana, was an ambitious former concubine who schemed to promote the succession of her own first-born son, Selim II (the Sot) by murdering several other potential successors to the throne, including another of her sons.

Mehmet II, known as the Conqueror

DECLINE AND FALL

The Ottoman economy was fundamentally a war one, bolstered and held in place by conquests and territorial expansion. Under imprudent, sometimes reckless, government, it began to crumble under its own weight. By 1700, the Ottomans had lost some of their European holdings, and by the 1800s, Greece, Egypt, Lebanon and other territories were agitating for autonomy. Dissent then stirred in the sultan's elite and unswerving army, the Janissaries, who were brutally put down in 1826.

By this time, Western Europeans controlled much of the Ottoman economy, at the same time enjoying the gaiety and intrigue of 'Con', as they called

Constantinople/İstanbul. They gradually tightened their grasp and influence, and this left the last sultans as effective pawns to foreign conspirators.

In 1854, the empire was saved from Russian domination by the French and British, who sided with the Turks during the Crimean War. Despite the passing of significant reforms between 1839 and 1876 that were designed to curtail the dissolution of the Ottoman Empire (the Tanzimat Reforms), sultan Mahmut II was under the sway of the European powers who had rallied to his defence in Crimea. His authority was diluted and this only served to weaken and undermine the empire further.

The final spasms of the empire saw a last-ditch effort at pomp and power in the frenzied building of flamboyant and costly Baroque buildings that they could ill afford, like the Dolmabahçe Palace. The first great political challenge to the sultans' power came from the Committee of Union and Progress (CUP), known as the Young Turks, whose three pashas, Enver, Cemal and Talaat, led a revolution in 1908 to force elections and the reopening of Parliament. The party, with its pan-Turkic ideology, represented the beginning of active Turkish nationalism.

The empire lost more territory in the Balkan Wars of 1912–13 and in the aftermath of World War I, in which Turkey sided with Germany and the Axis, ending up on the losing side. Involvement in the latter resulted in the loss of millions of lives, with disaster following disaster. The situation in the remote eastern provinces, where many Armenian nationalists sided with tsarist Russia or France on the promise of future independence, was considered especially critical. Already suspicious of the loyalties of resident Christian, Jewish and Greek Ottoman subjects, the CTP authorities ordered the deportation of all Armenian civilians, except those in İzmir and İstanbul, on 24 April, 1915. Hundreds of thousands were rounded up and marched towards detention camps in Mesopotamia; few made it there, the majority being killed at the outset or falling victim to disease or starvation. Around 1.5 million Armenians are thought to have perished and their part in Turkish history expunged from the official record. Referrals to this mass 'deportation' as

The Crimean War, as depicted here, was a small but bloody conflict

being a genocide are hotly contested by Turkey today and the issue remains a deeply contentious one.

BIRTH OF A NATION

Following the war, France, Germany, Britain and Italy all had designs (or mandates) on choice parts of the Empire. But in 1919, a young lieutenant who had excelled at Gallipoli in 1914, Mustafa Kemal, rallied his friends, fellow officers and former politicians to form an independence movement, bringing Turkey almost to the brink of civil war in the process, as many Ottomans believed their future lay with the religious Caliphate. In April 1920, he called the first meeting of the Grand National Assembly, and by 1922 his armies had forced the Greeks out of Anatolia in a war for the survival of Turkey. To rid Anatolia of foreign influence once and for all, a bizarre exchange of populations took place in 1923 expelling Greek and other Christian Ottomans to Greece, and sending Muslim Greeks to Turkey.

Few wars left such a durable national cult leader than the 1921–2 Turkish War of Independence (Kurtuluş Savaşı). Kemal, taking the name Atatürk, became the president of the new Turkish Republic in 1923 and a national father figure. In short order, he ushered in changes to undo centuries of tradition and create a secular, rather than Muslim, state. Polygamy was abolished, alcohol legalised, the fez and turban prohibited, education for women made mandatory, dervish orders outlawed, the Muslim calendar replaced and, fundamentally, a new Turkish language using the European Latin script was

A bust of Atatürk, the father of the modern state

creating, precluding newer generations of Turks from reading documents or history written in Ottoman script.

Atatürk founded not just a nation but a whole social system. His reforms, however, largely failed to reach eastern Anatolians, most of whom were remote from his new capital, Ankara, and preferred the pastoral life and their Muslim faith. Many of these were Kurds who were the first to challenge Atatürk's secular dictates in 1925. This was the first large-scale resistance movement of Kurds in Turkey.

After Atatürk's premature death in 1938, Turkey mourned but drifted unguided. Neutral during World War II, the country managed to play opposing sides off against each other. It was not until 1983, when the pious but visionary Turgut Özal became Prime Minister, that Turkey began to open up to the world. Export potential was realised and taxes were introduced to increase revenue, while tourism began to show promise as a money-spinner

The Turkish Army, always in the background of politics, took a leading role in 1960, 1971 and in 1981, staging coups to reaffirm Atatürk's indivisible state edicts with themselves as guardians. In 1997, they flexed their muscles by pressuring Turkey's first democratically elected Islamic party and its prime minister to step down.

Weary of squabbling politicians, inept coalition governments, an economy in recession and sky-high inflation, voters elected the moderately Islamic Recep Tayyip Erdoğan as Prime Minister in 2003. By 2005, Turkey had proclaimed a long-term desire to join the European Union and completed the *acquis* process and accession talks. Over 25 years, the country has achieved great progress in industrialisation and technology. However, unemployment is now stubbornly high and Turkey's much vaunted youthful and dynamic population lacks high-level skills. Progress has been interrupted by exaggerated fears of dissolution, enemies at the door, and an overwhelming emphasis on homogeneity as vital to state security. Minorities are feared as disloyal and unpatriotic, although the Kurdish language, long repressed, is now broadcast on state media.

To comply with EU norms of freedoms and rights, Turkey has had to enact tough reforms and Prime Minister Erdoğan is making much headway in restructuring Turkey's outmoded constitution, dating from 1981. Ultra-nationalists, anxious of forfeiting their entrenched, privileged status and determined not to lose their grip on the (secular) status quo, fear their authority may be diluted if they join the European club. Another stumbling block is the issue of northern Cyprus, divided since 1974; a nationalistic prime minister elected in April 2010 has dimmed hopes of uniting the troubled island.

Since 2008, Turkey's armed forces have been under legal scrutiny for allegedly plotting against the country they have pledged to protect, to ensure the country retains its secular bylines. It has been unprecedented at any other time to question the legacy of Atatürk or the right of the military to safeguard it. Questions of integrity are being asked of Turkey's judiciary, also ripe for reform. This 'Ergenekon' trial has riveted Turks and observers who perceive the winds of change blowing for Turkey, whether in or out of the EU.

The current prime minister, Recep Tayyip Erdoğan

Historical Landmarks

6500BC
Neolithic peoples settle near Konya

1250BC
Fall of Troy

1100BC
First Greeks settle on Aegean coast

800BC
Phrygian, Lydian and Lycian cultures begin to flourish

546BC
Persians, under Cyrus the Great, invade

334BC
Alexander the Great conquers the Persians

130BC
Romans create province of Asia Minor

AD40
St Paul begins preaching Christianity

325
Christian Council held at Nicaea (İznik)

330
Constantinople becomes capital of eastern Roman Empire

1071
Seljuks establish an empire

1203
Crusaders sack Constantinople

14TH CENTURY
Rise of the Ottomans begins

1453
Mehmet II conquers Constantinople, ending Byzantine Empire

1520–66
Sultanate of Süleyman the Magnificent

1571
Ottoman Navy is crushed at Lepanto

1680–75
Ottomans lose much of their European territory

1839–76
Overdue reforms enacted to restructure the Ottoman Empire

1877
Young Turks sow first seeds of Turkish nationalism

1912–13
Ottomans lose remaining European territories in Balkan Wars

1914–18
Turks enter World War I as German allies

1919–21
Turkish War of Independence

1923
Turkish Republic is established with Atatürk as its president

1938
Atatürk dies

1950
Turkey embraces a multi-party system, setting off a train of coalition governments

1952
Turkey becomes a member of NATO

1974
Turkey invades northern Cyprus, countering Greek expansion aspirations

2005
Acquis talks begin on Turkey's membership in the EU

2007
Stirrings of subversion within the Army

2010
First serious attempts made to revise Turkey's 1981 Constitution

Culture

For those expecting an orientalist time warp, the first impression of Turkey and its modern, upbeat persona, with buzzing İstanbul as a particularly animated gateway, is perhaps something of a surprise. But indeed, much of western Turkey, the part that most visitors see, is accessible and familiar. Women work in banks, government offices and in the police. In the cities and resort areas, slick transport networks and happening nightclubs reveal an upwardly mobile populace.

Traditions remain important, though, and hospitality is a sacrosanct principle. You will find that Turkish people consider it rude not to offer a guest something to eat or drink. Being a good host or hostess is a seriously important part of life and, as a Turkish saying goes, sharing a cup of coffee brings 40 friendships.

THE TURKISH PEOPLE

Initially visitors may think that Turks have an inferiority complex due to being on the losing (Axis) side of World War I. But closer examination reveals that the uniquely Turkish concepts of history and heritage have, instead, given Turks a superior mentality. The founder of the Turkish Republic, Atatürk, devised a new concept of nationhood that erased centuries of Ottoman rule and imbued Turks with a remarkable sense of national pride. In 1921 Turks won their own War of Independence, an achievement of immense significance to them that is still resonant to

this day. Turkey's official nationalistic history lays down that Turks are an elite race with a language that was the genesis for all other languages. To emphasise the point, the Turkish military regularly and ceremoniously visits schools to remind young minds of their exclusive destiny and loyalty to their founding father, Atatürk.

Because Turkey has been so isolated and it has only been in the last 10 or so years that they could travel abroad freely, one of the Turkish people's best traits is their curiosity. While the 'Hello Lady, where are you from?' queries can become tiring, generally visitors find Turks to be wonderfully congenial and friendly. They tend to want to know all about you, asking your age, how much you weigh, your salary and, especially, all about your family. But national

The importance of tea-drinking for sociability should not be underestimated

Playing cards in a *çaybahçe*

solidarity runs deep: even wealthier Turks who have gone abroad for education or to gain a postgraduate degree will tell you that 'a Turk has no friend but another Turk.'

MULTICULTURALISM

Turkey is also home to a mass of additional ethnic groups. The origins of the Kurdish population are obscure, but what is certain is that they have inhabited a region stretching from Syria through Iraq, Iran and eastern Turkey since antiquity. The Black Sea region boasts numerous Caucasian cultures such as the Laz, a unique people that traces its ancestry to the ancient kingdom of Colchis in the Caucasus. Greeks have lived in Asia Minor since about the 8th century BC. The south coast is full of Hellenistic antiquities and, away from rhetoric from Ankara and Athens, Turks and Greeks like each other. Many Greek islanders off Turkey's shores are

welcomed as comrades when they arrive semi-officially at weekly farmers' markets in Turkey (produce for them is often cheaper and fresher than waiting for the ferry to arrive from Athens or Rhodes).

Midyat in southeast Turkey is the home of a few remaining Suriyanis who still speak Aramaic, the language of the Bible. Once, over one million Armenians lived in Turkey and were skilled, creative architects, stone masons and jewellers, prior to their enforced exodus in 1915; however, about 80,000 Armenians live in Turkey today. Alevis, who are a liberal Shiite Muslim sect making up at least a quarter of Turkey's population, are barely acknowledged in the shadow of the Sunni majority. Many Jewish scholars were accommodated here during World War II, before most moved to Israel from 1948.

In general, Christian minorities in Turkey live furtively on the margins of society, often wary of being blamed for undermining the nation's security. Almost all of Turkey's famous historical churches have been anointed museums to discourage non-Muslim worship. The many thousands of ex-pats who have now retired to Turkey often wish to have their own church and Sunday services, but authorities view this as undermining the unity of the nation. Proselytising is highly dangerous.

Despite this appearing quite a cosmopolitan melting pot, the prevailing view is that anybody who lives in Turkey is a Turk. Whilst multiculturalism flourished in Ottoman times, nowadays minorities officially do not exist. Turks are not likely to redefine themselves as a diverse and harmonious cultural mosaic, despite decrees about freedom to worship and freedom of speech being woven into the Turkish Constitution. It is also worth noting that it is borderline illegal to insult Turkey or Turkishness.

Modern Turkish women in the big cities have similar freedoms to those in Europe

Similarly, Turks only accept one language. It was only in 2010 after concerted efforts that Kurdish was allowed on some media and for use in elections. Language is certainly a point where Turks exhibit strong feelings. Turkish is a very difficult language for foreigners to learn but Turks often feel that they need not learn a language: it is more a matter of 'You are in Turkey now; so let's speak Turkish', although this is certainly less the case in major tourist centres. Many of Turkey's prominent politicians, however, do not speak another language despite aspirations of EU membership.

CONTEMPORARY ISSUES

Where foreigners and tourists really will see divides in Turkey is between the eastern and western regions of the country. Atatürk's reforms, enshrined in law and culture from 1923, did not reach Turkey's eastern provinces. Many people here cling to clannish values and family honour and integrity are above the law of the land. The drive to eradicate the radical Kurdish wing has all but decimated many parts of Turkey's eastern towns and villages; tensions continue to simmer. Furthermore, Turkey has many divides between haves and have-nots, but it is most dramatically noticeable between the eastern and western provinces.

Recently, there has been a great deal of worry about the country's high unemployment rates, which are probably double the official rate of about 14 percent. Many are concerned that Turkey's education system has turned out an unsustainable number of students who are unemployable.

The wearing of headscarves continues to be contentious in ostensibly secular Turkey

The country is still struggling to make income tax, not VAT, its biggest tax base; a vast grey economy thrives. But none of this diminishes the cheerful and easy-going Turkish attitude. In the direst of situations, a smile, a shrug and the ubiquitous phrase '*İşte, burası Türkiye!*' (So, this is Turkey for you) wafts a thousand troubles to the wind.

Few topics reveal the differences between Muslim and other nations more clearly than the status of women. Western visitors are often surprised to see Turkish women sitting in a bar enjoying a cocktail after a hard day's work in their chosen profession, such as law or medicine. Equally, many modern urban Turkish women are appalled when they visit their rural sisters, slaving in the kitchen after a day's hard labour in the field while their husbands return to yet another game of cards or backgammon at the local teahouse. In Turkish divorce law, it is perfectly acceptable to cite mere 'incompatibility' as a reason to separate or divorce.

However, even at the elite level, the traditional Islamic ethic concerning female submission to male authority continues to pervade much of modern Turkish society. Relatively recent changes to the Turkish Civil Code have officially allowed married women to keep their maiden name, work without the permission of their husbands, and to be the legal head of the household, but in most cases the man is still legally regarded as the head of the family, and his opinions generally hold more sway in the courts. Planned new legislation will finally abolish references to any head of the family, grant women complete equality in family matters and the right to 50 percent of the family home on divorce.

Nothing has caused more controversy and garnered more attention than the issue of women wearing headscarves or Islamic dress in universities, government offices, courts and at government functions, officially banned on the grounds of Turkey's state being strictly secular, with religious symbols banned. It may seem trivial or repressive to outsiders to legislate whether a woman can or cannot wear a headscarf as an emblem of her faith, but the underlying sentiment is heavily political and reinforced by the firmly secular military. The tension is compounded by ironies such as Prime Minister Erdoğan's daughter being able to wear her headscarf unconstrained when attending university in the US.

Culture

Customs and Etiquette

- Turks love to know how much you love their country, food and cultural riches. Concentrate on the positive: they will keep you at arm's length if you criticise or seem condescending.

- It is wise to avoid making jokes about Atatürk or insulting Turkey generally, including defacing the flag or currency; this is perceived as a crime.

- Feet should not be put on the table or where someone might sit. Turks remove shoes before entering any house. You may be offered a pair of house slippers. Showing the soles of your feet even with shoes on is considered impolite.

- Non-Muslims should not enter a mosque during the five daily prayer times. Otherwise, you will be welcome, and an interest in Islam is seen as a compliment.

- Both men and women should dress modestly. For women this means a long(ish) skirt or trousers, and covered shoulders. For men, shorts are frowned upon other than in resort areas. The key is to be respectful of local protocol.

- In a traditional Turkish bath the sexes are segregated. Some tourist hamams allow mixed bathing, but you will pay more. Both men and women should keep their underwear on and use the wrap provided (peştemel) to cover themselves.

- Keep public displays of affection to a minimum, particularly in rural areas or in Turkey's more conservative eastern reaches. Even hand-holding between husband and wife is infrequently seen, apart from in beachside resorts.

LIFESTYLE

The pace of life in Turkey will seem very slow and leisurely compared to the USA or UK. Turkey does not have the GDP, foreign investment or wealth of some other G-nations but does boast a high proportion of the super-rich. If you are staying in a holiday resort or are on a package holiday, you will probably not notice much difference in lifestyles, but if you are travelling around the country seeing various areas, you will note that religion and family play a significant role in society, considerably more so than in western countries.

MUSIC

Turkish music has been influencing the world for hundreds of years but indigenous music styles vary wildly, from strident sentimental pop and mystical Sufi reed flutes to cutting-edge jazz and the wailing arabesque. There are the aşık troubadours whose roots go back to the 15th century, but whose laments for justice and equality are at the centre of most Turkish political folk music today, and the frenetic, almost Celtic bagpipe-and-fiddle dance music of the Black Sea. Meanwhile, jazz has been fashionable among the urban elite since the 1950s.

Don't be content with tourist-trail belly-dance music; watch for posters directing you to urban jazz clubs or punk dives, and check for the music festivals that take place in almost all Turkish towns today. An opera in the Byzantine church Aya Irini in İstanbul is never forgotten; nor is an aşık performance in an Anatolian teahouse.

Clogs at the Çağaloğlu Hamam; *see Hamams and Spas, p.46*, for etiquette tips

Superb Turkish 'alternative' music has developed on the urban scene, as the vast volume of Turkish young people tune in to techno and DJ mixes and begin to mix their own. Tarkan has become the first Turkish pop star to make it internationally, partly due to his singing the 2002 Turkish World Cup anthem, and partly due to a cover of one of his songs by Australian soap star Holly Valance. On the club scene, Mustafa Sandal has a growing reputation for good, honest dance music. Most recently, established local star Sertab Erener won the 2003 Eurovision song contest – the first Turkish win in 47 years.

The Atlantic record label was founded by a US-based Turk, Ahmet Ertegün, and his brother, Nesuhi, who later became a partner. Today, their commitment to contemporary music is being upheld by an increasing number of avant-garde musicians and indigenous record companies inspired by the New York club scene and black American blues and jazz, mixed with the 500-year-old Anatolian troubadour rhythms. The blues influence has been linked with young Turkish musicians finding an international expression of class conflict, which also combines the arabesque underbelly of Anatolia with the revival of *Raï* in urban Europe.

Traditional Sufi ritual music is slow and ponderous, an ideal backdrop for the dance of the whirling dervishes, while arabesque is the Anatolian equivalent of Country and Western, replete with references to laments for village life left behind in the pursuit of money in the big city. King of the genre, İbrahim Tatlıses, has Elvis Presley-level pop status in Turkey. His output includes an enormous number of melodramatic films that are hugely popular. The themes always touch on enduring love, forbidden love and retribution, and are not dissimilar to India's glittering Bollywood genre.

The best-known Sufi flute (*ney*) player today is probably Süleyman Erguner, who gives frequent performances all over Turkey and also collaborates on international experimental projects. However, Sufi music of all types is being widely recorded, and it is possible to hear it live at the traditional whirling dervish rituals in İstanbul through the summer and during the Mevlâna Festival in Konya in mid-December. Some of these compositions date back to the early 15th century and include instruments such as the *küdüm* (small drums), *kanun* (zither) and *rebab*, a type of violin accompanying the religious chants. However, the *ney*, or panpipe, is the principal instrument, considered by mystic sects to be God's voice. According to the position of the head and the force of breath, it is possible to play an extension of three octaves.

Music often forms a prominent part of local festivals

Aşık means a wandering minstrel, but Turkish troubadour songs are predominantly about spiritual or political yearning rather than romantic pursuit. Generally, the *aşık* is a solo performer accompanying himself on a *saz*, a simple long-necked wooden lute. Most of the bards belong to the Bektaşi and Alevi sects, known for their liberal egalitarianism, and the music is accompanied by the plaintive lyrics of medieval mystic poets such as Yunus Emre and Pir Sultan Abdul.

FILM

In recent years, Turkish cinema has moved beyond local borders and in many ways abandoned the more social and migratory themes that dominated national films in the 1960s and 1970s. Ferzan Özpetek's *Hamam* was a major influence in introducing new Turkish themes and interpretation to foreign audiences; the film duly won awards at major international festivals. Many more people now know about Nuri Bilge Ceylan, one of Turkey's most influential directors, best known for his film

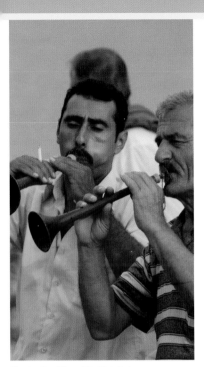
Playing traditional Turkish flutes

Uç Maymun (Three Monkeys), which deals with hardship and turmoil with unique twists and which won the Best Director award at the 2008 Cannes Film Festival. The Golden Orange International Film Festival in Antalya each October is bringing in more and more big names to help launch Turkish films on the international circuit.

LITERATURE

Were it not for language differences, it is likely that Turkish authors and literature would be far more widely known. Turkey's original folk literature had its roots in Central Asian nomadic traditions, but today scholars mostly read Ottoman Turkish. Twentieth-century and other contemporary authors like Yaşar Kemal have had novels translated into English and readers get a realistic glimpse of life in Turkey's small villages on the Çukurova plains in books like *Mehmet, My Hawk*. Kemal was a staunch leftist, something that gained him exposure outside of Turkey.

Novelist Elif Şafak has had her works translated into English, but she also has written in English and German. Her best-known books include the *Forty Rules of Love: a Novel of Rumi*, *Flea Palace* and her most controversial novel, *The Bastard of İstanbul*. She deals with themes of Islam, women and mysticism and cleverly juxtaposes traditional Turkish themes with a worldly vision.

No other author has put Turkey on the literary map as soundly as Orhan Pamuk, the winner of the 2006 Nobel Prize for Literature. His books translated into English include *The Red Book*, *My Name is Red*, *Snow*, *İstanbul* and, most recently, *The Museum of Innocence*. His themes deal with deeply Turkish sentiments and are influenced by undercurrents of melancholy and sombre emotions stemming from his middle-class upbringing in an eccentric family. Pamuk has been repeatedly prosecuted under Turkey's censorship laws for 'insulting the Republic' and his references to Armenian massacres. He has not lived in Turkey since 2008.

Whether it is music, film, theatre, dance or just the people, Turkey's cultural life is so energetic, it is no wonder that visitors return time and time again to delve deeper into it.

Culture

Food and Drink

NATIONAL CUISINE

Turkish cuisine is seen as one of the world's finest *(see Unique Experiences, p.52)*, although the nation has moved away from Ottoman delicacies and towards a Mediterranean diet over the centuries. Emphasis is on the taste of the fresh produce: fruit, vegetables, meat and fish, produced country-wide and year-round. Traditional dishes, usually of meat cooked with vegetables, bring out the simplicity and pure taste of the ingredients. You'll rarely see a savoury dish cooked with a fancy sauce à la France; cooks will more likely use rich olive oil, fresh herbs and spices (although rarely hot ones).

Most main dishes are meat-based, based on small chunks of chicken or lamb cooked with vegetables or beans, where the beloved tomatoes, peppers and aubergine are never far away. On the coast, freshly caught fish is on the menu (often pricey), sold by weight rather than portion, usually served grilled and served with fresh lemon. Each region has its specialist kebap, although larger cities and resorts will have many choices available. Olive oil laces most delicacies in the northern regions. İstanbul and Ankara city types tend to avoid spicy, garlicky dishes, which changes further southeast, with a heavy use of cumin and hot red pepper. Bread also changes, from the mainstream crusty white loaf, like a plump baguette, to Middle Eastern unleavened *pide* bread, closer to an Indian naan.

There's always a salad *(salatlar)* with every meal, most commonly the shepherd's salad *(çoban salatası)*, of finely chopped tomato, cucumber and onion. Rocket *(roka)* appears in the south, delicious with lemon juice and olive oil eaten with fish, and purslane *(semizotu)*, a fleshy, spinach-type leaf. Poured over salads, especially in the south, is *nar*, a sour pomegranate sauce which gets the taste buds tingling.

SEASONAL FOODS

Certain fresh produce comes into its own at certain times of the year and there might be local festivals to celebrate their harvest. Basics like tomatoes, potatoes, onion and peppers are available year-round.

Fresh fruit is a joy when in season. Look out for strawberries in June, grown in Bartın on the Black Sea. Malatya's delicious apricots, exported worldwide, are around in June – look

Turkey grows great amounts of fresh produce

Fresh *pide* bread, straight from the oven

out for the sun-dried variety with an intensely sweet, concentrated flavour. If you have a choice, look for the ones which are dark orange rather than the bright yellow-orange. In Antalya, citrus fruits, especially oranges (*portakal*) and grapefruit (*greyfrut*), fill the trees, and small bananas are popular further east, towards Alanya. The watermelons of Diyarbakır are famous – so much so that they are the city's emblem. Huge, juicy and sweet, the season is around September, celebrated with a lively festival and prizes for the heaviest one – which can reach up to 50kg.

FEASTING ALL DAY LONG

The day starts with Turkish breakfast (your hotel will serve anything from basic to elaborate) consisting of crumbly or creamy feta cheese, with crusty white bread in thick slices. Jam, butter and a hard-boiled egg, plus a small dish of olives, tomato and cucumber, are usually plonked on the plate. A step above might see pide bread, delicious when hot, and yellow *kaşar* cheese. If you're having breakfast in a café, look out for *menemen*, eggs cooked with tomato, peppers and cheese served in the round copper dish in which they were prepared. A plate of börek is also a common way to start the day.

Lunch is usually a quick meal at a *lokanta*, or a bowl of *mercemek çorbası* with mounds of bread. Sundays see family groups out for the day, so expect restaurants to be busy at lunch time.

The main meal is served in the evening. A typical dinner starts with a selection of appetisers or *meze*, a spread of dips, salads, stuffed vegetables and hot savoury pastries. Eating with a large group gives you the chance for

What Time is Food?

Meal times don't vary hugely from the UK or USA. Breakfast is often on the run if on the way to work or school; however, a more leisurely breakfast at weekends can start around 10am. Lunch time for state employees is pretty much fixed from around 12.30pm, otherwise in busy cities lunch can be taken as late as 3pm. Turks love to eat out, and the later the better – even with young kids in tow – from around 9pm. Sunday lunch times and evenings are busy times in restaurants, especially with families.

the most variety; order around two per person if you're having a main course. Contrary to European or American meals, soup (*çorba*) is rarely served for dinner. Whether you're dining at a smart restaurant or a lively meyhane, main courses are usually meat-based – the ubiquitous kebap in its myriad forms. A *mayhane* will usually have a fish option, especially in coastal resorts, of whatever is the catch of the day.

EATING ESTABLISHMENTS

Certain venues specialise in just one item. The *börek salonu* tempts you in with trays of freshly made *börek* (savoury pastries) in the window, often made on site early in the morning, cut into squares and served as one portion. A *pide salonu* sells, you've guessed it, pide bread with cheese or meat cooked on top, in what tourist-friendly cafés will often list as 'Turkish pizza'. A *büfe* is a simple stall or café selling juice and often *tost* (cheese or meat toasted sandwich). The *lokanta*, a canteen-style self-service café, specialises in *hazir yemek*, 'ready food', trays of usually meat-based dishes in a watery gravy, ideally served on a bed of rice or with mounds of bread to mop it up. In such places, vegetarians will often find *fasulye*, beans, but check if they have been cooked in meat.

Stepping up a gear is the *ocakbaşı*, a mid-standard informal barbecue-cum-grill house specialising in various forms of *şiş kebaps*, with little else on offer apart from mounds of fresh salad and flatbread. Dinner at a *meyhane* (traditional 'tavern') may be accompanied by traditional *fasil* (folk)

Food and Drink

Stirring a vat of *dondurma*, a popular street food, similar to ice-cream

music from musicians who wander between your tables (tip expected!). Some *meyhanes* only offer a set-price deal, including assorted *meze*, a main course and salad, bread and mineral water, and rounded off with seasonal fresh fruit (*meyve*). Alcohol may or may not be included.

For an alcohol-free date, courting couples favour the *pastane*, literally sweet house, with a range of baklava, and puddings including traditional *aşure* and *sütlaç*, a milky rice pudding. Branches of **Özsüt** (most towns and cities) have tempting sweet choices plus cakes, ice cream and coffee.

INTERNATIONAL TASTES

Turkish is obviously the way to dine, but for those craving variety then İstanbul is the best city for that, with a decent standard of international cuisines. Tourist areas and resorts might well attempt to cater to unadventurous foreigners, but Turkey's cultural capital genuinely makes a good attempt at cuisines from around the world (albeit pricey). Some of the best include sushi, Thai and Italian (at most top hotels). Around the country, the best hotels will make a decent stab at foreign cuisine, although unless desperate for a taste of something different, it's best to stick to local dishes.

SNACKS

Throughout the country, informal eateries dot the street with snacks and street food, which can be meals in themselves – it's perfectly possible to fill up and never enter a restaurant. Some street snacks are eaten on the run on the way to work; others (such as *Iskembe*) very much at the end of a long night. The following is a small selection *(for kebaps, see p.54)*.

Börek

Flaky pastry parcels filled with white cheese, potato, spinach or meat are usually bought and eaten at a *börek salonu*. Its variation *su böreği* has layers of boiled pastry, resembling pasta, with similar fillings.

Simit

Served from a glass-fronted barrow, the *simitci* sells these sesame-covered crispy bread rings from dawn, usually served in a paper napkin.

Işkembe

This soup, made from sheep or cow tripe, is a popular 3am post-drinking speciality – it's a hangover remedy and perhaps preventative also. Boiled in enormous vats, with lemon, garlic and vinegar added, it's usually eaten in an informal *paçacılar* salon.

Dondurma

This ice cream is made from *salep* (tubers of wild orchids) and mastic resin, making a chewy, sinewy frozen treat. Vendors love putting on a show when serving it up, often dressed in Ottoman garb, using a huge wooden paddle to stir and churn, and dollop it into your cone or cup like a thick length of elastic.

Gozleme

Anatolian women in peasant garb (nostalgic Turks love being reminded of their past) often sit in restaurant windows making these filled pancakes, fried and then rolled up to serve. Choose from cheese, meat, potato or spinach fillings for a delicious filling snack.

Tasty baklava, the ultimate Turkish sweet treat

Strong, sweet Turkish coffee is usually sipped after a meal

LOCAL DRINKS

Non-alcoholic

Ayran, a yoghurt drink whisked up with water and salt, is a local favourite, sold either by the individual carton or freshly made. Refreshing on a hot day and easy on the stomach. *Şira* is a traditional, slightly fermented grape drink, while a more acquired taste is required for *boza*, a centuries-old cold drink made from fermented millet. For either, try **Vefa Bozacisi** café (104 Katip Çelebi Caddesi, Fatih) in İstanbul which has been making and churning them out since 1876.

All foreign brands of canned fizzy drinks (*meşrubat*) are everywhere. Turkish varieties include **Yedigün**, an orange fizzy drink, and **Cola Türka**, local competition to the US brands which is as much a political statement as a new beverage.

Local varieties of fruit juices (*meyve suyu*) include sour cherry (*vişne*) and peach (*şeftali*), sold in cartons and glass bottles in *bakkals* (grocers). Street vendors make freshly squeezed orange juice (*taze portakal suyu*), a hundred times nicer than its cartoned cousin.

You'll be hard pushed to avoid tea (*çay*), seemingly drunk all day, and Turkish coffee (*Türk kahvesi*). Making a recent appearance in trendy city café culture are varieties of coffee including Americano, cappuccino, latte and the like. Branches of Western coffee shops are adored by locals – for those that can afford them. *Sahlep* is a traditional milky-looking winter drink made from a powdered orchid root, mixed with hot water and served warm in tiny glasses, most commonly in traditional teahouses. Herbal tea (*meyve çayı* – usually teabags) comes in varieties including

---

Water Water Everywhere

In most parts of Turkey, tap water isn't drinkable – even locals buy huge containers of filtered drinking water at home. In upmarket restaurants and hotels it's safe to drink their 'open water' – *acık suyu* – which is filtered. Otherwise stick to bottled, usually brought to your table automatically. In street cafés or *lokanta* it might be in a small carton, or bottle.

ihlamur (linden flower) and mint (*nane*). *Ada çay* (literally 'island tea') is made from dried sage leaves, a bunch of which makes a lightweight and lovely gift to take home.

Alcoholic Drinks

Alcohol is legal and acceptable in most parts of the country, although drinking isn't part of mainstream culture. **Efes Pilsner** is the ubiquitous Turkish beer (*bira*), available as regular, lite, dark and extra (strong). That and **Tuborg** are typically served by the bottle, but some bars will have it on draught (slightly cheaper). Expect to pay from around 6TL for a large local beer (500ml), more in fashionable venues and for imported brands.

Turkish wines (*şarap*) have made an increasing impact in the world market. This is the world's fourth-largest grape-growing area and wine has been produced here since Neolithic times. If a restaurant serves wine, most likely the menu will include safe bets like **Villa Doluca** and **Çankaya**, and hearty reds **Yakut** and **Dikmen**. Or look out for scented newcomers like **Okuzgozu**. The cheapest bottle of local wine in a restaurant starts at about 40TL, a medium-quality one from around 60TL.

Up another gear are spirits, although not a widespread choice for Turks. Local brands of whisky (*viski*), vodka, gin (*cin*) and brandy are rough and not advisable – the bad hangover the next morning will warn you off. If you yearn for an exported brand, expect high prices due to taxation. Spirit of choice for most locals is their very own *rakı* – best drunk

alongside a meal, rather than downed in bars – and usually mixed with water which turns it milky.

Because liquor licences are costly and cumbersome, it's only mid- and upper-priced restaurants that serve alcohol; some may only be allowed to sell nothing stronger than beer.

In tourist areas, especially coastal resorts like Antalya, Kuşadası and Bodrum, bars and clubs are lively and the focus of a heady nightlife. In off-the-beaten-track or small-town venues you might be able to find a bar, but forget nightclubs. Some are pretty basic, like a *birakhanesi* (literally 'beer house'), which tends to be male-only and a tad seedy, and unaccompanied foreign women may find the atmosphere uncomfortable. Be aware that *gazinos* tend to be frequented by prostitutes and hopeful men and you might find that your bill comes with some nasty surprises.

In some conservative regions like Diyarbakır, Konya and Kayseri, alcohol is not permitted or else highly disapproved of. You'd be hard pushed to find a legal tipple, except in the top hotels.

Food and Drink

PHRASE BOOK

Phrase Book

The abrupt replacement of the Ottoman Arabic alphabet by a Latin one in 1928 had a profound effect on literacy and modern Turkish. A difficult language for foreigners, Turkish is based on vowel harmony and the use of suffixes. Some English and French words have infiltrated the vocabulary but most local Turks know minimal English. Regional dialects exist and Kurds speak their own language, while languages like Georgian or Arabic intermingle more in border areas. Learning just a few key survival phrases and idioms in Turkish will win local friends.

PRONUNCIATION

This section is designed to familiarise you with the sounds of Turkish using our simplified phonetic transcription. You'll find the pronunciation of the Turkish letters explained below, together with their 'imitated' equivalents. To use this system, found throughout this section of the book, simply read the pronunciation as if it were English, noting any special rules below.

Letters underlined in the transcriptions should be read with slightly more stress than the others, but don't overdo this as Turkish is not a heavily stressed language.

Consonants

Letter	Approximate Pronunciation	Symbol	Example	Pronunciation
c	like j in jam	j	**ceket**	jeh • _keht_
ç	like ch in church	ch	**kaç**	kahch
g	like g in ground	g	**gitmek**	geet • _mehk_
ğ	1. at the end of a word, it lengthens the preceding vowel		**dağ**	dah*
	2. a silent letter between vowels		**kağıt**	kah • _iht_
	3. after e, like y in yawn	y	**değer**	deh • _yehr_
h	like h in hit	h	**mahkeme**	mah • keh • _meh_
j	like s in pleasure	zh	**bagaj**	bah • _gahzh_
r	trilled r	r	**tren**	trehn

s	like s in sit	s	**siyah**	see • _yahh_
ş	like sh in shut	sh	**şişe**	shee • _sheh_

Letters b, d, f, k, l, m, n, p, t, v, y and z are pronounced as in English.
*Bold indicates a lengthening of the sound, an extra emphasis on the vowel sound.
Turkish consonants are typically shorter and harder-sounding than English consonants.
When reading Turkish words, be sure to pronounce all the letters.

Vowels

Letter	Approximate Pronunciation	Symbol	Example	Pronunciation
a	like a in father	ah	**kara**	kah • _rah_
e	like e in net	eh	**sene**	seh • _neh_
ı	similar to i in ill	ih	**tatlı**	taht • _lih_
i	like ee in see	ee	**sim**	seem
o	like o in spot	oh	**otel**	oh • _tehl_
ö	similar to ur in fur	ur	**börek**	bur • _rehk_
u	like oo in cool	oo	**uzak**	oo • _zahk_
ü	like ew in few	yu	**üç**	yuch

Turkish vowels are quite different from English vowels. As with consonants, they are
generally shorter and harder than English vowels. In the pronunciation guide, certain
vowels are followed by an 'h' to emphasise the shortness of the sound.

Diphthongs

Letters	Approximate Pronunciation	Symbol	Example	Pronunciation
ay	like ie in tie	ie	**bay**	bie
ey	like ay in day	ay	**bey**	bay
oy	like oy in boy	oy	**koy**	koy

Turkish differs from English in two important ways. First, affixes take the place of
many words that, in other languages, would be written separately (such as pronouns,
negatives and prepositions); these affixes are attached to a base word. Second, it
features 'vowel harmony'; this restricts which vowels may appear within a word. So,
while affixes in their standard forms have the vowel 'i' or 'e', this may change when the
affix is attached to another word. For example, the suffix **in** (´s) stays **in** in **evin** (the
house's), but becomes **un** in **memurun** (the official's) and **ün** in **gözün** (the eye's).

English	Turkish	Pronunciation
How much?	**Ne kadar?**	_neh_ kah • dahr

Turkish words and phrases appear in bold. A simplified pronunciation guide follows each Turkish phrase; read it as if it were English, giving the underlined letters a little more stress than the others. Among the English phrases, you will find some words included in square brackets; these are the American-English equivalents of British-English expressions.

General

0	**sıfır** _sih_ • fihr	100	**yüz** yyuz	
1	**bir** beer	500	**beşyüz** _behsh_ yyuz	
2	**iki** ee • _kee_	1,000	**bin** been	
3	**üç** yuch	1,000,000	**bir milyon** _beer_ meel • yohn	
4	**dört** durrt	Monday	**Pazartesi** pah • _zahr_ • teh • see	
5	**beş** behsh	Tuesday	**Salı** sah • _lih_	
6	**altı** ahl • _tih_	Wednesday	**Çarşamba** chahr • shahm • _bah_	
7	**yedi** yeh • _dee_	Thursday	**Perşembe** pehr • shehm • _beh_	
8	**sekiz** seh • _keez_	Friday	**Cuma** joo • _mah_	
9	**dokuz** doh • _kooz_	Saturday	**Cumartesi** joo • _mahr_ • teh • see	
10	**on** ohn	Sunday	**Pazar** pa • _zar_	
Hello.			**Merhaba.** _mehr_ • hah • bah	
Hi!			**Selam!** seh • _lahm_	
How are you?			**Nasılsınız?** _nah_ • sihl • sih • nihz	
Fine, thanks.			**İyiyim, teşekkürler.** ee • _yee_ • yeem teh • shehk • kyur • _lehr_	
Excuse me!			**Afedersiniz!** _ahf_ • eh • dehr • see • neez	
Do you speak English?			**İngilizce biliyor musunuz?** een • gee • _leez_ • jeh bee • _lee_ • yohr moo • soo • nooz	
What's your name?			**İsminiz nedir?** ees • mee • _neez neh_ • deer	
My name is...			**İsmim...** ees • _meem_...	
Pleased to meet you.			**Tanıştığımıza memnun oldum.** tah • nihsh • tih • ih • mih • _zah_ mehm • _noon_ ohl • doom	
Where are you from?			**Nerelisiniz?** _neh_ • reh • lee • see • neez	
I'm from the UK.			**Birleşik Krallıktanım.** beer • leh • _sheek_ krahl • lihk • _tah_ • nihm	
What do you do?			**Ne iş yapıyorsunuz?** _neh_ eesh yah • _pih_ • yohr • soo • nooz	
I work for...			**...için çalışıyorum.** ...ee • _cheen_ chah • lih • _shih_ • yoh • room	
I'm a student.			**öğrenciyim.** ur • rehn • _jee_ • eem	
I'm retired.			**Emekliyim.** eh • mehk • _lee_ • yeem	
Do you like...?			**...sever misiniz?** ...seh • _vehr_ mee • see • neez	
Goodbye. (said by departing persons)			**Hoşçakalın.** hosh • _chah_ kah • lihn	
Goodbye. (said by persons staying behind)			**Güle güle.** gyu • _leh_ gyu • _leh_	
See you later.			**Tekrar görüşmek üzere.** tehk • _rahr_ gur • ryush • _mehk_ yu • zeh • reh	

Arrival and Departure

I'm here on holiday [vacation]/business.	**Tatil/İş için buradayım.** *tah • teel/eesh ee • cheen boo • rah • dah • yihm*
I'm going to...	**...gidiyorum.** *...gee • dee • yoh • room*
I'm staying at the...Hotel.	**...otelinde kalıyorum.** *...oh • teh • leen • deh kah • lih • yoh • room*

Money and Banking

Where's...?	**...nerede?** *...neh • reh • deh*
– the ATM	– **Paramatik** *pah • rah • mah • teek*
– the bank	– **Banka** *bahn • kah*
– the currency exchange office	– **Döviz bürosu** *dur • veez byu • roh • soo*
I'd like to change dollars/pounds into lira.	**Dolar/İngiliz Sterlini bozdurmak istiyorum.** *doh • lahr/ een • gee • leez stehr • lee • nee bohz • door • mahk ees • tee • yoh • room*

Transport

How do I get to town?	**Şehire nasıl gidebilirim?** *sheh • hee • reh nah • sıhl gee • deh • bee • lee • reem*
Where's...?	**...nerede?** *...neh • reh • deh*
– the airport	– **Havaalanı** *hah • vah • ah • lah • nıh*
– the railway [train] station	– **Tren garı** *trehn gah • rih*
– the bus station	– **Otobüs garajı** *oh • toh • byus gah • rah • jih*
– the underground [subway] station	– **Metro istasyonu** *meht • roh ees • tahs • yoh • noo*
How far is it?	**Ne kadar uzakta?** *neh kah • dahr oo • zahk • tah*
Where can I buy tickets?	**Nereden bilet alabilirim?** *neh • reh • dehn bee • leht ah • lah • bee • lee • reem*
A single [one-way]/return [round-trip] ticket.	**Sadece gidiş/gidiş dönüş bileti.** *sah • deh • jeh gee • deesh/ gee • deesh dur • nyush bee • leh • tee*
How much?	**Ne kadar?** *neh kah • dahr*
Which...?	**Hangi...?** *hahn • gee...*
– gate?	– **kapı?** *kah • pih*
– lane?	– **hat?** *haht*
– platform?	– **peron?** *peh • rohn*
Where can I rent a car?	**Nereden bir araba kiralayabilirim?** *neh • reh • dehn beer ah • rah • bah kee • rah • lah • yah • bee • lee • reem*
Can I have a map?	**Bir harita alabilir miyim?** *beer hah • reeh • tah ah • lah • bee • leer • mee • yeem*

Accommodation

Can you recommend a hotel?	**Bir otel tavsiye edebilir misiniz?** *beer oh • tehl tahv • see • yeh eh • deh • bee • leer • mee • see • neez*
I have a reservation.	**Yer ayırtmıştım.** *yehr ah • yihrt • mihsh • tihm*
My name is...	**İsmim...** *ees • meem...*
Do you have a room...?	**...odanız var mı?** *...oh • dah • nihz vahr mih*
– for one/two	– **Bir/İki kişilik** *beer/ee • kee kee • shee • leek*

– with a bathroom	– **Banyolu** bahn • yoh • _loo_
– with air conditioning	– **Klimalı** _klee_ • mah • lih
For tonight.	**Bu gecelik.** _boo_ geh • jeh • leek
For two nights.	**İki geceliğine.** ee • _kee_ geh • jeh • lee • yee • _neh_
For one week.	**Bir haftalığına.** _beer_ hahf • tah • lih • ih • _nah_
How much?	**Ne kadar?** neh kah • dahr
Do you have anything cheaper?	**Daha ucuz yer var mı?** dah • _hah_ oo • jooz yehr _vahr_ mih

294

Internet and Communications

Where's an internet cafe?	**İnternet kafe nerede?** een • tehr • _neht_ kah • _feh_ neh • reh • deh
Can I access the internet here?	**Burada internete girebilir?** _boo_ • rah • dah een • tehr • neh • _teh_ gee • reh • bee • _leer_
Hello, this is...	**Merhaba, ben...** _mehr_ • hah • bah behn...
I'd like to speak to...	**...ile konuşmak istiyorum.** ...ee • leh koh • noosh • _mahk_ ees • _tee_ • yoh • room
Can you repeat that, please?	**Tekrar eder misiniz lütfen?** tehk • _rahr_ eh • _dehr_ mee • see • neez _lyut_ • fehn
I'll call back later.	**Daha sonra arayacağım.** dah • _hah_ sohn • rah ah • rah • yah • _jah_ • ihm
Where is the post office?	**Postane nerede?** pohs • tah • _neh_ neh • reh • deh
I'd like to send this to...	**Bunu...göndermek istiyorum.** boo • _noo_...gurn • dehr • _mehk_ ees • _tee_ • yoh • room

Sightseeing

Where's the tourist office?	**Turist danışma bürosu nerede?** too • _reest_ dah • nihsh • _mah_ byu • roh • soo _neh_ • reh • deh
What are the main points of interest?	**Başlıca ilginç yerler nelerdir?** bahsh • _lih_ • jah eel • geench yehr • _lehr_ neh • _lehr_ • deer
Do you have tours in English?	**İngilizce turlarınız var mı?** een • geh • _leez_ • jeh toor • lah • rih • _nihz vahr_ mih
Can I have a map/guide?	**Harita/Rehber alabilir miyim?** hah • _ree_ • tah/reh • _ber_ ah • lah • bee • _leer_ mee • yeem

Shopping

Where is the market/shopping centre [mall]?	**Market/Alış veriş merkezi nerede?** mahr • _keht_/ah • _lihsh_ veh • _reesh_ mehr • keh • _zee neh_ • reh • deh
I'm just looking.	**Sadece bakıyorum.** _sah_ • deh • jeh bah • _kih_ • yoh • room
Can you help me?	**Bana yardım edebilir misiniz?** bah • nah yahr • _dihm_ eh • deh • bee • _leer_ mee • see • neez
I'm being helped.	**Yardım alıyorum.** yahr • _dihm_ ah • _lih_ • yoh • room
How much?	**Ne kadar?** neh kah • dahr
I'll pay in cash/by credit card.	**Nakit/Kredi kartı ile ödeyeceğim.** nah • _keet_/kreh • _dee_ kahr • tih ee • leh ur • deh • yeh • jeh • yeem
A receipt, please.	**Fatura lütfen.** _fah_ • too • rah _lyut_ • fehn

Culture and Nightlife

What is there to do in the evenings?	**Geceleri ne yapılır?** geh • jeh • leh • ree neh yah • pih • lihr
What's playing at the cinema [movies] tonight?	**Bu gece hangi filmler oynuyor?** boo geh • jeh hahn • gee feelm • lehr oy • noo • yohr
Where's…?	**…nerede?** …neh • reh • deh
– the city-centre [downtown area]	– **Kent merkezi** kehnt mehr • keh • zee
– the bar	– **Bar** bahr
– the dance club	– **Diskotek** dees • koh • tehk
Is there a cover charge?	**Giriş ücretli mi?** gee • reesh yuj • reht • lee mee

Business Travel

I'm here on business.	**İş için burdayım.** eesh ee • cheen boor • dah • yihm
Here's my business card.	**Buyrun kartvizitim.** booy • roon kahrt • vee • zee • teem
I have a meeting with…	**…ile bir randevum var.** …ee • leh beer rahn • deh • voom vahr
Where's…?	**…nerede?** …neh • reh • deh
– the business centre	– **İş merkezi** eesh mehr • keh • zee
– the convention hall	– **Kongre salonu** kohng • reh sah • loh • noo
– the meeting room	– **Toplantı odası** tohp • lahn • tih oh • dah • sih

Travel with Children

Is there a discount for children?	**Çocuklar için indirim var mı?** choh • jook • lahr ee • cheen een • dee • reem vahr mih
Can you recommend a babysitter?	**Bir çocuk bakıcısı önerebilir misiniz?** beer choh • jook bah • kih • jih • sih ur • neh • reh • bee • leer mee • see • neez
Could we have a child's seat/highchair?	**Çocuk sandalyesi/Yüksek sandalye alabilir miyiz?** choh • jook sahn • dahl • yeh see/yyuk • sehk sahn • dahl • yeh ah • lah • bee • leer mee • yeez
Where can I change the baby?	**Bebeğin altını nerede değiştirebilirim?** beh • beh • yeen ahl • tih • nih neh • reh • deh deh • yeesh • tee • reh • bee • lee • reem

Disabled Travellers

Is there…?	**…var mı?** …vahr mih
– access for the disabled	– **Engelli girişi** ehn • gehl • lee gee • ree • shee
– a wheelchair ramp	– **Tekerlekli sandalye rampası** teh • kehr • lehk • lee sahn • dahl • yeh rahm • pah • sih
– a disabled-[handicapped-] accessible toilet [restroom]	– **Özürlü tuvaleti** ur • zyur • lyu too • vah • leh • tee
I need…	**…ihtiyacım var.** …eeh • tee • yah • jihm vahr
– assistance	– **Yardımcıya** yahr • dihm • jih • yah
– a lift [an elevator]	– **Asansöre** ah • sahn • sur • reh
– a ground-floor room	– **Zemin-kat odasına** zeh • meen • kaht oh • dah • sih • nah

Emergencies

Help!	**İmdat!** eem • daht
Stop thief!	**Durdurun, hırsız!** door • doo • roon hihr • sihz

Get a doctor!	**Bir doktor bulun!** *beer dohk • tohr boo • loon*
Fire!	**Yangın!** *yahn • gihn*
I'm lost.	**Kayboldum.** *kie • bohl • doom*
Can you help me?	**Bana yardım edebilir misiniz?** *bah • nah yahr • dihm eh • deh • bee • leer mee • see • neez*
Call the police!	**Polis çağırın!** *poh • lees chah • ih • rihn*
Where's the police station?	**Karakol nerede?** *kah • rah • kohl neh • reh • deh*
There has been an accident/attack.	**Bir kaza/saldırı oldu.** *beer kah • zah/sahl • dih • rih ohl • doo*
My child is missing.	**Çocuğum kayıp.** *choh • joo • oom kah • yihp*
I need…	**…ihtiyacım var.** *…eeh • tee • yah • jihm vahr*
– an interpreter	– **Tercümana** *tehr • jyu • mah • nah*
– to contact my lawyer	– **Avukatımla görüşmeye** *ah • voo • kah • tihm • lah gur • ryush • meh • yeh*
– to make a phone call	– **Telefon görüşmesi yapmaya** *teh • leh • fohn gur • ryush • meh • see yahp • mah • yah*

Health

I'm ill [sick].	**Hastayım.** *hahs • tah • yihm*
I need an English-speaking doctor.	**İngilizce konuşan bir doktora ihtiyacım var.** *een • gee • leez • jeh koh • noo • shahn beer dohk • toh • rah eeh • tee • yah • jihm vahr*
It hurts here.	**Burası acıyor.** *boo • rah • sih ah • jih • yohr*
I have a stomachache.	**Mide ağrım var.** *mee • deh ah • rihm vahr*
Where's the nearest chemist [pharmacy]?	**En yakın eczane nerede?** *ehn yah • kihn ehj • zah • neh neh • reh • deh*
What time does the chemist [pharmacy] open/close?	**Eczane ne zaman açılıyor/kapanıyor?** *ehj • zah • neh neh zah • mahn ah • chih • lih • yohr/kah • pah • nih • yohr*
What would you recommend for…?	**…için ne önerirdiniz?** *…ee • cheen neh ur • neh • reer • dee • neez*
How much should I take?	**Ne kadar almalıyım?** *neh kah • dahr ahl • mah • lih • yihm*
I'm allergic to…	**…alerjim var.** *…ah • lehr • jeem vahr*

Eating Out

A table for…, please.	**…kişi için bir masa lütfen.** *…kee • shee ee • cheen beer mah • sah lyut • fehn*
Where are the toilets [restrooms]?	**Tuvalet nerede?** *too • vah • leht neh • reh • deh*
A menu, please.	**Menü lütfen.** *meh • nyu lyut • fehn*
I'd like…	**…istiyorum.** *…ees • tee • yoh • room*
The bill [check], please.	**Hesap lütfen.** *heh • sahp lyut • fehn*
Is service included?	**Servis dahil mi?** *sehr • vees dah • heel mee*
Thank you.	**Teşekkür ederim.** *teh • shehk • kyur eh • deh • reem*
I'd like a bottle/glass of red/white wine.	**Bir şişe/bardak kırmızı/beyaz şarap istiyorum.** *beer shee • sheh/bahr • dahk kihr • mih • zih/beh • yahz shah • rahp ees • tee • yoh • room*
A coffee/tea, please.	**Kahve/Çay lütfen.** *kah • hveh/chie lyut • fehn*

baklava <u>bahk</u> • lah • vah	filo pastry filled with honey and pistachio nuts	**kadayıf** kah • dah • <u>yihf</u>	shredded wheat dessert, similar to baklava
balık çorbası bah • <u>lihk</u> chohr • bah • sih	fish soup	**kafeini alınmış** kah • feh • ee • <u>nee</u> ah • lihn • <u>mihsh</u>	decaffeinated
beyaz peynir beh • <u>yahz</u> pay • neer	white cheese	**kahve** kah • <u>hveh</u>	coffee
beyaz şarap beh • <u>yahz</u> shah • rahp	white wine	**kalamar** kah • lah • <u>mahr</u>	squid
biber bee • <u>behr</u>	pepper	**karides** kah • ree • <u>dehs</u>	prawn [shrimp]
bira bee • <u>rah</u>	beer	**kavun** kah • <u>voon</u>	melon
bonfile bohn • fee • <u>leh</u>	steak	**kazandibi** kah • <u>zahn</u> • dee • bee	oven-browned milk pudding
börek bur • <u>rehk</u>	hot filo pastries	**kırmızı biber** kih • mih • <u>zih</u> bee • <u>behr</u>	chili
çay chie	tea	**kırmızı şarap** kihr • mih • <u>zih</u> shah • <u>rahp</u>	red wine
çiğ köfte chee kurf • <u>teh</u>	raw meatballs made from ground meat and cracked wheat	**kuzu** koo • <u>zoo</u>	lamb
dana dah • <u>nah</u>	veal	**lahana** lah • <u>hah</u> • nah	cabbage
deniz tarağı deh • <u>neez</u> tah • rah • ih	clams	**lokum** loh • <u>koom</u>	Turkish delight
dolma dohl • <u>mah</u>	stuffed grape leaves	**meyve suyu** may • <u>veh</u> soo • yoo	fruit juice
domates doh • mah • <u>tehs</u>	tomato	**midye** meed • <u>yeh</u>	mussels
domuz doh • <u>mooz</u>	pork	**patates** pah • tah • <u>tehs</u>	potato
ekmek ehk • <u>mehk</u>	bread	**patlıcan** paht • lih • <u>jahn</u>	aubergine [eggplant]
ev şarabı <u>ehv</u> shah • rah • bih	house wine	**sığır eti** sih • <u>ihr</u> eh • tee	beef
gazlı gahz • <u>lih</u>	carbonated water	**sosis** soh • <u>sees</u>	sausage
gazsız gahz • <u>sihz</u>	non-carbonated water	**şarap listesini** shah • <u>rahp</u> <u>lees</u> • teh • see	wine list
havuç hah • <u>vooch</u>	carrot	**tavuk** tah • <u>vook</u>	chicken
ıstakoz ihs • tah • <u>kohz</u>	lobster	**taze fasulye** tah • <u>zeh</u> fah • <u>sool</u> • yeh	green beans
içecek menüsünü ee • cheh • <u>jehk</u> meh • nyu • <u>syu</u>	drink menu	**ton balığı** <u>tohn</u> bah • lih • ih	tuna
içki eech • <u>kee</u>	drink	**tulum peyniri** too • <u>loom</u> pay • nee • <u>ree</u>	goat cheese
imam bayıldı ee • <u>mahm</u> bah • yihl • <u>dih</u>	aubergine [eggplant] stuffed with tomatoes and cooked in olive oil	**üzüm** yu • <u>zyum</u>	grapes
jambon jahm • <u>bohn</u>	ham	**yumurta** yoo • <u>moor</u> • tah	egg

297

Phrase Book

Index

Accommodation Index

Credits for Berlitz Handbook Turkey

Written by: Suzanne Swan and Emma Levine
Series Editor: Tom Stainer
Commissioning Editor: Sarah Sweeney
Cartography Editor: Zoë Goodwin
Map Production: APA Cartography Dept.
Production: Linton Donaldson
Picture Manager: Steven Lawrence
Art Editors: Richard Cooke and Ian Spick
Photography: All images APA/Frank Noon except: Istockphoto 2L, 3L,/R, 4TR, 14, 24, 33, 60/61, 93T, 95, 101, 102, 103, 134, 140, 146, 180, 184, 197/T, 200, 201, 202, 203/T, 205, 209, 211, 239T, 251; Alamy 26, 32, 35, 36, 37, 46, 47, 48, 91, 111/T, 137, 142, 157T, 187, 194, 199, 206, 208, 224, 238, 239; Art Archive 269; Scala 270; APA Rebecca Erol 4TL, 5TL, 7MR, 38, 41, 44, 65B,/T, 68, 69, 70, 71, 72, 73, 74, 75,/B, 76, 78, 79, 80, 81, 82, 83, 87, 88, 246/247, 252, 253, 259, 274, 276, 277, 279, 286, 288/289; Courtesy W Hotel 86; Getty Images 6MR, 20/21, 27, 34, 99B, 272; Corbis 6TL, 22, 99T, 128, 266; Turkish Tourism 7B, 8T, 9TL, 10/11, 267; Courtesy Aependos International Opera; Giray 28, 29; Courtesy Les Ottomans 49; Courtesy Cagaloglu Hamami 51; Ed Clayton 56; Ming yen Hsu 96; Erdine 98; Courtesy Kent Otel 106; Courtesy Imbat Hotel 138; Courtesy Hotel berk 168; Courtesy Swiss Hotel Gocek 169; Ajos A.S. 175; Amir Farshad Ebraimi 183; Feloidea 185T; Maderibeyza 192; Courtesy Caval Hotel 207; Courtesy Swiss Hotel 192; Courtesy mardin hotel 242; Courtesy Admar Hotel 248; Courtesy Hotel Ibrahim Pasha 249; Courtesy Pensiyon Rehberi 250
Cover: Four Corners Images (front); Istock
Printed by: CTPS-China

First Edition 2011
Reprinted 2011

Contact Us: We strive to keep our guides as accurate and up to date as possible, but if you find anything that has changed, or if you have any suggestions on ways to improve this guide, please write to Berlitz Publishing, PO Box 7910, London SE1 1WE, UK, or email: berlitz@apaguide.co.uk

Worldwide: APA Publications GmbH & Co. Verlag KG (Singapore branch), 7030 Ang Mo Kio Ave 5, 08-65 Northstar @ AMK, Singapore 569880; tel: (65) 570 1051; email: apasin@singnet.com.sg
UK and Ireland: GeoCenter International Ltd, Meridian House, Churchill Way West, Basingstoke, Hampshire, RG21 6YR; tel: (44) 01256-817 987; email: sales@geocenter.co.uk
United States: Ingram Publisher Services, One Ingram Blvd, PO Box 3006, La Vergne, TN 37086-1986; email: customer.service@ingrampublisherservices.com
Australia: Universal Publishers, PO Box 307, St Leonards, NSW 1590; tel: (61) 2-9857 3700; email: sales@universalpublishers.com.au

www.berlitzpublishing.com